# Eating Disorders
# SOURCEBOOK

## Health Reference Series

*First Edition*

# Eating Disorders SOURCEBOOK

*Basic Consumer Health Information about Eating Disorders, Including Information about Anorexia Nervosa, Bulimia Nervosa, Binge Eating, Body Dysmorphic Disorder, Pica, Laxative Abuse, and Night Eating Syndrome*

*Along with Information about Causes, Adverse Effects, and Treatment and Prevention Issues, and Featuring a Section on Concerns Specific to Children and Adolescents, a Glossary, and Resources for Further Help and Information*

*Edited by*
**Dawn D. Matthews**

*Omnigraphics*

615 Griswold Street • Detroit, MI 48226

## Bibliographic Note

Because this page cannot legibly accommodate all the copyright notices, the Bibliographic Note portion of the Preface constitutes an extension of the copyright notice.

Each new volume of the *Health Reference Series* is individually titled and called a "First Edition." Subsequent updates will carry sequential edition numbers. To help avoid confusion and to provide maximum flexibility in our ability to respond to informational needs, the practice of consecutively numbering each volume has been discontinued.

## Edited by Dawn D. Matthews

## Health Reference Series

Karen Bellenir, *Series Editor*
Peter D. Dresser, *Managing Editor*
Maria Franklin, *Permissions Assistant*
Joan Margeson, *Research Associate*
Dawn Matthews, *Verification Assistant*
Carol Munson, *Permissions Assistant*
Jenifer Swanson, *Research Associate*

## Omnigraphics, Inc.

Matthew P. Barbour, *Vice President, Operations*
Laurie Lanzen Harris, *Vice President, Editorial Director*
Kevin Hayes, *Production Coordinator*
Thomas J. Murphy, *Vice President, Finance and Controller*
Peter E. Ruffner, *Senior Vice President*
Jane J. Steele, *Marketing Coordinator*

## Frederick G. Ruffner, Jr., Publisher

## Library of Congress Cataloging-in-Publication Data

Eating disorders sourcebook : basic consumer health information about eating disorders, including information about anorexia nervosa, bulimia nervosa, binge eating, body dysmorphic disorder, pica, laxative abuse, and night eating syndrome; along with information about causes, adverse affects, and treatment and prevention issues, and featuring a section on concerns specific to children and adolescents, a glossary, and resources for further help and information / edited by Dawn D. Matthews.--1st ed.
    p.cm. -- (Health reference series)
  Includes bibliographical references and index.
  ISBN 0-7808-0335-3
    1. Eating disorders. 2. Consumer education. I. Matthews, Dawn D. II. Health reference series (Unnumbered)
RC552.E18 E287 2001
616.85'26--dc21

                          2001034610

∞

# Table of Contents

## Part III: Causes and Adverse Affects

## Part IV: Treatment and Prevention

## Part V: Specific Concerns Related to Children and Adolescents

## Part VI: Additional Help and Information

# *Preface*

## About This Book

Every year millions of people in the United States are affected by serious and sometimes life-threatening eating disorders. More than 90 percent are adolescent and young adult women who desire the "ideal" figure. The consequences of eating disorders can be severe— one in ten cases of anorexia nervosa leads to death. Recognition of the problem is the first step toward treatment which can literally save someone's life.

*Eating Disorders Sourcebook* provides valuable information to individuals suffering from eating disorders as well as to family members and friends. It describes the symptoms of eating disorders, possible causes, treatment options, and how to take the first steps toward recovery. It includes a special section focusing on issues specific to adolescents and also offers a resource section for readers who require additional help and information.

## How to Use This Book

This book is divided into parts and chapters. Parts focus on broad areas of interest. Chapters are devoted to single topics within a part.

*Part I: Introduction to Eating Disorders* offers an overview of general information about eating disorders as well as statistical information and a chapter with frequently asked questions.

*Part II: Types of Eating Disorders* explains the different types of eating disorders, including anorexia nervosa, bulimia, and binge eating disorder. It also includes a chapter on lesser-known eating disorders.

*Part III: Causes and Adverse Effects* gives information about the causes of eating disorders and discusses who is at risk. It addresses how eating disorders affect athletes, pregnancy, and people with diabetes.

*Part IV: Treatment and Prevention* contains advice for the treatment of eating disorders as well as information for those seeking to help a friend or loved one. It contains chapters on questionable dieting behaviors and offers advice for healthy dieting.

*Part V: Specific Concerns Related to Adolescents* gives helpful information to parents and educators about their role in the treatment of eating disordered children. It offers strategies to enhance self-esteem in adolescents and discusses school-based programs for preventing eating disorders.

*Part VI: Additional Help and Information* includes a glossary of important terms, links to internet websites related to eating disorders, and a directory of resources for further help and information.

## *Bibliographic Note*

This volume contains documents and excerpts from publications issued by the following government agencies: National Institute of Diabetes and Digestive and Kidney Diseases (NIDDK); U.S. Department of Health and Human Services (DHHS); and the U.S. Federal Trade Commission (FTC).

In addition, this volume contains copyrighted articles from American Academy of Child and Adolescent Psychiatry; American Academy of Family Physicians; American Diabetes Association Inc.; American Dietetic Association; American Medical Association; American School Health Association; ANRED, Anorexia Nervosa and Related Eating Disorders, Inc.; Brown University; Clinical Reference Systems Ltd.; Hearst Corporation; Maclean Hunter (Canada); Medical Economics Publishing; Nursecom, Inc.; Project Innovation; SIRS Mandarin, Inc.; and the Weekly Reader Corporation.

Full citation information is provided on the first pa ge of each chapter. Every effort has been made to secure all necessary rights to reprint the copyrighted material. If any omissions have been made, please contact Omnigraphics to make corrections for future editions.

## Acknowledgements

Thanks go to Carol Munson and Maria Franklin for their patience during this process and to Karen Bellenir for her help and advice.

## Note from the Editor

This book is part of Omnigraphics' *Health Reference Series*. The series provides basic information about a broad range of medical concerns. It is not intended to serve as a tool for diagnosing illness, in prescribing treatments, or as a substitute for the physician/patient relationship. All persons concerned about medical symptoms or the possibility of disease are encouraged to seek professional care from an appropriate health care provider.

## Our Advisory Board

The *Health Reference Series* is reviewed by an Advisory Board comprised of librarians from public, academic, and medical libraries. We would like to thank the following board members for providing guidance to the development of this series:

Dr. Lynda Baker,
Associate Professor of Library and Information Science,
Wayne State University, Detroit, MI

Nancy Bulgarelli,
William Beaumont Hospital Library, Royal Oak, MI

Karen Imarasio,
Bloomfield Township Public Library, Bloomfield Township, MI

Karen Morgan,
Mardigian Library, University of Michigan-Dearborn,
Dearborn, MI

Rosemary Orlando,
St. Clair Shores Public Library, St. Clair Shores, MI

## Health Reference Series *Update Policy*

The inaugural book in the *Health Reference Series* was the first edition of *Cancer Sourcebook* published in 1992. Since then, the Series has been enthusiastically received by librarians and in the medical community. In order to maintain the standard of providing high-quality health information for the layperson the editorial staff at Omnigraphics felt it was necessary to implement a policy of updating volumes when warranted.

Medical researchers have been making tremendous strides, and it is the purpose of the *Health Reference Series* to stay current with the most recent advances. Each decision to update a volume will be made on an individual basis. Some of the considerations will include how much new information is available and the feedback we receive from people who use the books. If there is a topic you would like to see added to the update list, or an area of medical concern you feel has not been adequately addressed, please write to:

Editor
*Health Reference Series*
Omnigraphics, Inc.
615 Griswold St.
Detroit, MI 48226

The commitment to providing on-going coverage of important medical developments has also led to some format changes in the *Health Reference Series*. Each new volume on a topic is individually titled and called a "First Edition." Subsequent updates will carry sequential edition numbers. To help avoid confusion and to provide maximum flexibility in our ability to respond to informational needs, the practice of consecutively numbering each volume has been discontinued.

# Part One

# Introduction to Eating Disorders

# Chapter 1

# *Eating Disorders: An Overview*

Eating disorders are complex, chronic illnesses largely misunderstood and misdiagnosed. The most common eating disorders—anorexia nervosa, bulimia nervosa, and binge eating disorder—are on the rise in the United States and worldwide. No one knows exactly what causes eating disorders. However, all socioeconomic, ethnic and cultural groups are at risk.

More than ninety percent of those with eating disorders are women. Further, the number of American women affected by these illnesses has doubled to at least five million in the past three decades.

Eating disorders are one of the key health issues facing young women. Studies in the last decade show that eating disorders and disordered eating behaviors are related to other health risk behaviors, including tobacco use, alcohol use, marijuana use, delinquency, unprotected sexual activity, and suicide attempts. Currently, 1-4% of all young women in the United States are affected by eating disorders.[1] Anorexia nervosa, for example, ranks as the third most common chronic illness among adolescent females in the United States.[2]

Eating disorders have numerous physical, psychological and social ramifications, from significant weight preoccupation, inappropriate eating behavior, and body image distortion. Many people with eating disorders experience depression, anxiety, substance abuse, and childhood sexual abuse, and may be at risk for osteoporosis and heart

U.S. Department of Health And Human Service's Office On Women's Health (DHHS), 2000.

problems. Moreover, death rates are among the highest for any mental illness.

## Types of Eating Disorders

### Anorexia Nervosa

Anorexia nervosa is a dangerous condition in which people can literally starve themselves to death. People with this disorder eat very little even though they are already thin. They have an intense and overpowering fear of body fat and weight gain, repeated dieting attempts, and excessive weight loss. This particular eating disorder affects from 0.5% to 1% of the female adolescent population with an average age of onset between 14 and 18 years.[3] Anorexia is identified in part by refusal to eat, an intense desire to be thin, repeated dieting attempts, and excessive weight loss. To maintain an abnormally low weight, people with anorexia may diet, fast, or over exercise. They often engage in behaviors such as self-induced vomiting or the misuse of laxatives, diuretics, or enemas. People with anorexia believe that they are overweight even when they are extremely thin. Often, the beginning of illness will occur after a stressful life event such as initiation of puberty or moving out of the parents' home.

Those with anorexia are often characterized as perfectionists and overachievers who appear to be in control. In reality, they suffer from low self-esteem and confidence and overly criticize themselves. They are also very concerned about pleasing others.

The most severe and noticeable consequences of anorexia nervosa resemble those of starvation. The body reacts to the lack of food by becoming extremely thin, developing brittle hair and nails, dry skin, lowered pulse rate, cold intolerance, and constipation as well as occasional diarrhea. In addition, mild anemia, reduced muscle mass, loss of menstrual cycle and swelling of joints often accompany anorexia.

Beyond experiencing the immediate effects of anorexia nervosa, individuals suffer long-term consequences throughout the life cycle, regardless of treatment. In addition to the risks of recurrence, malnutrition may cause irregular heart rhythms and heart failure. Lack of calcium places anorexics at increased risk for osteoporosis both during their illness and in later life. A majority of anorexics also have clinical depression while others suffer from anxiety, personality disorders or substance abuse, and many are at risk for suicide. Approximately 1 in 10 women afflicted with anorexia will die of starvation, cardiac arrest, or other medical complication, making its death rate among the highest for a psychiatric disease.[4]

## *Bulimia Nervosa*

Individuals suffering from bulimia nervosa follow a routine of secretive, uncontrolled or binge eating (ingesting an abnormally large amount of food within a set period of time) followed by behaviors to rid the body of food consumed. This includes self-induced vomiting and/or the misuse of laxatives, diet pills, diuretics (water pills), excessive exercise or fasting. Bulimia afflicts approximately 1%-3% of adolescents in the US with the illness usually beginning in late adolescence or early adult life.[3] As with anorexia nervosa, those with bulimia are overly concerned with food, body weight, and shape. Because many individuals with bulimia "binge and purge" in secret and maintain normal or above normal body weight, they can often hide the disorder from others for years. Binges can range from once or twice a week to several times a day and can be triggered by a variety of emotions such as depression, boredom, or anger. The illness may be constant or occasional, with periods of remission alternating with recurrences of binge eating Individuals with bulimia are often characterized as having a hard time dealing with and controlling impulses, stress, and anxieties. Bulimia nervosa can and often does occur independently of anorexia nervosa, although half of all anorexics develop bulimia.

Most medical complications attributed to bulimia nervosa result from electrolyte imbalance and repeated purging behaviors. Loss of potassium due to vomiting, for example, damages heart muscle, increasing the risk for cardiac arrest. Repeated vomiting also causes inflammation of the esophagus and possible erosion of tooth enamel as well as damage to the salivary glands. Some individuals with bulimia struggle with addictions such as drugs and alcohol, and compulsive stealing. Like those with anorexia, many people with bulimia suffer from clinical depression, anxiety, obsessive-compulsive disorder and other psychiatric illnesses.

## *Binge Eating Disorder (BED)*

Binge eating disorder (BED) is the newest clinically recognized eating disorder. BED is primarily identified by repeated episodes of uncontrolled eating. The overeating or bingeing does not typically stop until the person is uncomfortably full. Unlike anorexia nervosa and bulimia nervosa, however, BED is not associated with inappropriate behaviors such as vomiting or excessive exercise to rid the body of extra food. The illness usually begins in late adolescence or in the early 20s, often coming soon after significant weight loss from dieting. Some researchers believe that BED is the most common eating disorder, affecting 15%-50% of participants in weight control programs. In these programs, women are more likely to have BED than males. Current findings suggest that BED affects 0.7%-4% of the general population.[3]

To the lay person, BED can be difficult to distinguish from other causes of obesity. However, the overeating in individuals with BED is often accompanied by feeling out of control and followed by feelings of depression, guilt, or disgust.

People with BED are often overweight because they maintain a high calorie diet without expending a similar amount of energy. Medical problems for this disorder are similar to those found with obesity such as increased cholesterol levels, high blood pressure, and diabetes, as well as increased risk for gallbladder disease, heart disease, and some types of cancer. Researchers have shown that individuals with BED also have high rates of depression.

### Eating Disorder not Otherwise Specified (EDNOS)

The Eating Disorder Not Otherwise Specified (EDNOS) category is for disorders of eating that do not meet the criteria for any specific eating disorder. In EDNOS, individuals engage in some form of abnormal eating but do not exhibit all the specific symptoms required to diagnose an eating disorder. For instance, an individual with EDNOS may meet all the criteria of anorexia nervosa but manage to maintain normal weight while someone else may engage in purging behavior with less frequency or intensity than a diagnosed bulimic.

### Disordered Eating

Far more common and widespread than defined eating disorders are atypical eating disorders, or disordered eating. Disordered eating refers to troublesome eating behaviors, such as restrictive dieting, bingeing, or purging, which occur less frequently or are less severe than those required to meet the full criteria for the diagnosis of an eating disorder. Disordered eating can be changes in eating patterns that occur in relation to a stressful event, an illness, personal appearance, or in preparation for athletic competition. The 1997 Youth Risk Behavior Surveillance Study found that over 4% of students nationwide had

taken laxatives, diet pills o                             se weight or to
keep from gaining weight.[5]                             n lead to weight
loss or weight gain and t                             .ems, it rarely requires in depth professi                   __ __e other hand, disordered
eating may develop ir                   g disorder. If disordered eating becomes sustained, di   .ssing, or begins to interfere with everyday
activities, then it may require professional evaluation.

## Diagnosis

Because of the secretive habits of many individuals with eating disorders, their conditions often go undiagnosed for long periods of time. In the cases of anorexia nervosa, signs such as extreme weight loss are more visible. Bulimics who maintain normal body weight, on the other hand, may be able to hide their condition to the casual observer. Family members and friends might notice some of the following warning signs of an eating disorder.

A person with anorexia may:

- Eat only "safe" foods, usually those low in calories and fat
- Have odd rituals, such as cutting food into small pieces
- Spend more time playing with food than eating it
- Cook meals for others without eating
- Engage in compulsive exercising
- Dress in layers to hide weight loss
- Spend less time with family and friends, become more isolated, withdrawn, and secretive

A person with bulimia may:

- Become very secretive about food, spend a lot of time thinking about and planning the next binge
- Take repeated trips to the bathroom, particularly after eating
- Steal food or hoard it in strange places
- Engage in compulsive exercising

If an individual is displaying any of these characteristics, they should be taken to a physician, nutritionist, or other professional with expertise in diagnosing eating disorders.

## Treatment and Recovery

Eating disorders are most successfully treated when diagnosed early. The longer abnormal eating behaviors persist, the more difficult it is to overcome the disorder and its effects on the body. In some cases, long-term treatment and hospitalization is required. Families and friends offering support and encouragement can play an important role in the success of the treatment program.

Presently, there is no universally accepted standard treatment for anorexia nervosa, bulimia nervosa, or binge eating disorder. Ideally, an integrated approach to treatment would include the skills of nutritionists, mental health professionals, endocrinologists and other physicians. Various types of psychotherapy may be employed, including cognitive-behavioral therapy, interpersonal therapy, and family and group therapy. Self-esteem enhancement and assertiveness training may also be helpful. Antidepressants and other drugs have been part of some therapeutic regimes.

The status of eating disorders as curable diseases has been controversial, since relapse rates for disturbed eating patterns can be very high.

## Etiology

No exact cause of eating disorders has yet been found. However, some characteristics have been shown to have influence in the development of the illnesses.

### Personality Factors

Most people with eating disorders share certain personality traits: low self-esteem, feelings of helplessness, and a fear of becoming fat. In anorexia, bulimia, and binge eating disorder, eating behaviors seem to develop as a way of handling stress.

### Genetic and Environmental Factors

Eating disorders appear to run in families, with female relatives most often affected. However, there is growing evidence that a girl's immediate social environment, including her family and friends, can emphasize the importance of thinness and weight control. For example, regular discussion of weight and dieting may normalize societal pressure to be thin. Weight related teasing by peers and family is related to low body esteem and eating disturbances in young girls.

The National Institute of Mental Health (NIMH) reports that girls who live in families that tend to be strict and place strong emphasis on physical attractiveness and weight control are at an increased risk for inappropriate eating behaviors.[4]

Additionally, people pursuing professions or activities that emphasize thinness—like modeling, dancing, gymnastics, wresting, and long distance running—are more susceptible to the problem.

### Body Image

The idealization of thinness has resulted in distorted body image and unrealistic measures of beauty and success. Cultural and media influences such as TV, magazines, and movies reinforce the belief that women should be more concerned with their appearance than with their own ideas or achievements. Body dissatisfaction, feelings of fatness, and drive for thinness has led many women to become overly concerned about their appearance. Research has shown that many normal weight and even underweight girls are dissatisfied with their body and are choosing inappropriate behaviors to control their appetite and food intake. The American Association of University Women found that adolescent girls believe physical appearance is a major part of their self-esteem and that their body image is a major part of their sense of self.[6]

### Biochemistry

Recent studies have revealed a connection between biological factors associated with clinical depression and the development of anorexia nervosa and bulimia nervosa. Stress hormones such as cortisol are elevated in those with eating disorders, while neurotransmitters such as serotonin may not function correctly. Research continues to better understand this relationship.

## Population Differences

### Gender Differences

Eating disorders are much more prevalent in females than in males. However, recent studies have shown that incidence and prevalence rates are increasing among males. Currently, there is approximately one male case to ten female cases. Further, up to one in four children referred to an eating disorders professional for anorexia is a boy. Many boys with eating disorders share the same characteristics as their female counterparts, including low self-esteem, the need to be accepted, an inability to cope with emotional pressures, and family and relationship. Males with eating disorders are most commonly seen in specific subgroups. For instance, males who wrestle show a disproportionate increase in eating disorders, rates seven to ten times the normal. Additionally, homosexual males have an increased rate of eating disorders.[7]

### Cultural Variation

Eating disorders are often perceived to be an affliction of Caucasian girls and young women in middle and upper socio-economic classes. Nevertheless, increasing numbers of cases are being seen in men and women of all different ethnic and cultural groups.[3]

Girls and women from all ethnic and racial groups may suffer from eating disorders and disordered eating. The specific nature of the most common eating problems, as well as risk and protective factors, may vary from group to group, but no population is exempt. Research findings regarding prevalence rates and specific types of problems among particular groups are limited, but it is evident that disturbed eating behaviors and attitudes occur across all cultures.

### Age

While eating disorders tends to peak between adolescence and early adulthood, the incidence and prevalence has shown an increase in all age groups. For instance, eating disorders are increasing rapidly among pre-pubertal girls. Disordered eating habits and weight concerns are beginning at earlier ages and concerns of body weight and image emerge in girls as young as 9 years of age. A recent study found that 70% of sixth grade girls surveyed report that they first became concerned about their weight between the ages of 9 and 11.[8]

Eating disorders are also becoming more common among elderly women. This is in part due to patients maintaining their illness into old age. Also, elderly women have been shown to initiate weight control practices, such as bingeing and purging.[9]

## Prevention

Increasing interest and concern about eating disorders has been demonstrated in both the public and private sectors but research into prevention has been limited. Although many risk factors for developing

10

eating disorders have been identified, efforts at prevention have so far been disappointing. A few studies have attempted to intervene in high-risk groups with mixed results. Attitudes that lay the groundwork for developing eating disorders occur as early as fourth or fifth grade or younger, making prevention a major challenge. Better success has been accomplished in early detection and treatment of individuals with eating disorders.

## Actions by the Department of Health and Human Services

Consistent with its mission to protect and advance the Nation's health, the Department of Health and Human Services (DHHS) undertakes various activities to advance the understanding and education of eating disorders.

### *Office on Women's Health*

The Office on Women's Health is sponsoring "BodyWise," an educational campaign on eating disorders. The goal of the program is to increase knowledge of eating disorders, including their signs and symptoms, steps to take when concerned about students, and ways to promote healthy eating and reduce preoccupation with body weight and size. An information packet has been developed that includes materials emphasizing the links among healthy eating, positive body image, and favorable learning outcomes.

OWH also sponsors the National Women's Health Information Center, a one-stop gateway to Federal and private sector information resources on a variety of women's health topics including eating disorders, nutrition, and body image. OWH also a supports the Girl Power! campaign which provides positive messages, accurate health information, and support for girls ages 9 to 14 years. BodyWise information packets can be accessed on the National Women's Health Information Center (http://www.4woman.gov) as well as the Girl Power! Website (http://www.girlpower.gov).

### *National Institutes of Mental Health*

The National Institute of Mental Health (NIMH) conducts and supports research on mental illness and mental health, seeking to improve basic, clinical and service delivery knowledge concerning any aspect of behavioral and mental disorders. The NIMH is also concerned with the speedy dissemination and implementation of this knowledge in practice and service delivery systems. As part of this effort, scientists funded by NIMH are actively studying ways to better treat and understand eating disorders.

### *Food and Drug Administration*

The Food and Drug Administration (FDA) provides information for women and adolescents on diet and nutrition. Information can be downloaded from: http://www.fda.gov/womens/informat.html

FDA Consumer magazine also periodically runs articles with important health information for teenagers, ranging from eating disorders and nutrition to sun safety and attention deficit disorder. These "Teen Scene" articles are available electronically at http://www.fda.gov/opacom/7teens.html and some are available as reprints. To order single copies, call toll-free 1-888-INFO-FDA (1-888-463-6332).

### *National Institute of Diabetes and Diseases of the Kidney Weight—Control Information Network*

The National Institute of Diabetes and Diseases of the Kidney (NIDDK) provides consumers and health professionals with information on nutrition and obesity. Fact sheets can be found at: http://www.niddk.nih.gov/health/health.htm

NIDDK also sponsors the Weight-control Information Network (WIN). WIN was established in 1994 to provide health professionals and consumers with science-based information on obesity, weight control, and nutrition. WIN has also developed the "Sisters Together: Move More, Eat Less" program that encourages black women to achieve a healthy weight by making changes in their lifestyle.

## *Endnotes*

1. Yager J, Andersen A, Devin M, Mitchell J, Powers P, Yates A. American Psychiatric Association practice guidelines for eating disorders. *Am J Psychiatry* 1993;150:207-28

2. Fisher M, Golden NH, Katzman DK, et al. Eating disorders in adolescents: A background paper. *J Adolesc Health* 1995;16: 420-437.

3. American Psychiatric Association: *Diagnostic and Statistical Manual of Mental Disorders, Fourth Edition*. Washington, DC, American Psychiatric Association, 1994.

4. National Institute Of Mental Health, National Institutes of Health. *"Eating Disorders,"* 1994.

5. Kann L, Kinchen SA, Williams BI, et al. *Youth Risk Behavior Surveillance – United States, 1997.* Centers for Disease Control and Prevention. August 14, 1998 / 47(SS-3);1-89.

6. American Association of University Women Education Foundation (1991): *Shortchanging Girls, Shortchanging America.* Washington, DC, American Association of University Women Educational Foundation Press, 1991.

7. Andersen AE. Eating disorders in males. In Brownell KD, Fairburn CG (eds.): *Eating Disorders and Obesity; A Comprehensive Handbook.* Guilford Press, New York, 1995.

8. Shisslak CM, Crago M, McKnight KM, Estes LS, Gray N, Parnaby OG. Potential risk factors associated with weight control behaviors in elementary and middle school girls. *J Psychosomatic Research 1998*;44:301-313.

9. Hsu LK, Zimmer B. Eating disorders in old age. *Intl J of Eating Disorders* 1988;7:1:133-138.

# Chapter 2

# *Frequently Asked Questions about Eating Disorders*

This chapter contains a list of miscellaneous questions about different aspects of eating disorders and related topics.

## How long have eating disorders been around? What is their history?

There are descriptions of disorders very like what we now call anorexia nervosa and bulimia nervosa in ancient Egyptian hieroglyphics and Persian manuscripts. Scrolls originating in early Chinese dynasties also mention behaviors similar to the starving and stuffing of today's eating disorders. Ancient Romans overindulged at lavish banquets and then relieved themselves in a vomitorium (lavatory chamber that accommodated vomiting) so they could return to the feast and continue eating.

African tribal lore contains stories of individuals who refused to eat during times of famine so their children might have extra food. They were much admired by peers who could not exercise the same rigid self-denial. When the famine passed, a few of the voluntary restrictors continued to refuse to eat and were in danger of dying. Some were healed by shamans who induced trance states similar to what we now know as hypnotherapy.

In Europe, the first formal description of anorexia nervosa in medical literature was made by Richard Morton in London in 1689. He is credited with first describing an anorexic patient as "a skeleton clad only with skin." Two other physicians, Lasegue in 1873 in France and Gull in 1874 in England, wrote the first two articles about anorexia nervosa in modern medical literature.

At first anorexia nervosa was thought to be a form of tuberculosis or a manifestation of some other physical disease or disorder, perhaps related to hormone imbalance or endocrine deficiency. It was not until the 1930s that researchers began to believe that the causes of self-starvation were psychological and emotional. Today clinicians believe that eating disorders represent the final outcome when emotional distress interacts with physiological imbalance (including the imbalances caused by dieting) in a vulnerable individual. Effective treatment, of course, will address both physical and psychological factors.

## What's the most effective treatment for someone with an eating disorder who is also abusing alcohol and other drugs?

In most cases, effective treatment means tackling the substance abuse first. When people are clean and sober, they don't use substances. Period. That same kind of abstinence is not possible with food, so in some ways recovery from substance abuse is easier than recovery from an eating disorder where the person must face the trigger substance (food) three or four times a day.

After nine to twelve months of sobriety, most people have become stable enough to move on to treatment of the eating disorder. If they are truly committed to sobriety, they won't switch coping behaviors back to alcohol and other drugs when the going gets rough. If, however, they begin by working on the eating disorder, without a commitment to sobriety, they almost always escalate substance abuse as they decrease the disordered eating behaviors.

Of course if the person is in medical danger because of the eating disorder, some intervention should be made early on to preserve life. A physician and treatment team must make this judgment call. Many substance abuse treatment centers have an eating disorders track for their dual-diagnosis patients.

## Why about eating disorder support groups?

For someone who has recently begun to starve or stuff, especially someone young in years, we recommend formal treatment to quickly break disordered eating patterns and restore physical and psychological health. If people find friends and acceptance in a support group, they may begin to define their identity as "eating disordered" so they can continue to belong and participate. That makes recovery much harder.

On the other hand, not everyone will get into treatment, and of those who do, not everyone will make progress and recover in a timely manner. For these more chronic sufferers, a support group can provide valuable encouragement and a safe place to problem solve and talk about challenges. Informal groups led by parents or people who themselves are still recovering from an eating disorder, are a concern. Experience shows, the most effective groups are led or supervised by a professional mental health therapist as part of an integrated treatment program. Without the involvement of an experienced professional, groups tend to deteriorate into subtle competitions to see who can be the thinnest and who can produce the most alarming story. Without supervision, the group's focus tends to shift from developing more effective behaviors to caretaking and noncritical acceptance of even the most irresponsible choices and decisions.

Also, if a lay leader is not confirmed in his or her own recovery, there will be temptation to relapse when group dynamics become intense and the focus remains on food and weight behaviors instead of on problem solving.

For these reasons, cautious avocation of support groups is wise. While many people have found much help in well-run groups, in too many cases unsupervised support groups have led to problems and even crises when no experienced professional was present to defuse problems before they escalated.

## I'm anorexic, not bulimic. Why are my teeth decaying at the gumline?

People who have anorexia often have saliva deficient in the buffers that protect teeth from the effects of acid manufactured by bacteria in the mouth. There is also significant acid in many of the low-cal foods and soft drinks that anorexics favor.

Normal saliva contains buffers that protect teeth from acid. The body makes those buffers in part from materials found in fatty foods. If you don't eat enough dietary fat, your body can't protect your teeth adequately. Tell your dentist what's going on. There are steps you can take to prevent or minimize further damage.

## *How do I figure out my ideal weight?*

Your "right" body weight is that weight at which you are strong, energetic, and healthy. Everybody's body is different. Don't rely on charts, tables, or complex formulas involving body measurements to determine what's right for you. Instead, eat a balanced, moderate, and varied diet that includes lots of fruits, vegetables, and whole grains. Low-fat or non-fat dairy products contribute to healthy bones. Go easy on high-fat and high-sugar foods, but allow yourself to enjoy moderate amounts to satisfy your body's need for the nutrients they provide and so you don't feel deprived and vulnerable to bingeing.

Regular, moderate exercise helps stabilize weight, and it also gives you a whole host of long- and short-term health benefits.

You are at your ideal weight when you have enough strength and energy to lead a healthy, normal life. You know you are on the right track when your blood pressure, cholesterol, and blood sugar levels are normal, and when you have no back or joint pain because of undernutrition (loss of minerals from bones) or extra weight.

## *How do the media encourage or combat eating disorders?*

Most people in westernized countries are flooded by media words and images. We watch hours of TV every day. We read magazines and go to movies. We notice, perhaps without even noticing that we notice, that happy, successful people are almost always portrayed by actors and models who are young, toned, and thin. The vast majority are stylishly dressed and have spent much time on hair styles and makeup.

In contrast, evil, stupid, or buffoonish people are portrayed by actors who are older, frumpier, unkempt, perhaps physically challenged, and/or fatter.

Most people want to be happy and successful. These states require hard work and lots of discipline. The media, especially ads and commercials, suggest that we can shortcut by making our bodies into mirror images of the icons of success. Think about a commercial for some personal product. If you read between the lines, it probably tells you that you are not acceptable the way you are. The only way you can become acceptable is to buy the product, but you know from past experience that you will never look like the model who is six feet tall and wears size four jeans (and is probably anorexic), so you are left feeling inadequate no matter what you do.

The differences between media images of happy, successful men and women are interesting. The women, with few exceptions, are young and thin. Thin is desirable. The men are young or older, but the heroes and good guys are strong and powerful, physically, in the business world, and socially. For men in the media, thin is not desirable. Thin men are seen as skinny, and skinny men are often depicted as sick, weak, frail, or deviant.

These differences are reflected in male and female approaches to self-help. When a man wants to improve himself, he often begins to lift weights to become bigger, stronger, and more powerful. When a woman wants to improve herself, she usually begins with a diet, which if continued will leave her smaller and weaker.

Many people believe this media stereotyping helps explain why 90-95% of people with eating disorders are women and only 5-10% are men.

In recent years it has become politically correct for the media to put forth some effort to combat eating disorders. We have seen magazine articles and TV shows featuring the perils and heartbreak of anorexia and bulimia, but these efforts seem weak and ineffective when they are presented in the usual context. For example, how can one believe that a fashion magazine is truly motivated to combat anorexia when their articles about that subject are surrounded by advertisements featuring anorexic-looking models? How can one believe that the talk show hostess is truly in favor of strong, healthy female bodies when she frequently prods her stick-like thighs and talks about how much she wants to lose weight from her already scrawny body?

In May 1999 new research that emphasizes the media's unhealthy affect on women's self-esteem and body awareness was found. Four years ago, before television came to their island, the people of Fiji thought the ideal body was round, plump, and soft. Then, after 38 months of Melrose Place, Beverly Hills 90210, and similar western shows, Fijian teenage girls showed serious signs of eating disorders.

Those who regularly watch TV three or more nights per week are fifty percent more likely than non-watchers to feel "too big" or "too fat." About two-thirds of the TV-watching female teens dieted in the month preceding the survey. Fifteen percent admitted vomiting to control their weight.

TV shows like the two mentioned are fantasies, but all over the world young women, and some not so young, accept them as instructions on how to look and act. That's really a shame.

One last thought: When you look at a magazine, movie, or TV show, ask yourself if the images are giving you a window on the real world, or are they holding up to you a fun house mirror in which the reflections of real people are distorted into impossibly tall, thin sticks (or impossibly muscular, steroid-dependent action figures if you are male) that are supposed to represent ideal images. Be a wise consumer of visual images.

### I read in a book that bingeing can permanently distend one's stomach. Is this true?

For some people, bingeing does indeed stretch and distend the abdomen, making it look poochy. Eating a large meal and then falling asleep, when all the muscles relax, can have the same effect. Some folks tighten up when they stop bingeing, others do not in spite of crunches and other exercises.

### I am trying to eat, but when I do, I feel bloated for hours. It's not body image distortion, but a real, physical feeling of being too full. Help!

One of the common consequences of an eating disorder is slowed gastric motility. That means that food stays in your stomach and intestines longer than it did before you began to diet. Your GI tract does not pass digesting food along as rapidly as it did before. Of course you then feel stuffed.

If you persist in eating normal amounts of normal foods, your body should gradually return to normal. In the beginning it may help to limit really greasy foods and other items that are harder to digest. As you progress in recovery, you can add back reasonable portions of these foods so your body can learn to handle them once again. In addition, small frequent meals may be easier for your body to handle than three large ones.

In cases like this, it's always a good idea to check with a physician to rule out the possibility of a medical problem. Serious problems are rare, but they do happen. If loss of gastric motility is causing undue distress, your doctor can prescribe medications for temporary use that will speed up the digestive process. These meds, however, should not be used indefinitely. The goal is to achieve normal digestion without artificial aids.

### Are there different degrees of eating disorders?

Yes. Because of unrealistic cultural demands for thinness, probably most of us are more concerned about body shape and size than a totally healthy person would be. It's a long way, however, from an occasional, brief diet and fleeting dissatisfaction about body shape and size to the rigid preoccupations and ever-present obsessions about food and weight manifested by people who have clinical eating disorders.

There are also differences in mental, physical, and emotional impairment between someone who has just begun an eating disorder and someone else who has starved or stuffed for many years. Likewise, there are differences between people whose symptoms are less severe and those who are in crisis.

The problem with all of this is that, without treatment, eating disorders tend to get worse, not better. It is not unusual for someone to begin an eating disorder with seemingly minor behaviors that quickly progress to threaten life and future happiness. If you are concerned about yourself or your minor child, arrange for medical and psychological evaluations right away. If you are concerned about a friend, urge her/him to seek professional advice before the problem becomes intractable.

## I used to have an eating disorder, and now I want to help other people. What can I do?

First you must decide if you want to make helping people a career or a volunteer activity. If you want a career, prepare yourself by getting at least a masters degree in psychology, counseling, psychiatric nursing, or clinical social work. If you want more training, you could become a psychiatrist or a clinical psychologist. The people in your campus academic counseling center can help you arrange the classes you need for these options. Be aware that you will need to meet licensing requirements in most states in the U.S.

If you want to do volunteer work, we recommend you get involved with EDAP, Eating Disorders Awareness and Prevention. They have several programs across the United States. Visit their Web site for details on how you can combat eating disorders in your own community.

Wanting to help others is admirable, but make sure your recovery is solid before you begin. Focusing on disordered eating behaviors and the painful underlying issues may undermine your own progress unless your are comfortable with your body, enjoying a wide variety of normal foods, and aware of and on top of the issues that brought you to starving or stuffing in the first place. You must decide if it would be wisest for you to move on or if you are indeed strong enough to help others.

## *How can I manage my life so I don't relapse. What are some ways to handle daily occurrences and stresses, emotional and otherwise, that previously triggered my behaviors?*

You are wise to plan ahead because most people who eventually make full recoveries have at least one slip or relapse.

Remember that a slip doesn't have to lead to a full-blown relapse, and a relapse doesn't have to lead to total collapse. Make plans now, while your life is relatively calm, so when the inevitable stresses and problems come, with all their chaotic feelings, you will have well-thought-out ways to deal with them.

Often recovery is sabotaged by a "just this once" or "just a little bit won't hurt" kind of thinking. Just this once I'll binge and vomit. Losing just five pounds won't hurt. Unfortunately incidents like these often prove to be slippery slopes leading right back into the eating disorder. If you do slip, don't do the behavior again. Just because you ate ten Oreos doesn't mean you have to finish the package. Just because you finished the package doesn't mean you have to vomit (really, it doesn't). Just because you binged and purged yesterday, doesn't mean you have to do it again today. Consider the incident a learning experience. What was going on in your life that stressed you so that you resorted to your old familiar coping device? Then deal with the stressor directly instead of trying to defuse it by starving or stuffing. Stressors tend to fall into one of the following categories.

### *Physical Stresses*

Did you let yourself get too hungry so that you were vulnerable to a binge? Hunger is the strongest binge trigger there is. Did you not allow yourself enough sleep? Have you been getting too much, or not enough, exercise? Have you been using too much alcohol or other drugs? Some intoxicants lead to overeating and others contribute to lack of appetite.

### *Relationship Stresses*

Are you lonely? Some people eat to comfort themselves if they have no close friends or intimates. Are you in an unsatisfying relationship? Are you experiencing interpersonal conflict? Some folks starve or stuff in an ineffective effort to deal with loneliness, anger, sadness, and frustration.

## *Power and Control Issues*

Do you feel in charge of your life, or does it seem that other people and circumstances are conspiring to manipulate you and make you do what they want you to do? Do you feel like you are an effective person who can make things happen, or does it seem that you are a pawn, dancing not to your own tune but to someone else's? Some people lose weight because it is the only thing they know how to do that gives them a feeling of effectiveness and competency. Weight loss is something they do better than most people, and they glory in it.

## *Freedom and Independence Issues*

Do you feel free to make your own choices and move through the world as you see fit? Are you free to build a life that is satisfying to you, that meets your needs, without interference or overwhelming demands from others? Some folks binge eat or refuse to eat out of defiance and rebellion. Those behaviors may be the only ways they have to express their need for independence and freedom from the constraints of others.

## *Problems with Relaxation and Fun*

Do you laugh? A lot? Everyday? Do you do things—hobbies, avocations, cultural pursuits, and so forth—that give you opportunities to relax and enjoy yourself? Some people have so tightly structured their time that they have to place in the day to let their hair down and play. Bingeing on junk food may become a self-indulgent substitute for play and fun. Starving and watching the numbers on the scale fall may take the place of more healthy games. Focusing on food may provide a way out of boredom that is not relieved in better ways.

Answers to these questions are self-evident. Some additional thoughts about preventing lapses and relapses include:

- Find something, or some things, that you truly enjoy doing. When you feel tempted to fall back into old behaviors, do the healthier, enjoyable thing instead.

- Stay away from temptation. If ice cream is a major binge trigger, don't even keep it in the house until you are stronger.

- Don't deprive yourself either. If ice cream is part of your normal, healthy meal planning (and it can be), go to the soda shop and have a single scoop cone. Don't deprive yourself of anything healthy. Deprivation, especially hunger, is the most powerful binge trigger we know of.

- Wait out the urge. Postpone a binge for thirty minutes. Start the diet tomorrow. In the meantime, figure out what stressor is triggering the urge, and come up with better ways of dealing with it.

- Cultivate friendships. Always have available someone you can trust with your doubts, fears, hopes, dreams, and other feelings. Call these resource people when you feel lonely or upset. Talking with someone who understands and cares about you is much more satisfying that eating or not eating.

- Find something to do that you enjoy and learn to do it well. Give yourself permission to take pride in your work and achievements.

This information is not a substitute for medical treatment or psychological care. For help with the physical and emotional problems associated with eating and exercise disorders, talk to your physician and a competent mental health professional.

# Chapter 3

# *Eating Disorders— Still a Threat*

Anorexia nervosa, bulimia, and binge eating disorder—as much cultural diseases as they are medical conditions—continue to take their largest toll on young women. You'll need sharp assessment and management skills to help these patients survive.

In case you have any doubts about America's obsession with being thin, consider the statistics:[1]

- Most of today's fashion models weigh at least 15% less than the average woman of the same age and height.

- Many look thin enough to be considered anorectic. Super model Kate Moss, for instance, looks so thin that people have been scribbling "Feed this woman" on board photos of her.[2]

- Overweight women are 20% less likely to get married than thinner women—and they earn about $6,700 less.[1]

With such messages, it's little wonder that so many patients are at risk for eating disorders. Although you can't change the cultural atmosphere, understanding the nature of these disorders will allow you to help patients overcome them.

---

© 1996 Medical Economics, Montvale, NJ, from *RN*, June 1996, Vol. 9, No. 6, Pg. 30(4); reprinted with permission.

## *Defining the Problem, Recognizing It's Symptoms*

The three eating disorders you are most likely to see are anorexia nervosa, bulimia, and binge eating disorder.

Anorexia nervosa is a misnomer because patients usually don't lose their appetite, they just refuse to eat. That refusal often results in weight loss that's severe enough to warrant hospitalization.

Although anorexia has received a great deal of publicity, it may not be the epidemic that some reports suggest. Several surveys focusing on the years after 1980 have found that as many as 11% of girls between the ages of 10 and 19 have the disorder.[3] But experts point out that when strict criteria are used to diagnose the condition, the percentage drops to 1% or less.[4] Still, that's a significant increase over the number of cases that occurred between the 1950s and 1970s.

According to the *Diagnostic and Statistical Manual of Mental Disorders (DSM-IV)*, four traits mark the anorectic patient:

- She refuses to eat enough to maintain her weight. Typically she weighs less than 85% of what's normal for her age and height. To remain slender, she may exercise obsessively. Many anorectics avoid family meals or dramatically change their diet. They may eliminate all meats or high-calorie foods, for instance. Or they'll handle food in a very ritualistic way, cutting part of the meal into smaller portions and spreading it around the plate.

- She has an abnormal fear of gaining weight.

- She has a distorted physical self-image. Instead of seeing an emaciated body when she looks in the mirror, she may see herself as obese. Or she may perceive certain parts of her body as fat. Some patients acknowledge that they're not actually fat but still feel as though they are. And their sense of self-worth depends on their ability to avoid food.

- She has not menstruated in the last three months. More often than not, menstruation stops because malnutrition has caused estrogen levels to drop too low.

Bulimia nervosa is sometimes called the binge/purge disorder. Patients consume huge amounts and then try to rid themselves of the calories by inducing vomiting, taking laxatives or diuretics, exercising excessively, or using a combination of these various methods.

As with anorexia nervosa, some studies have suggested a bulimia epidemic, with nearly one in five young women reporting they have the condition.[5] Using well-defined diagnostic criteria, however, experts estimate that no more than 3% of teenage and young adult women suffer from the disorder.[4]

In trying to distinguish bulimic patients from those who simply eat too much, again keep in mind the *DSM-IV* diagnostic criteria. A patient with full-blown bulimia consumes very large amounts—as much as 20,000 calories—in a short period of time, usually within two hours. She must be eating this way at least twice a week for three months or more. Most patients overindulge in sweets.

Another signpost for bulimia is secretive eating. Because patients are embarrassed by their problem, they try to hide it from friends and relatives—and will probably try to hide it from you as well.

Bulimics report feeling out of control when they embark on an eating orgy. Typically stress triggers the episode: The patient may have had a fight with her mother, or been reprimanded by her boss. Or, she may have fasted for 24 hours or more, then started binging when she became ravenous. As with anorexia nervosa, a bulimic's self-image is closely linked to her weight and shape.

Among the physical signs to look for are eroded dental enamel and abrasions on the backs of the hands. The damaged teeth result from the constant regurgitation of stomach acid. The hand injuries develop when the patient sticks her fingers down her throat to induce vomiting. Some patients use ipecac for this purpose, though, so hand abrasions aren't always present.

Binge eating disorder—a newly defined condition just added to the *DSM-IV* on a provisional basis—is similar to bulimia. Patients consume huge amounts, claiming they can't stop eating once they begin. But unlike bulimia, patients don't compensate for the excess intake by purging.

Using strict diagnostic standards, as many as 4% of Americans suffer from binge eating disorder. Among women in weight-control programs, the prevalence may be as high as 50%.[4]

While statistics for these three disorders—1%, 3%, and 4%—are relatively low, the figures can be misleading. They don't take into account the many patients with subclinical eating disorders. These young women—and occasionally young men—may not have all the signs and symptoms needed to meet the *DSM* criteria, but they often have enough of them to make their lives miserable.

Although there's no foolproof way to detect eating disorders in their early, less threatening stages, you may be able to get some hint of what's going on. Researchers at Boston University Medical Center, for instance, have found that patients who answer No to "Do you eat in secret?" and Yes to "Are you satisfied with your eating patterns?" probably don't have bulimia.[6] While the opposite responses don't prove that someone has the disorder, they do warrant a more in-depth evaluation.

## What's at the Root of Eating Disorders?

While the exact causes of anorexia nervosa, bulimia, and binge eating disorder remain elusive, investigators suspect a combination of social, interpersonal, and biochemical factors.

At least one researcher maintains that Americans' prejudice against fat has fostered attitudes that make it hard for people even slightly above average in weight to feel good about themselves. To wit: To be thin is to be beautiful, in control, fit, and content. To be overweight is to be ugly, helpless, lazy, and unhappy.[7]

Certain personality traits or psychiatric conditions, combined with societal influences, can escalate the risk of developing an eating disorder. Many clinicians report, for instance, that patients with eating disorders are often perfectionists, people pleasers, or have very poor self-esteem.

One theorist believes that low self-esteem is a prerequisite for eating disorders.[8] Thus, someone who thinks poorly of herself may notice that thin people are often admired and conclude that if she loses weight, she'll be appreciated more and feel better about herself.

That may in fact happen. But some people lose weight and still feel emotionally empty, prompting them to resort to long-term fasts or vomiting in an attempt to lose even more weight.

Fear of sexual maturity and intimacy is another underlying issue. Some anorectics believe that staying small and emaciated will help keep them childlike. And many patients with binge eating disorder want to remain obese, say the experts, because they realize excess body fat will turn the boys off. But more than psychological factors may be at play. Eating disorder patients may have a physiological defect that makes it difficult to interpret the sensations of hunger and fullness.[9] Those who can't recognize hunger may eat so little that they become anorectic. Similarly, the inability to sense satiety may encourage eating huge amounts at one sitting.

In fact, scientists recently discovered an obesity gene that generates a hormone that in turn produces an appropriate sense of fullness. Compulsive eaters may have a mutation in this gene.[10]

## *Complications and Treatment Options*

Although the causes of eating disorders still aren't fully understood, the effects are painfully clear—except, all too often, to the patients themselves.

Teach anorectic patients about the dangers of malnutrition. Point out, for example, that not getting enough protein and calories can lower their resistance to infection and cause constipation, hallucinations, and liver damage. Since they're concerned about body image, mention the possibility of dry, lifeless skin and hair, or even increased body hair, which is referred to as lanugo.

Warn them, too, that not getting enough potassium, chloride, sodium, and magnesium can threaten an anorectic's life, causing cardiac arrhythmias, severe muscle spasms, and sudden death.[11]

Bulimics face a similar threat from electrolyte imbalances, due in large part to laxative and diuretic abuse and self-induced vomiting. Both bulimics and patients with binge eating disorder run the risk of gastric rupture, the result of consuming huge amounts of food at one sitting. More than 80% of patients who have a rupture don't survive.[11]

Self-induced vomiting can also cause enamel erosion, cavities, gum abscesses, mouth ulcers, and loose fillings. While it's important to make patients aware of the dangers, never overemphasize the negative. These patients have a great deal of emotional work ahead of them. While most of that work usually has to be supervised by a mental health professional, you can still offer some guidance.

Cognitive therapy is one of the more effective forms of treatment for patients with bulimia and binge eating disorder. While it may not be very useful for anorectic patients during acute hospitalization it will likely help recovering anorectics.[9]

Explain to your patient that during cognitive therapy, she will learn to identify some of the irrational thoughts and beliefs that have been contributing to her disorder. The therapist will then offer rational alternatives, a process called retraining. Many psychotherapists also stress the importance of family therapy. Helping parents come to grips with any guilt they may have, for instance, can improve the patient's environment. That in turn may improve her eating behavior.

Assuming you can convince the patient of the need for treatment— no easy task—your responsibility does not end with her referral to a psychiatrist, nutritionist, or specialist. She still needs your support.

With that in mind, try to establish a written contract that lays down some ground rules. You want to get an anorectic to agree to reach and maintain a minimum acceptable weight—no less than 70% of her ideal weight for her height—or be re-hospitalized if she doesn't.[12]

An anorectic patient should gain no more than about 2 pounds a week. Gaining more weight outside a hospital setting poses the risk of edema and congestive heart failure. While encouraging weight gain, assure patients that the regimen will not make them overweight.

If the patient was referred to a psychotherapist, get her to agree in writing to see that specialist. Then provide a copy of the contract to the therapist.

A patient's weight, vital signs, and electrolytes should be monitored weekly for changes. All patients should agree in writing to be hospitalized if their electrolyte readings drop dangerously low.

Finally, eating disorder patients should take a multivitamin/mineral supplement and at least 1,000 mg of calcium a day, unless it's contraindicated by some preexisting medical condition.

## Does Medication Have a Role?

To date, researchers have not been able to find any medication that clearly benefits patients with anorexia nervosa. However, many bulimics respond well to tricyclic antidepressants such as imipramine (Janimine, Tipramine, Tofranil) and desipramine (Norpramin).[9]

Fluoxetine (Prozac), a member of a relatively new family of antidepressants called serotonin re-uptake inhibitors, has also been found helpful. In fact, an FDA advisory board recently recommended adding bulimia to the list of indications for which fluoxetine is approved.[13] Studies also suggest that fluoxetine and desipramine may benefit patients who have binge eating disorder.[14]

At least one antidepressant—bupropion (Wellbutrin)—is contraindicated for eating disorder patients because it may precipitate seizures.

If the patient is started on an antidepressant, monitor for adverse effects and teach the patient how to use the drug properly. Above all, emphasize the need for patience. These drugs usually take between two and four weeks to have a therapeutic effect. And, with the benefits often come side effects. Tricyclics frequently cause dry mouth, blurred vision, constipation, and urinary hesitancy. The drugs should also be used cautiously in patients with urinary retention and narrow-angle glaucoma. Other possible adverse effects to look for include sinus tachycardia, arrhythmias, restlessness, tremor, and sedation.

Instruct patients on tricyclics to take them with food or right after eating to reduce gastric irritation. If drowsiness becomes a problem, suggest they take a single dose at bedtime, with the physician's approval.

Among the more common side effects of fluoxetine are nausea, headache, nervousness, anxiety, diarrhea, and insomnia. To minimize the risk of insomnia, instruct a patient taking a single dose to take it in the morning. If she is taking divided doses, the second one should be taken at noon.[16]

While medication and psychotherapy have their place, don't underestimate the value of peer support. Organizations that can provide you with information on eating disorders and support groups are listed in the end section of this book.

Although there may not be an epidemic of eating disorders in this country, a number of your patients probably suffer from these disorders. Identifying patients and guiding them into treatment can end years of misery and make the dining room table a pleasant place to be again.

## References

1. Staff. (1994). Special report: You've come a long way, baby, or have you? *Tufts University Diet & Nutrition Letter*, 11(12), 6.

2. Elliott, S. (1994, April 26). Ultrathin models in Coca Cola and Calvin Klein campaigns draw fire and boycott call. *N.Y. Times*, p. D18.

3. Lucas, A. R. (1992). The eating disorders "epidemic": More apparent than real? *Pediatric Annals*, 21(11), 746.

4. American Psychiatric Association. (1994). *Diagnostic and statistical manual of mental disorders (4th ed.)*. Washington, DC: Author.

5. Kaplan, H. I., & Sadock, B. J. (1992). *Comprehensive Textbook of Psychiatry* (Vol. 2), (5th ed.). Baltimore: Williams & Wilkins.

6. Freund, K., Graham, S., et al. (1993). Detection of bulimia in a primary care setting. *J. Gen. Intern. Med.* 8(5), 236.

7. Fontaine, K. L. (1991). The conspiracy of culture: Women's issues in body size. *Nurs. Clin. North. Am.*, 26(3), 669.

8. Silverstone, P. H. (1992). Is chronic low self-esteem the cause of eating disorders? *Med. Hypotheses*, 39, 311.

9. American Psychiatric Association. (1993). Practice guidelines for eating disorders. *Am. J. Psychiatry*, 150(2), 212.

10. Rink, T. J. (1994). In search of a satiety factor. *Nature*, 372(6505), 406.

11. Hall, R. C., & Beresford, T. (1990). Medical complications of anorexia and bulimia. In R. C. Hall (Ed.), *Clinical diagnosis and management of eating disorders* (pp. 165-203). Longwood, FL: Ryandic Publishing, Inc.

12. Halmi, K., Mitchell, J., et al. (1993). Anorexia and bulimia: You can help. *Patient Care*, 27(6), 24.

13. Eli Lilly and Company. (April 26, 1994). FDA Advisory Committee unanimously supports the use of Prozac for bulimia.

14. Marcus, M.D. (1993). Binge eating in obesity. In C. Fairburn & G. Wilson (Eds.), *Binge eating: Nature, assessment, and treatment* (pp. 77-96). New York: Guilford Press.

15. *Physicians' Desk Reference*. (1994). Montvale, NJ: Medical Economics.

16. Wilson, B. A., Shannon, M. T., et al. (1995). *Nurses Drug Guide*. Norwalk, CT: Appleton and Lange.

*—by Arla Amara and Paul L. Cerrato*

# Chapter 4

# *The Statistics of Eating Disorders*

## *How many people have eating and exercise disorders?*

### *Anorexia, Bulimia, Obesity, and Binge Eating Disorder*

Research suggests that about one percent (1%) of female adolescents have anorexia. That means that about one out of every one hundred young women between ten and twenty are starving themselves, sometimes to death.

Research also suggests that about four percent (4%), or four out of one hundred, college-aged women have bulimia. About 50% of people who have been anorexic develop bulimia or bulimic patterns.

Only about five to ten percent (5-10%) of people with anorexia and bulimia are male. This gender difference may reflect our society's opposite expectations for men and women. Men are supposed to be strong and powerful. They feel ashamed of skinny bodies. Women, on the other hand, are supposed to be tiny, waif-like, and thin. They diet to lose weight, and if they lose control of the resulting hunger, or develop rigid and compulsive overcontrol, they can become anorexic, bulimic, or both.

Anorexia and bulimia affect primarily people in their teens and twenties, but clinicians report both disorders in children as young as six and individuals as old as seventy-six.

---

© 1998 ANRED, Anorexia Nervosa and Related Disorders, Inc.; reprinted with permission.

New studies suggest that over half of adult Americans, both male and female, are overweight. About one third (34%) are obese, meaning that they are 20% or more above normal, healthy weight. Many of these people have binge eating disorder.

A recent study reported in *Drugs and Therapy Perspectives* reports that about one percent of women in the United States have binge eating disorder, as to thirty percent of women who seek treatment to lose weight.

### What about compulsive exercising?

Because anorexia athletica is not a formal diagnosis, it has not been studied as rigorously as the eating disorders. We have no idea how many people exercise compulsively.

### Body Dysmorphic Disorder

Not yet an official diagnosis, but may achieve that status soon. BDD affects about two percent of people in the U.S. and strikes males and females equally, usually before age eighteen (70% of the time). Sufferers are excessively concerned about appearance, body shape, body size, weight, perceived lack of muscles, facial blemishes, and so forth. In some cases BDD can lead to steroid abuse, unnecessary plastic surgery, and even suicide. BDD is treatable and begins with an evaluation by a mental health care provider.

### Subclinical Eating Disorders

We can only guess at the vast numbers of people who have subclinical or threshold eating disorders. They are too much preoccupied with food and weight. Their eating and weight control behaviors are not normal, but they are not disturbed enough to qualify for a formal diagnosis.

## Mortality and Recovery Rates

Without treatment, up to twenty percent (20%) of people with serious eating disorders die. With treatment, that number falls to two to three percent (2-3%).

With treatment, about sixty percent (60%) of people with eating disorders recover. They maintain healthy weight. They eat a varied diet of normal foods and do not choose exclusively low-cal and non-fat items. They participate in friendships and romantic relationships.

They create families and careers. Many say they feel they are stronger people and more insightful about life in general and themselves in particular than they would have been without the disorder.

In spite of treatment, about twenty percent (20%) of people with eating disorders make only partial recoveries. They remain too much focused on food and weight. They participate only peripherally in friendships and romantic relationships. They may hold jobs but seldom have meaningful careers. Much of each paycheck goes to diet books, laxatives, jazzercise classes, and binge food.

The remaining twenty percent (20%) do not improve, even with treatment. They are seen repeatedly in emergency rooms, eating disorders programs, and mental health clinics. Their quietly desperate lives revolve around food and weight concerns, spiraling down into depression, loneliness, and feelings of helplessness and hopelessness.

Please note: The study of eating disorders is a relatively new field. We have no good information on the long-term recovery process. We do know that recovery usually takes a long time, perhaps on average five years of slow progress that includes starts, stops, slides backwards, and ultimately movement in the direction of mental and physical health.

If you believe you are in the forty percent of people who do not recover from eating disorders, give yourself a break. Get into treatment and stay there. Give it all you have. You may surprise yourself and find you are in the sixty percent after all.

## Miscellaneous Statistics

### From England

A 1998 survey done by Exeter University included 37,500 young women between twelve and fifteen. Over half (57.5%) listed appearance as the biggest concern in their lives. The same study indicated that 59% of the twelve and thirteen-year-old girls who suffered from low self-esteem were also dieting.

### Dieting Teens

More than half of teenaged girls are, or think they should be, on diets. They want to lose all or some of the forty pounds that females naturally gain between 8 and 14. About three percent of these teens go too far, becoming anorexic or bulimic.

## Determining Accurate Statistics Is Difficult

Because physicians are not required to report eating disorders to a health agency, and because people with these problems tend to be secretive, denying that they even have a disorder, we have no way of knowing exactly how many people in this country are affected.

We can study small groups of people, determine how many of them are eating disordered, and then extrapolate to the general population. The numbers are usually given as percentages, and they are as close as we can get to an accurate estimate of the total number of people affected by eating disorders.

# Chapter 5

# *Medical and Psychological Aspects of Eating Disorders*

## Warning Signs

Because everyone today seems concerned about weight, and because most people diet at least once in a while, it is hard to tell what is normal behavior and what is a problem that may escalate to threaten life and happiness. No one person will show all of the following characteristics, but people with eating disorders will manifest several.

In addition, the early stages of an eating disorder can be difficult to define. When does normative dieting become a health and emotional problem? When does weight loss cross the line and become pathological? Answering these questions is hard, especially when the person has not yet lost enough weight to qualify for a clinical diagnosis. Nevertheless, the questions are important. The sooner an eating disorder is treated, the easier it will be for the person to recover. If warning signs and symptoms are allowed to persist until they become entrenched behaviors, the person may struggle for years before he or she can turn matters around.

### *Food Behaviors*

- The person skips meals, takes only tiny portions, will not eat in front of other people, eats in ritualistic ways, and mixes strange food combinations. May chew mouthfuls of food but spits them out before swallowing. Grocery shops and cooks for the entire household, but will not eat the tasty meals. Always has an excuse not to eat: is not hungry, just ate with a friend, is feeling ill, is upset, and so forth.

- Becomes "disgusted" with former favorite foods like red meat and desserts. Will eat only a few "safe" foods. Boasts about how healthy the meals he or she does consume are. Becomes a "vegetarian" but will not eat the necessary fats, oils, whole grains, and the denser fruits and veggies (such as sweet potatoes and avocados) required by true vegetarianism. Chooses primarily low-fat items with low levels of other nutrients, foods such as lettuce, tomatoes, sprouts, and so forth.

- Always has a diet soda in hand. Drastically reduces or completely eliminates fat intake. Reads food labels religiously. If he or she breaks self-imposed rigid discipline and eats normal or large portions, excuses self from the table to vomit and get rid of the calories.

- Or, in contrast to the above, the person gorges, usually in secret, and empties cupboards and refrigerator. May also buy special binge food. If panicked about weight gain, may purge to get rid of the calories. May leave clues that suggest discovery is desired: empty boxes, cans, and food packages; foul smelling bathrooms; running water to cover sounds of vomiting; excessive use of mouthwash and breath mints; and in some cases, containers of vomit poorly hidden that invite discovery.

- Sometimes the person uses laxatives, diet pills, water pills, or "natural" products from health food stores to promote weight loss. May abuse alcohol or street drugs, sometimes to deaden appetite, sometimes to escape emotional pain, and usually in hopes of feeling better, at least temporarily.

## *Appearance and Body Image Behaviors*

- The person loses, or tries to lose, weight. Has frantic fears of weight gain and obesity. Wears baggy clothes, sometimes in layers, to hide fat, hide emaciation, and stay warm. Obsesses about clothing size. Complains that he or she is fat even though others truthfully say this is not so. He or she will not believe them.

- Spends lots of time inspecting self in the mirror and usually finds something to criticize. Detests all or specific parts of the body, especially breasts, belly, thighs, and buttocks. Insists he or she cannot feel good about self unless he or she is thin, and he or she is never thin enough to satisfy her/himself.

## Exercise Behaviors

- The person exercises excessively and compulsively. May tire easily, keeping up a harsh regimen only through sheer will power. As time passes, athletic performance suffers. Even so, he or she refuses to change the routine.

- May develop strange eating patterns, supposedly to enhance athletic performance. May consume sports drinks and supplements, but total calories are less than what an active lifestyle requires.

## Thoughts

- In spite of average or above-average intelligence, the person thinks in magical and simplistic ways, for example, "If I am thinner, I will feel better about myself." He or she loses the ability to think logically, evaluate reality objectively, and admit and correct undesirable consequences of choices and actions.

- Becomes irrational, argues with people who try to help, and then withdraws, sulks, or throws a tantrum. Wanting to be special, he or she becomes competitive. Strives to be the best, the smallest, the thinnest, and so forth.

- Has trouble concentrating. Obsesses about food and weight and holds to rigid, perfectionistic standards for self and others.

## Feelings

- Has trouble talking about feelings, especially anger. Denies anger, saying something like, "Everything is OK. I am just tired and stressed." Escapes stress by turning to binge food, exercise, or anorexic rituals.

- Becomes moody, irritable, cross, snappish, and touchy. Responds to confrontation and even low-intensity interactions with tears, tantrums, or withdrawal. Feels he or she does not fit in and therefore avoids friends and activities. Withdraws into self and feelings, becoming socially isolated.

## Social Behaviors

- Tries to please everyone and withdraws when this is not possible. Tries to take care of others when he or she is the person who needs care. May present self as needy and dependent or conversely as fiercely independent and rejecting of all attempts to help. Anorexics tend to avoid sexual activity. Bulimics may engage in casual or even promiscuous sex.

- Person tries to control what and where the family eats. To the dismay of others, he or she consistently selects low-fat, low-sugar non-threatening—and unappealing—foods and restaurants that in the past have provided these "safe" items.

- Relationships tend to be either superficial or dependent. Person craves true intimacy but at the same time is terrified of it. As in all other areas of life, anorexics tend to be rigidly controlling while bulimics have problems with lack of impulse control that can lead to rash and regrettable decisions about sex, money, stealing, commitments, careers, and all forms of social risk taking.

## Medical and Psychological Complications

### Medical Problems

If not stopped, starving, stuffing, and purging can lead to irreversible physical damage and even death. Eating disorders can affect every cell, tissue, and organ in the body. The following is a partial list of the medical dangers associated with anorexia, bulimia, and binge eating disorder.

- Irregular heartbeat, cardiac arrest, death

- Kidney damage, death

- Liver damage (made worse by substance abuse), death

- Destruction of teeth, rupture of esophagus, loss of muscle mass

- Disruption of menstrual cycle, infertility

- Weakened immune system

- Icy hands and feet

- Swollen glands in neck; stones in salivary duct. "Chipmunk cheeks."

- Excess hair on face, arms, and body.
- Dry, blotchy skin that has an unhealthy gray or yellow cast
- Anemia, malnutrition. Disruption of body's fluid/mineral balance
- Fainting spells, sleep disruption, bad dreams, mental fuzziness
- Permanent loss of bone mass, fractures and lifelong problems

Binge eating disorder adds the following:

- Increased risk of cardiovascular disease
- Increased risk of bowel, breast, and reproductive cancers
- Increased risk of diabetes
- Obesity can lead to arthritic damage to joints

### *Psychological Problems*

It is a sad paradox that the person who develops an eating disorder often began with a diet, believing that weight loss would lead to improved self-confidence, self-respect, and self-esteem. The cruel reality is that persistent undereating, binge eating, and purging have the opposite effect. Eating disordered individuals typically struggle with one or more of the following complications:

- Depression that can lead to suicide
- Person feels out of control and helpless to do anything about problems.
- Anxiety, self-doubt
- Guilt and shame
- Hypervigilant. Suspects others of wanting to interfer.
- Terrified of discovery
- Obsessive thoughts and preoccupations
- Compulsive behaviors. Rituals dictate most activities
- Feels alienated and lonely. "I don't fit in anywhere."
- Feels hopeless. May give up and sink into fatalism or denial.

Important: Eating disorders are treatable, and people do recover from them. The above complications, or threat of them developing, should encourage people to seek treatment, not give up and sink into despair. Sooner is better than later. The sooner treatment is begun, the sooner the person can develop personal strength and begin to create a life worth living.

# Part Two

# Types of Eating Disorders

# Chapter 6

# *Anorexia Nervosa*

Anorexia nervosa is a psychologic illness characterized by marked weight loss, an intense fear of gaining weight even though the patient is underweight, a distorted body image and amenorrhea. Anorexia primarily affects adolescent girls and occurs in approximately 0.2 to 1.3 percent of the general population. Complications of anorexia nervosa are numerous, involving almost every organ system, although most complications may be reversed when a healthy nutritional state is restored. Treatment may be administered on an inpatient or outpatient basis and involves nutritional and psychologic rehabilitation.

Dieting and weight loss are now common in males and females of all ages. Television, motion pictures and the print media portray a slender body as a way to obtain power, control, and success. Americans are exposed to the ideas of healthy eating and thinness at an early age, and by early childhood they are learning the power they wield over their bodies through weight loss. Disordered eating syndromes, which may include use of fad diets, fasting and specialized vitamin formulas, are not classified as eating disorders. Certain criteria must be met for diagnosis of eating disorders such as anorexia nervosa and bulimia.

Excerpted from "Anorexia Nervosa: An Overview." Used with permission from the Sept. 15, 1996, issue of *American Family Physician*, Vol. 54, No. 4, Pg. 1273(10). © 1996 American Academy of Family Physicians. All rights reserved.

## Epidemiology

Dieting is currently at epidemic proportions. By age 18, more than 50 percent of girls perceive themselves as too fat, despite having a normal weight.[1] Anorexia nervosa is estimated to occur in 0.2 to 1.3 percent of the population,[2-4] with an annual incidence of five to 10 cases per 100,000 population.[1] Prevalence and incidence rates of both anorexia nervosa and bulimia tend to be higher in certain populations, such as college sororities. In this type of environment, a high priority is placed on thinness, and dieting is a common practice. Anorexia nervosa is much more common in women than in men, although approximately 5 to 10 percent of patients with anorexia nervosa are men.[5,6]

The condition typically begins in adolescence to early adulthood, with onset at a mean of 17 years of age, although it has been reported in grade-school children and middle-aged persons.[7] Anorexia nervosa is common in industrialized societies such as Great Britain, Sweden and Canada, where food is easily obtained and a high priority is placed on slenderness. Anorexia nervosa seldom occurs in developing countries.

## Diagnosis and Clinical Features

The typical patient with anorexia nervosa is an adolescent female who is a high achiever. She usually has successful parents and feels compelled to excel. She is a perfectionist and a good student, involved in many school and community activities.[8] She is very performance-driven and berates herself for any performance she perceives as being less than perfect. Family members often perceive the patient with anorexia as being the "good girl" because she completes tasks and homework without having to be asked. She rarely engages in typical adolescent activities such as attending parties or dating.

Criteria for anorexia nervosa as defined in the *Diagnostic and Statistical Manual of Mental Disorders (DSM-IV)* are listed in Table 6.1.[9] Patients with anorexia maintain a body weight less than 85 percent of normal either through weight loss or by refusal to make expected weight gains during times of normal growth. Normal reference weights may be obtained from Metropolitan Life Insurance tables or from childhood growth charts. Alternatively, a diagnosis of anorexia may be determined by body mass index. A body mass index less than 17.5 kg is sufficient for diagnosis of anorexia nervosa in adolescents and young adults.[9]

46

Persons with anorexia nervosa have a disturbed perception of their own weight and body shape. Certain individuals perceive themselves as overweight even though they are emaciated, while others perceive only certain parts of their body as fat.

**Table 6.1.** *DSM-IV* Diagnostic Criteria for Anorexia Nervosa

**A.** Refusal to maintain body weight at or above a minimally normal weight for age and height (e.g., weight loss leading to maintenance of body weight less than 85 percent of that expected, or failure to make expected weight gain during a period of growth, leading to body weight less than B percent of that expected).

**B.** Intense fear of gaining weight or becoming fat, even though underweight.

**C.** Disturbance in the way in which one's body weight or shape is experienced, undue influence of body weight or shape on self-evaluation, or denial of the seriousness of the current low body weight.

**D.** In postmenarcheal females, amenorrhea, i.e., the absence of at least three consecutive menstrual cycles. (A woman is considered to have amenorrhea if her periods occur only following hormone, e.g. estrogen, administration.)

Specify Type:

*Restricting type:* During the current episode of anorexia nervosa, the person has not regularly engaged in binge-eating or purging behavior (i.e., self-induced vomiting or the misuse of laxatives, diuretics or enemas).

*Binge-eating/purging type:* During the current episode of anorexia nervosa, the person has regularly engaged in binge-eating or purging behavior (i.e., self-induced vomiting or the misuse of laxatives, diuretics or enemas).

From American Psychiatric Association. *Diagnostic and Statistical Manual of Mental Disorders. 4th Ed.* Washington, D.C.; American Psychiatric Association, 1994:544-5.

Anorexic patients have an intense fear of gaining weight, which paradoxically becomes more intense with greater weight loss. Their fear of weight gain is greater than the fear of dying from self-induced starvation. Instead of feeling relief once weight loss is achieved, the anorexic patient feels a greater fear of gaining weight as she becomes thinner.

Amenorrhea is a common finding in females with anorexia nervosa. Starvation places the body in a high-stress state, which causes cortisol levels to rise. High levels of cortisol feed back to the hypothalamus to turn off secretion of cortisol-releasing hormone and the pulsatile release of gonadotropin-releasing hormone (GnRH). Decreased pulsatile secretion of GnRH leads to decreased circulating levels of follicle-stimulating hormone (FSH) and luteinizing hormone (LH), which subsequently lead to amenorrhea.

The *DSM-IV* categorizes anorexia nervosa into two subtypes: restricting type and binge-eating/purging type.[9] Patients with absolute restricting patterns do not engage in binge eating or purging behaviors. Restrictive behaviors include under-eating and avoidance of high-calorie foods. Excessive strenuous exercise is a common feature of this subtype. The binge-eating/purging type of anorexia nervosa is characterized by regular binge eating and/or purging behaviors, such as self-induced vomiting and use of laxatives or diuretics. The distinction between anorexia nervosa and bulimia nervosa is based on the fact that bulimia patients do not become 15 percent underweight.

Features associated with anorexia nervosa, but not required for diagnosis, are listed in Table 6.2. Bulimic episodes (eating binges) may occur as a result of an inability to exert continuous control over food intake. For anorexic patients who routinely ingest less than 500 calories over a 24-hour period, "overeating" may consist of eating a cookie or a piece of fruit. This perceived loss of control perpetuates a feeling of self-loathing to which the person responds with increased starvation. Thus, a positive feedback loop is established that perpetuates the illness.

Obsessive-compulsive behaviors are common among patients with anorexia. Rituals encompass almost every aspect of their lives, from food to body shape to daily activities. Anorexic patients often conceal or hoard food, or cut up food into tiny pieces, and arrange and rearrange it on their plates to give the appearance that they have eaten. Anorexics tend to eat "safe," low-calorie foods. Many times, these foods must be consumed in specific quantities, for example, 10 green beans or one tablespoon of ketchup. Many anorexics go so far as to count the calories in chewing gum, medicines, and the glue on postage

**Table 6.2.** Features Associated with Anorexia Nervosa

| | |
|---|---|
| Bulimic episodes | Edema |
| Preparation of elaborate meals for others but self-limitation to a narrow selection of low-calorie foods | Lanugo |
| | Overactivity, exercise |
| Obsessive-compulsive behaviors | Early satiety |
| Denial or minimization of illness | Constipation |
| Delayed psychosexual development | Skin dryness |
| Hypothermia | Hypercarotenemia |
| Bradycardia | Hair loss |
| Hypotension | Dehydration |

stamps. Anorexics may use ritualistic behaviors to continually assess weight and body size, such as frequent daily weighings and measurement of body parts. These patients are obsessed with burning up calories, which leads to incessant exercising. Even when severely emaciated and malnourished, anorexic patients may vigorously exercise in an attempt to burn the few calories that they have consumed. Daily tasks such as bathing, homework and occupation are also often highly ritualized. Any deviation from the normal routine is a source of intense anxiety for patients with anorexia.

Anorexic patients frequently deny the severity of their illness, which makes therapy difficult. They perceive their thinking as being entirely rational and think that their families, friends, and health care providers are attempting to "fatten them up." They see the rest of the world as dysfunctional and themselves as having within reality.

Delayed psychosexual development is often present in patients with anorexia and may be caused by a variety of factors. Anorexic patients tend to socially isolate themselves as a result of both a lack of self-esteem and a fear of breaking out of their highly ritualistic lifestyle. Starvation represses female sex hormone secretion to a prepubertal level, and there is a loss of interest in sexuality.[10]

A common misperception is that patients with anorexia are not hungry, but in actuality, they always feel hunger. It is their ability to overcome this feeling of hunger that gives them a sense of power over their bodies. Anorexic patients are constantly preoccupied with food and have difficulty concentrating on subjects other than food, weight and dieting. It is not uncommon for these persons to have declining performances at work, at school and in relationships because of their inability to concentrate on issues unrelated to food. Depression is a common manifestation of the illness and is almost always alleviated by nourishment.

## Complications

The medical complications of anorexia nervosa are listed in Table 6.3. These complications are primarily side effects of starvation. Most physical complications are a result of the body's attempt to conserve

**Table 6.3.** Complications of Anorexia Nervosa

*Metabolic*
*Hypothermia*
*Dehydration*
*Electrolyte abnormalities:*
    hypokalemia
    hyponatremia
    hypochloremic alkalosis
    hypocalcemia
    metabolic acidosis secondary to ketosis
    hypercholesterolemia
    hypercarotenemia
    hypoglycemia
*Cardiovascular*
    bradycardia
    hypotension
    decreased heart size
    arrhythmias (atrial flutter, atrial fibrillation, premature ventricular contractions, right bundle branch block)
    superior mesenteric artery syndrome
    pericardial effusion
*Hematologic*
    pancytopenia
    hypocellular bone marrow
    decreased plasma proteins

energy and may be reversed with a return to a normal nutritional state.

Metabolic complications may be numerous and varied, depending on whether the patient engages in purging behaviors. Hypokalemia is especially common in patients who vomit, or take diuretics or laxatives and may acutely cause life-threatening arrhythmias and muscle cramping. Chronic purging and vomiting practices lead to hypokalemic nephropathy. Metabolic acidosis is a result of the ketotic state produced by starvation.[11]

Cardiac complications are fairly common and are the most frequent cause of death in patients with anorexia.[12] Bradycardia, as low as 40

**Table 6.3.** Complications of Anorexia Nervosa (continued)

*Renal*
> prerenal azotemia
> chronic renal failure

*Endocrine*
> decreased gonadotropins, estrogens, testosterone
> sick euthyroid syndrome
> increased cortisol and growth hormone
> amenorrhea, infertility, impotence

*Musculoskeletal*
> cramps, tetany, weakness
> osteopenia, stress fractures

*Gastrointestinal*
> swollen salivary glands, dental caries, erosion of tooth enamel
>    (with vomiting)
> delayed gastric emptying, constipation, bowel obstruction
> early satiety

*Dermatologic*
> dry, pale skin
> thinning hair
> lanugo

*Cognitive and Behavior*
> depression
> poor concentration
> food preoccupation
> impaired sleep
> decreased libido

beats per minute, occurs in an attempt to conserve energy by slowing the body's metabolic rate. Arrhythmias result from an altered metabolic state and from the effects of starvation.

Gastrointestinal complications are related to starvation and purging behaviors. Erosion of the enamel on teeth is extremely common in patients who vomit, and bulimia is often detected during a routine dental visit. Swollen parotid salivary glands, resulting from irritation of the gland by stomach acid, occur in patients who routinely vomit. Delayed gastric emptying and constipation are related to underuse, which leads to muscle atrophy and flaccidity of the gut.[1] This phenomenon, along with a reduced gastric capacity, leads to the early satiety often reported by anorexic patients. This sensation is falsely interpreted by anorexics as gaining weight, which may hinder recovery.

Dry skin and thinning scalp hair are caused by starvation and by decreased collagen. Lanugo, a fine downy coat of hair, develops on the torso and extremities. This phenomenon is analogous to an animal's fur thickening during the winter months in order to conserve heat.

Numerous other findings mainly result from a disruption of the hypothalamic-pituitary axis. Hypothermia develops secondary to a disruption of this axis and to the depletion of body fat stores. Often, patients with anorexia will wear layers of clothing in order to keep warm. Osteopenia is a manifestation of decreased dietary intake of calcium, hypercortisolemia, low serum concentration of estrogens and acid-base imbalance. The rate of bone resorption is increased, coupled with a decreased rate of formation. Consequently, stress fractures are frequent and occasionally are presenting signs.

## Treatment

Treatment of anorexia nervosa begins with a comprehensive history and physical examination to rule out concomitant psychiatric or medical disorders, and to assess medical complications of the illness. Table 6.4 lists areas that need to be addressed in the evaluation.[5]

Once the diagnosis of anorexia nervosa is confirmed, the initial goal of treatment is to prevent death by starvation. The family physician must provide the patient and family with information about the illness and negotiate the plan for treatment. The patient should be told that resumption of normal eating will decrease her preoccupation with food and the urge to binge, relieve fatigue and depression, and result in improved relationships with family and friends.[12] A trial of outpatient treatment may be attempted if the patient is not severely emaciated, has had the illness for less than six months, has no serious medical complications, is accepting her illness and is motivated to change, and has supportive and cooperative family and friends.

The first step in the treatment of anorexia nervosa is correction of the starvation state. A goal weight should be set and the patient's weight should be monitored once or twice a week in the office under standardized conditions. The patient should be referred to a dietitian for nutritional counseling and to a psychiatrist or a psychologist trained in the treatment of eating disorders for counseling. A caloric intake to provide a weight gain of 1 to 3 lb per week should be instituted. Initially, weight gain should be gradual to prevent gastric dilation, pedal edema and congestive heart failure.[5] Anorexic patients may attempt to give the impression that they have gained weight by drinking large amounts of liquids or by carrying weights in their pockets. The physician should be alert for these tactics. Often, a nutritional supplement is added to the regimen to augment dietary intake.

During the process of refeeding, weight gain as well as electrolyte levels should be strictly monitored. The disturbed eating behavior must be addressed in specific counseling sessions. Mealtimes should not be times when eating issues should be confronted and instead should be a time of social interaction. Immediately following meals, patients should be confined to sedentary activities and access to bathrooms should be denied to prevent purging. The physician must work closely with the patient's family in order to determine the patient's progress and to monitor complications of the illness that are undetectable in the office.

Inpatient treatment is indicated under certain circumstances: weight loss exceeds 30 percent of ideal weight; patient is having suicidal thoughts; patient is abusing laxatives, diuretics or diet pills, or outpatient treatment has failed.[5] Care of the anorexic patient in an inpatient unit is primarily overseen by a psychiatrist along with a treatment team comprising nurses, therapists and a dietitian. During inpatient treatment, the family physician should maintain frequent communication with the treatment team and family.

An inpatient program is most successful with a hospitalization of 10 to 12 weeks in order to achieve maximum physical and psychologic rehabilitation.[11] However, this duration of hospitalization may not be feasible, depending on the patients insurance. The patient should be educated about what constitutes a healthy diet. In rare cases, tube feeding and parenteral nutrition are used during hospitalization when rapid renourishment is required. These methods, however, are detrimental to the therapeutic relationship because the patient loses trust in the treatment team. The patient must feel comfortable with consumption of normal meals and maintenance of a healthy weight before discharge.[11]

Discharge from the hospital is often preceded by weekend home visits during which the patient is exposed to everyday family life to facilitate the patient's ability to deal with stressful situations before dismissal. On discharge, the patient should be involved in a regular follow-up program, continuing months and sometimes years after hospitalization.

The drug of choice for the treatment of anorexia nervosa is food. Depression, a common finding in anorexia nervosa, is usually alleviated with renourishment. In cases of depression refractory to proper nutrition, an antidepressant may be helpful. Tricyclic antidepressants have been used with success but cause sedation and anti-cholinergic and alpha-adrenergic side effects, which may limit effectiveness. At present, the use of serotonin-specific reuptake inhibitors (SSRIs) is

**Table 6.4.** Assessment of Eating Disorders

*History*
- Eating habits and rituals
- Body Image
- Weight, minimum and maximum weights, desired weight
- Menstrual pattern
- Use of laxatives, diuretics or diet pills
- Exercise participation
- Binging and purging behaviors
- Substance abuse, personality, mood and anxiety disorders, and suicidal thoughts
- Past medical history
- Family history of medical and psychiatric disorders

*Physical Examination*
- Mental status
- Complete physical examination
- Laboratory: complete blood count, electrolytes, blood urea nitrogen, creatinine, calcium, magnesium, phosphate, cholesterol, lipids, amylase, total protein, albumin, liver function tests, thyroid function tests, urinalysis, electrocardiogram
- Vital signs, and standard weight and height

common and has proved to alleviate the depressed mood and moderate obsessive-compulsive behaviors occurring in some individuals. Current research is directed toward exploring the role of altered function of the serotonergic system in anorexic patients and the effect of SSRIs in preventing relapse, changing distorted cognitive patterns and changing the disturbed perception of hunger and satiety.

Psychotherapy begins when the diagnosis is established and continues after the patient has returned to a normal weight. Generally, psychotherapy is provided by professionals trained in the treatment of eating disorders. Behavior therapies are commonly used in the treatment of anorexia nervosa, using a system of positive and negative reinforcements based on weight gain or loss. Weight gain is rewarded by attainment of desired activities such as participation in recreational activities, television privileges and home visits. Conversely, weight loss results in loss of privileges or confinement to bed rest.

Cognitive techniques center around understanding and changing dysfunctional thinking and teaching alternative coping strategies.[13] Family therapy is highly recommended, especially in younger patients. Anorexia is a disorder that affects the entire family, and family counseling facilitates recovery in the individual by addressing problems in the family environment.[14] Therapy often continues for years after return to a normal weight and, during this time, the family physician is often instrumental in ensuring that the patient's physical health does not regress. Bimonthly to monthly weighings and monitoring of electrolyte levels every six months aid in assessment of the patients recovery.

## Prognosis

The prognosis for anorexia nervosa is poor.[15] The course of the illness varies. An individual may suffer from a single episode or several episodes of starvation, or the illness may be unremitting until death. Most commonly, patients have the illness for years and have recurrent exacerbations interspersed with periods of normal weight. Unfortunately, in some patients, death occurs as a result of starvation, electrolyte abnormalities or suicide.[9]

Mortality rates for anorexia vary from 5 to 20 percent. Higher mortality rates have been found with longer duration of illness, extremely low weights, poor family support, purging behaviors and multiple relapses.[16]

Anorexia nervosa is a chronic illness, and patients may take years to recover, undergoing several hospitalizations and relapses. The family physician must develop a relationship of trust with the anorexic patient, while at the same time avoiding manipulation by the patient. The family physician must have realistic expectations for the patient's recovery and must make appropriate referrals. Although working with this patient population can be extremely frustrating and challenging, being a part of the recovery process can be extremely rewarding.

## References

1. Woodside, D.B. A review of anorexia nervosa and bulimia nervosa. *Curr Probl Pediatr* 1995;25(2):67-89.

2. Rastam, M.; Gillberg, C.; Garton, M.; Anorexia nervosa in a Swedish urban region. A population-based study. *Br J Psychiatry* 1989;155:642-6.

3. Rathner, G.; Messner, K.; Detection of eating disorders in a small rural town: an epidemiological study. *Psychol Med* 1993;23:175-84.

4. Whitaker, A.; Davies, M.; Shaffer, D.; Johnson, J.; Abrams, S.; Walsh, B.T., et al. The struggle to be thin: a survey of anorexic and bulimic symptoms in a non-referred adolescent population. *Psychol Med* 1989; 19:143-63.

5. Haller, E.; Eating disorders. A review and update. *West J Med* 1992;157:658-64.

6. Beumont, P.J.; Beardwood, C.J.; Russell, G.F. The occurrence of the syndrome of anorexia nervosa in male subjects. *Psychol Med* 1972;2:216-31.

7. Halmi, K.A.; Casper, R.C.; Eckert, E.D.; Goldberg, S.C.; Davis, J.M. Unique features associated with age of onset of anorexia nervosa. *Psychiatry Res* 1979; 1:209-15.

8. Hewitt, P.L.; Flett, G.L.; Ediger, E. Perfectionism traits and perfectionistic self-presentation in eating disorder attitudes, characteristics, and symptoms. *Int J Eat Disord* 1995;18(4):317-26.

9. American Psychiatric Association. *Diagnostic and statistical manual of mental disorders. 4th ed.* Washington, D.C.: American Psychiatric Association, 1994:539-45.

10. Neuman, P.A.; Halvorson, P.A. *Anorexia nervosa and bulimia: a handbook for counselors and therapists*. New York: Van Nostrand Reinhold, 1983.

11. Giannini, A.J.; Newman, M.; Gold, M. Anorexia and bulimia. *Am Fam Physician* 1990;41:1169-76.

12. Beumont, P.J.; Russell, J.D.; Touyz, S.W. Treatment of anorexia nervosa. *Lancet* 1993;341:1635-40.

13. Yager, J. Psychosocial treatments for eating disorders. *Psychiatry* 1994;57:153-64.

14. Robin, A.L.; Siegel, P.T.; Moye, A. Family versus individual therapy for anorexia impact on family conflict. *Int J Eat Disord* 1995;17(4):313-22.

15. Eckert, E.D.; Halmi, K.A.; Marchi, P.; Grove, W.; Crosby, R. Ten-year follow-up of anorexia nervosa: clinical course and outcome. *Psychol Med* 1995;25:143-56.

16. Hsu, GL. Critique of follow up studies. In: Halmi, K.A., ed. *Psychobiology and treatment of anorexia nervosa and bulimia nervosa*. Washington, D.C.: American Psychiatric Press, 1992:152-7.

*— by Wendy L. Hobbs and Cynda Ann Johnson*

Chapter 7

# Bulimia Nervosa

## What Is Bulimia?

Bulimia nervosa is an eating disorder. It is characterized by binge eating (eating large amounts of food in a short time) followed by self-induced vomiting and/or use of laxatives.

Although most bulimics have a normal weight, they feel a lack of control over their eating behavior. After binging, they induce vomiting or use laxatives or diuretics because they are fearful of becoming overweight. They often feel that their lives are controlled by conflicts about eating. Although the disorder can affect men, most people with bulimia nervosa are female adolescents or young women.

## How Does It Occur?

The exact cause of bulimia nervosa is not known. Some researchers believe that eating disorders may be related to malfunctioning of the part(s) of the brain regulating mood and appetite.

Factors that increase the risk of developing bulimia nervosa include:

* family history of bulimia nervosa or eating disorders

- a family or personal history of mood disorders, such as major depression or bipolar disorder (manic depression).

## What Are the Symptoms?

Symptoms of bulimia include:

- repeated episodes of binge eating
- strict dieting or fasting
- repeated weight loss and gain of more than 10 pounds
- dehydration
- weakness
- depression and guilt after binge eating
- damaged teeth from gastric acid contained in vomit
- swollen cheeks from repeated vomiting
- preoccupation with being thin
- depressed or anxious mood.

## How Is It Diagnosed?

The doctor takes a medical history and does a physical exam. The doctor will ask about eating patterns, looking for such behavior as:

- repeated episodes of binge eating followed by self-induced vomiting or use of laxatives
- alternate binging and fasting
- secret eating and binging
- exercising excessively to prevent weight gain.

## How Is It Treated?

People with this problem must recognize that they are suffering from a dangerous disorder. Treatment involves regulation of new eating habits. The doctor may recommend psychotherapy and family counseling and may prescribe medication used for mood disorders, such as antidepressants or mood stabilizers.

## How Long Will the Effects Last?

The risk of relapse exists for years after treatment ends. Without treatment, a person with bulimia may become depressed and suicidal.

Take care of yourself by:

- Eating well-balanced, nutritious meals.
- Schedule meals regularly, but not too rigidly. Avoid irregular eating habits and avoid fasting.
- Taking vitamin and mineral supplements.
- Avoiding use of laxatives and diuretics.
- Seeking professional help if you need to lose weight so you can lose weight slowly and to a reasonable level.
- Exercising regularly and in moderation.

## What Can Be Done to Help Prevent Bulimia?

Many bulimics do not feel good about themselves. You can raise your self-esteem and thus prevent or minimize bulimia if you:

- Try to resolve areas of conflict in your life.
- Try to achieve a balance of work, social activities, recreation, rest, and exercise in your life.
- Create a support group of good friends.
- Keep a positive outlook on life.
- Stop judging yourself and others.

Bulimia nervosa is a psychiatric syndrome with potentially serious consequences.[1,2] Relatively effective treatments for this disorder have been developed, and early intervention is more likely to facilitate eventual recovery.[2] Unfortunately, few health care professionals receive training in the assessment of bulimia nervosa. Therefore, they may be unable to identify and treat patients with the disorder.

Historically, patients with bulimia nervosa often were hospitalized until the most disruptive symptoms ceased. In today's health care environment, hospitalization for bulimia nervosa is infrequent and tends to take the form of brief admissions focused on crisis management.[3] Specialists in the field of eating disorders have responded to the present cost-containment measures by developing a combination of treatment modalities, including medication and individual and group psychotherapy, that can be used in the outpatient care of patients with bulimia nervosa. This chapter discusses the assessment and treatment of bulimia nervosa and considers how this disorder can best be handled in a managed care environment.

## Definitions and Etiology

Bulimia nervosa is a multifaceted disorder with psychologic, physiologic, developmental and cultural components.[1,2] There may be a genetic predisposition for the disorder. Other predisposing factors include psychologic and personality factors, such as perfectionism, impaired self-concept, affective instability, poor impulse control and an absence of adaptive functioning to maturational tasks and developmental stressors (e.g., puberty; peer and parental relationships, sexuality, marriage and pregnancy).

Biologic researchers suggest that abnormalities of central nervous system neurotransmitters may also play a role in bulimia nervosa.[4] Furthermore, several familial factors may increase the risk of developing this disorder. For example, researchers have discovered that first- and second-degree relatives of individuals with bulimia nervosa have an increased incidence of depression and manic-depressive illnesses, eating disorders, and alcohol and substance abuse problems.[5-7]

Regardless of the cause, once bulimia nervosa is present, the physiologic effects of disordered eating appear to maintain the core features of the disorder, resulting in a self-perpetuating cycle.

## Diagnostic Criteria

The diagnostic criteria for bulimia nervosa (Table 7.1) now include subtypes to distinguish patients who compensate for binge eating by purging (vomiting and/or the abuse of laxatives and diuretics) from those who use nonpurging behaviors (e.g., fasting or excessive exercising).[1]

A binge eating/purging subtype of anorexia nervosa also exists. Low body weight is the major factor that differentiates bulimia nervosa from this subtype of anorexia nervosa. Thus, according to the established diagnostic criteria,[1] patients who are 15 percent below natural bodyweight and binge eat or purge are considered to have anorexia nervosa.

Patients can, and frequently do, move between diagnostic categories as their symptom pattern and weight change over the course of the illness.

Some patients do not meet the full criteria for bulimia nervosa or anorexia nervosa. These patients may be classified as having an eating disorder "not otherwise specified" (Table 7.2).[1]

## Prevalence and Prognosis

Bulimia nervosa appears to have become more prevalent during the past 30 years. The disorder is 10 times more common in females than in males and affects 1 to 3 percent of female adolescents and young adults.[6]

**Table 7.1.** Diagnostic Criteria for Bulimia Nervosa

**A.** Recurrent episodes of binge eating. An episode of binge eating is characterized by both of the following:

1. Eating, in a discrete period of time (e.g., within a two-hour period), an amount of food that is definitely larger than most people would eat during a similar period of time and under similar circumstances.

2. A sense of lack of control over eating during the episode (e.g., a feeling that one cannot stop eating or control what or how much one is eating).

**B.** Recurrent inappropriate compensatory behavior in order to prevent weight gain, such as self-induced vomiting; misuse of laxatives, diuretics, enemas, or other medications; fasting or excessive exercise.

**C.** The binge eating and inappropriate compensatory behaviors both occur, on average, at least twice a week for three months.

**D.** Self-evaluation is unduly influenced by body shape and weight.

**E.** The disturbance does not occur exclusively during episodes of anorexia nervosa.

Specify type:

*Purging type:* during the current episode of bulimia nervosa, the person has regularly engaged in self-induced vomiting or the misuse of laxatives, diuretics, or enemas.

*Nonpurging type:* during the current episode of bulimia nervosa, the person has used other inappropriate compensatory behaviors, such as fasting or excessive exercise, but has not regularly engaged in self-induced vomiting or the misuse of laxatives, diuretics, or enemas.

From American Psychiatric Association. *Diagnostic and statistical manual of mental disorders. 4th ed.* Washington, D. C.: American Psychiatric Association, 1994:549-50.

Both anorexia nervosa and bulimia nervosa have a peak onset between the ages of 13 and 20 years. The disorder appears to have a chronic, sometimes episodic course in which periods of remission alternate with recurrences of binge/purge cycles. Some patients have bulimia nervosa that persists for 30 years or more.[8] Recent data suggest that patients with subsyndromal bulimia nervosa may show morbidity comparable to that in patients with the full syndrome.

The long-term outcome of bulimia nervosa is not known. Available research indicates that 30 percent of patients with bulimia nervosa rapidly relapse and up to 40 percent remain chronically symptomatic.[9]

**Table 7.2.** Diagnostic Criteria for Eating Disorder Not Otherwise Specified

1.  For females, all of the criteria for anorexia nervosa are met except that the individual has regular menses.

2.  All of the criteria for anorexia nervosa are met except that, despite significant weight loss, the individual's current weight is in the normal range.

3.  All of the criteria for bulimia nervosa are met, except that the binge eating and inappropriate compensatory mechanisms occur at a frequency of less than twice a week or for a duration of less than three months.

4.  The regular use of inappropriate compensatory behavior by an individual of normal body weight after eating small amounts of food (e.g., self-induced vomiting after the consumption of two cookies).

5.  Repeatedly chewing and spitting out, but not swallowing, large amounts of food.

6.  Binge-eating disorder: recurrent episodes of binge eating in the absence of the regular use of inappropriate compensatory behaviors characteristic of bulimia nervosa.

From American Psychiatric Association. *Diagnostic and statistical manual of mental disorders. 4th ed.* Washington, D.C. American Psychiatric Association, 1994:550.

## Psychiatric Comorbidity

Clinical and research reports[10-13] emphasize a frequent association between bulimia nervosa and other psychiatric conditions. Comorbid major depression is commonly noted (Table 7.3), although it is not clear if the mood disturbance is a function of bulimia nervosa or a separate phenomenon.[11]

Information concerning the comorbidity rates of bipolar disorders (e.g., manic depression, rapid cycling mood disorder) and bulimia nervosa is somewhat limited. However, recent epidemiologic data indicate an increased incidence of rapid cycling mood disorders in patients with more severe, chronic bulimia nervosa.[13]

The association between bulimia nervosa and other anxiety and substance-related disorders has been well documented.[7] For example, substance abuse or dependence, particularly involving alcohol and stimulants, occurs in one third of patients with bulimia nervosa. Thus, a comorbid substance-related disorder must be addressed before effective treatment for bulimia nervosa can be initiated.

Significant research has been devoted to the high frequency of personality disturbances in patients with bulimia nervosa. Overall, between 2 and 50 percent of women with bulimia nervosa have some type of personality disorder, most commonly borderline, antisocial, histrionic or narcissistic personality disorder.[10,14-16]

To ensure that the treatment approach is properly designed and effective, the physician must look carefully for symptoms of comorbid

**Table 7.3.** Psychiatric Conditions Commonly Coexisting with Bulimia Nervosa

| | |
|---|---|
| Mood disorders | Panic disorder |
| Major depression | Obsessive-compulsive disorder |
| Dysthymic disorder | Generalized anxiety disorder |
| Bipolar disorder | Post-traumatic stress disorder |
| Substance-related disorders | Personality disorders |
| Alcohol abuse | Borderline personality disorder |
| Stimulant abuse | Histrionic personality disorder |
| Polysubstance abuse | Narcissistic personality disorder |
| Anxiety disorders | Antisocial personality disorder |

psychiatric illness in patients with bulimia nervosa. Although further research is needed to determine the extent to which comorbid conditions influence the course of bulimia nervosa, the presence of these additional problems clearly complicates the treatment process.

## Medical Complications

The medical complications of bulimia nervosa range from fairly benign, transient symptoms, such as fatigue, bloating and constipation, to chronic or life-threatening conditions, including hypokalemia, cathartic colon, impaired renal function and cardiac arrest[17,18] (Table 7.4).

### Binge Eating

Binge eating alone rarely causes significant medical complications, Gastric rupture, the most serious complication, is uncommon.[17] More often, patients describe nausea, abdominal pain and distention, prolonged digestion and weight gain.

**Table 7.4.** Medical Complications of Bulimia Nervosa

| | |
|---|---|
| Binge eating | Heartburn and sore throat |
| Gastric rupture | Upper gastrointestinal tears |
| Nausea | Perforation of upper digestive tract, esophagus or stomach |
| Abdominal pain and distention | |
| Prolonged digestion | Excessive blood in vomitus and gastric pain |
| Weight gain | |
| Purging (most often, self-induced vomiting) | Electrolyte imbalances |
| | Hypokalemia |
| Dental erosion | Fatigue |
| Enlarged salivary glands | Muscle spasms |
| Oral/hand trauma | Heart palpitations |
| Esophageal/pharyngeal damage Irritation of esophagus and/or pharynx due to contact with gastric acids | Paresthesias |
| | Tetany |
| | Seizures |
| | Cardiac arrhythmias |

The combination of heightened anxiety, physical discomfort and intense guilt provokes the drive to purge the food by self-induced vomiting, excessive exercise or the misuse of ipecac, laxatives or diuretics. These purgative methods are associated with the more serious complications of bulimia nervosa.

## *Self-Induced Vomiting*

Self-induced vomiting, the most common means of purging, is used by more than 75 percent of patients with bulimia nervosa.[19] Most patients vomit immediately or soon after a binge. During the binge, they commonly drink excessive fluids to "float the food" and facilitate regurgitation.

Vomiting is induced by stimulation of the pharynx using a finger or a narrow object such as a toothbrush. Some patients describe the learned ability to vomit by pressure or contraction of the abdominal muscles. A minority of patients develop reflux following the consumption of virtually any amount of food or fluid. Treatment of this reflux is difficult and requires that the patient practice relaxation during food ingestion.

Self-induced vomiting can lead to a number of serious medical complications.

**Dental Erosion.** Gastric acids may cause deterioration of tooth enamel (perimolysis), particularly involving the occlusal surfaces of molars and the posterior surfaces of maxillary incisors. Since these effects are irreversible, patients with this complication need to have regular dental care.

**Enlarged Salivary Glands.** Frequent vomiting has been reported to cause swelling of the salivary glands in approximately 8 percent of patients with bulimia nervosa.[20] The exact etiology is unknown. The glandular enlargement is typically painless and may occur within several days of excessive vomiting. It appears to be a cosmetically distressing but medically benign condition. Other than cessation of vomiting, no specific treatment has been identified.

**Oral and Hand Trauma.** The induction of vomiting with a finger or an object can cause lacerations of the mouth and throat. Bleeding lacerations can also occur on the knuckles because of repeated contact with the front teeth. Some patients with bulimia nervosa develop a calloused, scarred area distal to their knuckles. Oral or hand trauma can provide evidence of vomiting even when patients deny bulimic, symptoms.

**Esophageal and Pharyngeal Complications.** Because of repeated contact with gastric acids, the esophagus or pharynx may become irritated. Heartburn and sore throats may occur and are best treated with antacids and throat lozenges, respectively.[17]

Blood in the vomitus is an indication of upper gastrointestinal tears, which are a more serious complication of purging. Most tears heal well with cessation of vomiting. Perforation of the upper digestive tract, esophagus or stomach is an extremely rare but potentially lethal complication. Patients with gastric pain and excessive blood in their vomitus should be evaluated on an urgent basis.[17]

**Electrolyte Imbalances.** Serious depletions of hydrogen chloride, potassium, sodium and magnesium can occur because of the excessive loss of fluids during vomiting. Hypokalemia represents a potential medical emergency, and serum electrolyte levels should be measured as part of the initial evaluation in all new patients. Patients who complain of fatigue, muscle spasms or heart palpitations may be experiencing transient episodes of electrolyte disturbance. Paresthesias, tetany, seizures or cardiac arrhythmias are potential metabolic complications that require acute care.[17] Chemistry profiles should be obtained regularly in patients who continue to vomit or abuse purgatives on a regular basis.

## Patient Evaluation

### Physical Features

Since bulimia nervosa has numerous medical complications, a complete physical examination is imperative in patients with this disorder. The examination should include vital signs and an evaluation of height and weight relative to age. The physician should also look for general hair loss, lanugo, abdominal tenderness, acrocyanosis (cyanosis of the extremities), jaundice, edema, parotid gland tenderness or enlargement, and scars on the dorsum of the hand.

Routine laboratory tests in patients with bulimia nervosa include a complete blood count with differential, serum chemistry and thyroid profiles, and urine chemistry microscopy testing. Depending on the results of the physical examination, additional laboratory tests, such as a chest radiograph and an electrocardiogram, may be indicated.

Finally, patients who engage in self-induced vomiting should be referred for a complete dental examination.

## Psychiatric Assessment

Because of the multifaceted nature of bulimia nervosa, a comprehensive psychiatric assessment is essential to developing the most appropriate treatment strategy. Patients should be referred to a mental health professional with specific expertise in this area. Frequently, student health programs or university medical centers have personnel who are experienced in the evaluation and treatment of eating disorders.

The most appropriate course of treatment can usually be determined on the basis of a thorough evaluation of the patient's medical condition, associated eating behaviors and attitudes, body image, personality, developmental history and interpersonal relationships. In the present managed care environment, hospitalization for patients with bulimia nervosa is no longer readily available. It has become especially important to determine a treatment approach that will be effective as quickly as possible.[3] The physician needs to know when inpatient treatment is or is not indicated. A comprehensive evaluation provides the rationale for this judgment and includes the following:

1. Standardized testing to document the patient's general personality features, characterologic disturbance and attitudes about eating, body size and weight.

2. A complete history of the patient's body weight, eating patterns and attempts at weight loss, including typical daily food intake, methods of purging and perceived ideal weight.

3. An investigation of the patient's interpersonal history and functioning, including family dynamics, peer relationships, and present or past physical, sexual or emotional abuse.

4. An evaluation of medical and psychiatric comorbidity, as well as documentation of previous attempts at treatment.

## Treatment

Considerable research has been devoted to identifying the most effective pharmacologic and psychologic treatments for bulimia nervosa, including the effects of different medications (e.g., tricyclic antidepressants and selective serotonin reuptake inhibitors) and the benefits of different psychotherapy approaches (e.g., behavioral treatment versus cognitive-behavioral therapy and individual versus group therapies). In addition, a few studies have compared the efficacies of different combinations of medications and psychotherapy.

### *Pharmacologic Interventions*

**Tricyclic Antidepressants.** A number of placebo-controlled, double-blind studies[21-27] have examined the effectiveness of tricyclic antidepressants in patients with bulimia nervosa. Several of these studies[23,25-27] found that desipramine, 150 to 300 mg per day, was clearly superior to placebo. Two parallel studies[21,24] reported that imipramine, 176 to 300 mg per day, was also more beneficial than placebo. Amitriptyline, 150 mg per day, was shown to be more effective than placebo in reducing binge eating (72 percent versus 52 percent) and vomiting (78 percent versus 53 percent).[22] Overall, short-term placebo-controlled trials in patients with bulimia nervosa have reported that tricyclic antidepressants reduce binge eating by 47 to 91 percent and vomiting by 45 to 78 percent.

**Monoamine Oxidase Inhibitors.** Phenelzine, 60 to 80 mg per day, has been found to be more effective than placebo in reducing binge eating (64 percent versus 5 percent).[28] Isocarboxazid, 60 mg per day, has also been superior to placebo in controlling binge eating.[29] However, the monoamine oxidase inhibitors have considerable side effects and therefore are not recommended as initial pharmacologic therapy for bulimia nervosa.

**Other Antidepressants.** Several atypical antidepressants have been investigated in placebo-controlled double-blind studies. Bupropion, 25 to 450 mg per day, can effectively diminish the frequency of binge eating, but an increased rate of seizures discourages the use of this medication in patients with bulimia.[30] Binge eating has been reduced by 31 percent in patients treated with trazodone, 400 to 650 mg per day.[31]

**Selective Serotonin Reuptake Inhibitors.** The most promising results have been reported in studies investigating the use of fluoxetine in the treatment of bulimia nervosa.[32,33] In the most comprehensive drug trial to date,[33] 382 patients were evaluated in a multicenter study comparing 20- and 60-mg dosage of fluoxetine with placebo. At the 20-mg dosage, fluoxetine therapy resulted in a 45 percent reduction in binge eating, compared with a 33 percent reduction with placebo. Vomiting was reduced by 29 percent in patients treated with fluoxetine and by 5 percent in those who received placebo. Notably, the patients who received fluoxetine in a dosage of 60 mg per day showed the best treatment response, demonstrating a 67 percent reduction in binge eating and a 56 percent reduction in vomiting.[33] A smaller study[32] replicated these findings, reporting a 51 percent reduction of binge eating in patients treated with fluoxetine at 60 mg per day, compared with a 17 percent reduction in those who were given placebo. The U.S. Food and Drug Administration has recently approved the use of fluoxetine for the treatment of bulimia nervosa.

**Other Medications.** In one placebo-controlled crossover study,[34] no improvement in bulimic symptoms was noted in patients treated with naltrexone, 50 mg per day. Likewise, a brief placebo-controlled trial of lithium[35] resulted in no significant differences between groups in the reduction of binge eating frequency.

## *Psychotherapy*

Despite differences in the application of techniques, the skill level of clinicians and the duration of the illness, controlled studies have clearly established the superiority of cognitive-behavioral therapy for the treatment of bulimia nervosa. Based on comparative studies, this therapy used alone or in combination with another technique has resulted in the most significant reductions of binge eating and/or purging.

Cognitive-behavioral therapy principally involves a systematic series of interventions aimed at addressing the cognitive aspects of bulimia nervosa, such as the preoccupation with body, weight and food, perfectionism, dichotomous thinking and low self-esteem. This therapy also addresses the behavioral components of the illness, such as disturbed eating habits, binge eating, purging, dieting and ritualistic exercise.

The initial goal of cognitive-behavioral therapy is to restore control over dietary intake. Caloric restriction and dieting efforts that set patients up to binge are avoided. Patients typically record their food intake and feelings. They then receive extensive feedback concerning their meal plan, symptom triggers, caloric intake and nutritional balance. Patients are also instructed in cognitive methods for challenging rigid thought patterns, methods for improving self-esteem, assertiveness training, and the identification and appropriate expression of feelings. A thorough explanation of cognitive-behavioral therapy for the treatment of bulimia nervosa is available elsewhere.[36]

The relative benefits of medications and cognitive-behavioral therapy have been assessed and compared. Study results indicate that cognitive-behavioral therapy is superior to medication alone and that the combination of cognitive-behavioral therapy and medication is more effective than the use of medication alone.[37]

Similarly, the durable effects of cognitive-behavioral therapy have been well documented. In contrast, there has been only one study of the long-term effectiveness of pharmacologic treatment. In that study, six months of desipramine therapy produced lasting improvement, even after the medication was withdrawn.[38]

Although cognitive-behavioral therapy is the first-line treatment of choice for bulimia nervosa, its effectiveness is limited. Approximately 50 percent of patients who receive this therapy stop binge eating and purging. The remaining patients show partial improvement, but a small number do not benefit at all.[37] A comorbid personality disorder is associated with a poorer response not only to cognitive-behavioral therapy but also to alternative therapies.

The approach to take when cognitive-behavioral therapy is not effective remains unclear. Some patients may not respond to additional pharmacologic or psychologic therapy. However, the hope is that some treatment is better than no treatment at all. Thus, no patient should be dismissed as "chronic and untreatable."

## References

1. *American Psychiatric Association. Diagnostic and statistical manual of mental disorders. 4th ed.* Washington, D.C.: American Psychiatric Association, 1994:539-50.

2. American Psychiatric Association. Practice guidelines for eating disorders. *Am J Psychiatry* 1993; 150:212-28.

3. Kaye, W. Can we manage managed care? *Eating Disord Rev* 1995;6(1):1-4.

4. Kaye, W. Neuropeptide abnormalities. In: Halmi KA, ed. *Psychobiology and treatment of anorexia nervosa and bulimia nervosa.* Washington, D.C.: American Psychiatric Press, 1992.

5. Lilenfeld, L.R.; Strober, M.; Kaye, W. Genetics and family studies of anorexia nervosa and bulimia nervosa. In: Kaye, W.;

Jimerson, D.C., eds. *Eating disorders*. London: Balliere's Tindal (In press).

6.  Herzog, D.; Agras, W.S.; Marcus, M.D.; Mitchell, J.; Walsh, B.T. Eating disorders: recent advances. Symposium of the American Psychiatric Association, May 20, 1995.

7.  Holderness, C.C.; Brooks-Gunn, J.; Warren, M.P. Co-morbidity of eating disorders and substance abuse: review of the literature. *Int J Eating Disord* 1994;16:1-34.

8.  Agras, W.S. Disorders of eating: anorexia nervosa, bulimia nervosa and binge eating disorder. in: Shader RI, ed. *Manual of psychiatric therapeutics*. 2d ed. Boston: Little, Brown, 1994.

9.  Ferbe, K.J.; Marsh, S.R.; Coyne, L. Comorbidity in an inpatient eating disordered population: clinical characteristics and treatment implications. *Psychiatr Hosp* 1993;24(1/2):3-8.

10. Gartner, A.F.; Marcus, R.N.; Halmi, K.; Loranger, A.W. DSM-III-R personality disorders in patients with eating disorders. *Am J Psychiatry* 1989;146:1585-91.

11. Strobe, M.; Katz, J.L. Depression in the eating disorders: a review and analysis of descriptive, family, and biological findings. In: Garner DM, Garfinkel PE, eds. *Diagnostic issues in anorexia nervosa*. New York: Brunner/Mazel, 1988.

12. Yeary, J.R.; Heck, C.L. Dual diagnosis: eating disorders and psychoactive substance dependence. *J Psychoactive Drugs* 1989;21:239-49.

13. Mury, M.; Verdoux, H.; Bourgeois, M. Comorbidity of bipolar and eating disorders. Epidemiologic and therapeutic aspects [French]. *Encephale* 1995;21: 545-53.

14. Ames-Frankel, J.; Devlin, M.J.; Walsh, B.T.; Strasser, T.J.; Sadik, C.; Oldham, J.M., et al. Personality disorder diagnoses in patients with bulimia nervosa: clinical correlates and changes with treatment. *J Clin Psychiatry* 1992;53:90-6.

15. Herzog, D.B.; Keller, M.B.; Lavori, P.W.; Kenny, G.M.; Sacks, N.R. The prevalence of personality disorders in 210 women with eating disorders. *J Clin Psychiatry* 1992;53:147-52.

16. Wonderlich, S.A.; Swift, W.J.; Slotnick, H.B.; Goodman, S. DSM-III-R personality disorders in eating disorder subtypes. *Int J Eating Disord* 1990;9:607-16.

17. Sansone, R.A.; Sansone, L.A. Bulimia nervosa: medical complications. In: Alexander-Mott L, Lumsden DB, eds. *Understanding eating disorders: anorexia nervosa, bulimia nervosa, and obesity.* Washington, D.C.: Taylor & Francis, 1994:181-201.

18. Kaplan, A.S.; Garfinkel, P.E., eds. *Medical issues and the eating disorders: the interface.* New York: Brunner/Mazel, 1993.

19. Fairburn, C.G. *Overcoming binge eating.* New York: Guilford, 1995.

20. Jacobs, M.B.; Schneider, J.A. Medical complications of bulimia: a prospective evaluation. *Q J Med* 1985; 54:177-82.

21. Pope, H.G., Jr.; Hudson, J.I.; Jonas, J.M.; Yurgelun-Todd, D. Bulimia treated with imipramine: a placebo-controlled, double-blind study, *Am J Psychiatry* 1983; 140:554-8.

22. Mitchell, J.E.; Groat, R. A placebo-controlled, double-blind trial of amitriptyline in bulimia. *J Clin Psychopharmacol* 1984;4:186-93.

23. Hughes, P.L.; Wells, L.A.; Cunningham, C.J.; Ilstrup, D.M. Treating bulimia with desipramine. A double-blind, placebo-controlled study. *Arch Gen Psychiatry* 1986;43:182-6.

24. Agras, W.; Dorian, B.; Kirkely, B.; Arnow, B.; Bachman, J. Imipramine in the treatment of bulimia: a double-blind controlled study. *Int J Eating Disord* 1987; 6:29-38.

25. Barlow, J.; Blouin, J.; Blouin, A.; Perez, E. Treatment of bulimia with desipramine: a double-blind crossover study. *Can J Psychiatry* 1988;33:129-33.

26. Blouin, A.; Blouin, J.; Perez, E.; Bushnik, T.; Zuro, C.; Mulder, E. Treatment of bulimia with fenfluramine and desipramine. *J Clin Psychopharmacol* 1988;8: 261-9.

27. Walsh, B.T.; Hadigan, C.M.; Devlin, M.J.; Gladis, M.; Roose, S.P. Long-term outcome of antidepressant treatment for bulimia nervosa. *Am J Psychiatry* 1991;148:1206-12.

28. Walsh, B.T.; Gladis, M.; Roose, S.P.; Stewart, J.W.; Stetner, F.; Glassman, A.H. Phenelzine vs placebo in 50 patients with bulimia. *Arch Gen Psychiatry* 1988; 45:471-5.

29. Kennedy, S.H.; Piran, N.; Warsh, J.J.; Prendergast, P.; Mainprize, E.; Whynot, C., et al. A trial of isocarboxazid in the treatment of bulimia nervosa. *J Clin Psychopharmacol* 1988;8:391-6 [Published erratum appears in *J Clin Psychopharmacol* 1989;9:3].

30. Horne, R.L.; Ferguson, J.M.; Pope, H.G., Jr.; Hudson, J.I.; Lineberry, C.G.; Ascher, J., et al. Treatment of bulimia with bulpropion: a multicenter controlled trial. *J Clin Psychiatry* 1988;49:262-6.

31. Pope, H.G., Jr.; Keck, P.E., Jr.; McElroy, S.L.; Hudson, J.I. A placebo-controlled study of trazodone in bulimia nervosa. *J Clin Psychopharmacol* 1989;9:254-9.

32. Goldstein, D.J.; Wilson, M.G.; Thompson, V.L.; Potvin, J.H.; Rampey, A.H., Jr. Long-term fluoxetine treatment of bulimia nervosa. *Br J Psychiatry* 1995;166:660-6.

33. Fluoxetine Bulimia Nervosa Collaborative Study Group. Fluoxetine in the treatment of bulimia nervosa. A multicenter, placebo-controlled, double-blind trial. *Arch Gen Psychiatry* 1992;49:139-47.

34. Mitchell, J.E.; Christenson, G.; Jennings, J.; Huber, M.; Thomas, B.; Pomeroy, C., et al. A placebo-controlled, double-blind crossover study of naltrexone hydrochloride in outpatients with normal weight bulimia. *J Clin Psychopharmacol* 1989;9:94-7.

35. Hsu, L.K.; Clemen, L.; Santhouse, R.; Ju, E.S. Treatment of bulimia nervosa with lithium carbonate. A controlled study. *J Nerv Ment Dis* 1991; 179:351-5.

36. Fairburn, C.; Marcus, M.; Wilson, G. Cognitive behavior therapy for binge eating and bulimia nervosa: a treatment manual. In: Fairburn, C.G.; Wilson, G.T., eds. *Binge eating: nature, assessment, and treatment*, New York: Guilford, 1993.

37. Wilson, G.T. Treatment of bulimia nervosa: when CBT fails. *Behav Res Ther* 1996;34:197-212.

38.   Agras, W.S.; Telch, C.F.; Arnow, B.; Eldredge, K.; Wilfley, D.; Raeburn, S.D., et al. Weight loss, cognitive-behavioral, and desipramine treatments in binge eating disorder: an additive design. *Behav Ther* 1994; 25:225-38.

*—by Phyllis G. Cooper*

Chapter 8

# Binge Eating Disorder

Binge eating disorder is a newly recognized condition that probably affects millions of Americans. People with binge eating disorder frequently eat large amounts of food while feeling a loss of control over their eating. This disorder is different from binge-purge syndrome (bulimia nervosa) because people with binge eating disorder usually do not purge afterward by vomiting or using laxatives.

## How Does Someone Know If He or She Has Binge Eating Disorder?

Most of us overeat from time to time, and many people feel they frequently eat more than they should. Eating large amounts of food, however, does not mean that a person has binge eating disorder. Doctors are still debating the best ways to determine if someone has binge eating disorder. But most people with serious binge eating problems have:

- Frequent episodes of eating what others would consider an abnormally large amount of food.

National Institute of Diabetes and Digestive and Kidney Diseases (NIDDK), from http://www.niddk.nih.gov, National Institute of Health (NIH) Publication No. 94-3589, November, 1993; and © 1999 *Nutrition Research Newsletter*, Nov. 1999, Vol. 18, Issue 11, Pg. 3; reprinted with permission of John Wiley & Sons.

- Frequent feelings of being unable to control what or how much is being eaten.
- Several of these behaviors or feelings:
  1. Eating much more rapidly than usual.
  2. Eating until uncomfortably full.
  3. Eating large amounts of food, even when not physically hungry.
  4. Eating alone out of embarrassment at the quantity of food being eaten.
  5. Feelings of disgust, depression, or guilt after overeating.

Episodes of binge eating also occur in the eating disorder bulimia nervosa. Persons with bulimia, however, regularly purge, fast, or engage in strenuous exercise after an episode of binge eating. Purging means vomiting or using diuretics (water pills) or laxatives in greater-than-recommended doses to avoid gaining weight. Fasting is not eating for at least 24 hours. Strenuous exercise, in this case, is defined as exercising for more than an hour solely to avoid gaining weight after binge eating. Purging, fasting, and strenuous exercise are dangerous ways to attempt weight control.

## How Common Is Binge Eating Disorder, and Who Is at Risk?

Although it has only recently been recognized as a distinct condition, binge eating disorder is probably the most common eating disorder. Most people with binge eating disorder are obese (more than 20 percent above a healthy body weight), but normal-weight people also can be affected. Binge eating disorder probably affects 2 percent of all adults, or about 1 million to 2 million Americans. Among mildly obese people in self-help or commercial weight loss programs, 10 to 15 percent have binge eating disorder. The disorder is even more common in those with severe obesity.

Binge eating disorder is slightly more common in women, with three women affected for every two men. The disorder affects blacks as often as whites; its frequency in other ethnic groups is not yet known. Obese people with binge eating disorder often became overweight at a younger age than those without the disorder. They also may have more frequent episodes of losing and regaining weight (yo-yo dieting).

## What Causes Binge Eating Disorder?

The causes of binge eating disorder are still unknown. Up to half of all people with binge eating disorder have a history of depression. Whether depression is a cause or effect of binge eating disorder is unclear. It may be unrelated. Many people report that anger, sadness, boredom, anxiety or other negative emotions can trigger a binge episode. Impulsive behavior and certain other psychological problems may be more common in people with binge eating disorder.

Dieting's effect on binge eating disorder is also unclear. While findings vary, early research suggests that about half of all people with binge eating disorder had binge episodes before they started to diet. Still, strict dieting may worsen binge eating in some people.

Researchers also are looking into how brain chemicals and metabolism (the way the body burns calories) affect binge eating disorder. These areas of research are still in the early stages.

## What Are the Complications of Binge Eating Disorder?

The major complications of binge eating disorder are the diseases that accompany obesity. These include diabetes, high blood pressure, high cholesterol levels, gallbladder disease, heart disease, and certain types of cancer.

People with binge eating disorder are extremely distressed by their binge eating. Most have tried to control it on their own but have not succeeded for very long. Some people miss work, school, or social activities to binge eat. Obese people with binge eating disorder often feel bad about themselves, are preoccupied with their appearance, and may avoid social gatherings. Most feel ashamed and try to hide their problem. Often they are so successful that close family members and friends don't know they binge eat.

## Should People with Binge Eating Disorder Try to Diet?

People who are not overweight or only mildly obese should probably avoid dieting, since strict dieting may worsen binge eating. However, many people with binge eating disorder are severely obese and have medical problems related to their weight. For these people, losing weight and keeping it off are important treatment goals. Most people with binge eating disorder, whether or not they want to lose weight, may benefit from treatment that addresses their eating behavior.

## What Treatment Is Available for People with Binge Eating Disorder?

Several studies have found that people with binge eating disorder may find it harder than other people to stay in weight loss treatment. Binge eaters also may be more likely to regain weight quickly. For these reasons, people with the disorder may require treatment that focuses on their binge eating before they try to lose weight.

Even those who are not overweight are frequently distressed by their binge eating and may benefit from treatment.

Several methods are being used to treat binge eating disorder. Cognitive-behavioral therapy teaches patients techniques to monitor and change their eating habits as well as to change the way they respond to difficult situations. Interpersonal psychotherapy helps people examine their relationships with friends and family and to make changes in problem areas. Treatment with medications such as antidepressants may be helpful for some individuals. Self-help groups also may be a source of support. Researchers are still trying to determine which method or combination of methods is the most effective in controlling binge eating disorder. The type of treatment that is best for an individual is a matter for discussion between the patient and his or her health care provider.

If you believe you have binge eating disorder, it's important you realize that you are not alone. Most people who have the disorder have tried unsuccessfully to control it on their own. You may want to seek professional treatment.

### Drug Therapy and Diet Counseling in Binge Eaters

Obesity is a common disorder in the United States, with one-third of the female population and one-fifth of the male population being obese. Weight loss is an important issue among obese people, whether it is for health or aesthetic reasons. Some obese patients also engage in binge eating, which complicates the matter of weight loss even more.

Studies have shown that obese binge eaters report more depressive symptoms and more sexual and psychiatric complaints. As a result, trials using bicyclic antidepressants have shown that patients treated with one of these drugs plus behavioral modification exhibited more weight reduction than placebo-treated patients did. Imipramine is a tricyclic antidepressant that has also been studied in these patients. However, the long-term effects of these medications with diet counseling and psychological support have not been studied. A recent Swiss research team studied the effects imipramine had on the frequency of binge eating, body weight, and depression during an eight-week program. They also looked at whether any weight loss achieved by the drug therapy was maintained for a follow-up period of six months after cessation of imipramine, but with the continuation of psychological support and diet counseling.

For the first eight weeks of the study, fifteen patients were randomly assigned to the imipramine group and sixteen subjects received a placebo treatment. All patients were diagnosed as binge eaters by *DSM* criteria, were overweight or obese and aged 20-60 years. While receiving either the placebo or the drug, patients received a half-hour of individual diet counseling on a biweekly basis and were provided with regularly scheduled behavior-oriented psychological support. After the initial eight weeks of the study, the placebo and imipramine were discontinued. Patients were evaluated throughout the study by interviews, psychometric questionnaires, and medical appointments.

There were no significant differences between binge eater groups with respect to age, blood pressure, binge eating episodes, etc. The subjects on imipramine showed an individual mean weight loss of 2.2 kg, while the placebo-treated subjects' weight remained stable. Binge eating episodes were significantly reduced from 7.1 to 2.8 episodes per week in imipramine-treated subjects and from 7.1 to 5.4 in the controls. After discontinuation of the drug therapy, only the imipramine group showed a continued weight loss with the diet counseling and psychological support. In fact, the placebo-treated subjects showed a slight weight increase.

The results show that imipramine with the addition of diet counseling and psychological support had a positive impact on weight reduction. Since binge-eating episodes were also reduced, one might assume that either dependent or independent of the drug, there was also a selective change in eating behavior. With regard to the effects of imipramine, the researchers believe that its long-lasting effects on weight loss and reduction of binge eating last considerably longer than its known influence on mood improvement. However, it must not be forgotten that binge eaters binge for a reason, and while medication might help, psychological issues need to be addressed on a long-term basis as well.

## Binge Eating Disorder Programs

Behavioral Medicine
Stanford University School of Medicine
Department of Psychiatry TD209
Stanford, CA 94305
Tel: (650) 723-5868

COPE: Center for Overcoming Problem Eating
Western Psychiatric Institute and Clinic
3811 O'Hara Street
Pittsburgh, PA 15213
Tel: (412) 624-5420
Website: http://www.wpic.pitt.edu/clinical/CLINSERV/eating

Eating Disorders Clinic
New York State Psychiatric Institute
Columbia Presbyterian Medical Center
1501 Riverside Drive
New York, NY 10032
Tel: (212) 543-5316
Website: http://www.columbia.edu/~EA12

Eating Disorder Research Program
University of Minnesota
2450 Riverside Drive, South
Minneapolis, MN 55445
Tel: (612) 672-6134

Nutrition Research Clinic
Baylor College of Medicine
6535 Fannin Street
MS F700
Houston, TX 77030
Tel: (713) 798-5757

Rutgers Eating Disorders Clinic
GSAPP, Rutgers University
Box 819
Piscataway, NJ 08854
Tel: (732) 445-2292

Yale Center For Eating and Weight Disorders
P.O. Box 208205
New Haven, CT 06520
Tel: (203) 432-4610

Weight-Control Information Network
1 Win Way
Bethesda, MD 20892-3665

Phone: (202) 828-1025 or (877) 946-4627
Fax: (202) 828-1028
E-mail: win@info.niddk.nih.gov

The Weight-control Information Network (WIN) is a service of the National Institute of Diabetes and Digestive and Kidney Diseases (NIDDK), part of the National Institutes of Health, under the U.S. Public Health Service. Authorized by Congress (Public Law 103-43), WIN assembles and disseminates to health professionals and the public information on weight control, obesity, and nutritional disorders. WIN responds to requests for information; develops, reviews, and distributes publications; and develops communications strategies to encourage individuals to achieve and maintain a healthy weight.

# Chapter 9

# *Body Dysmorphic Disorder*

With her long strawberry-blond hair, large green eyes and beautiful complexion, 22-year-old Jennifer would be considered attractive by any standards. She reminded Katharine A. Phillips of the captain of a high school cheerleading squad, but there had been no crisp fall afternoons on the sidelines of the football field for Jennifer: She had dropped out of high school, and was steadily dropping out of public life.

"I'm too scared to go out—everyone will see how ugly I am," Jennifer told Phillips, the assistant professor of psychiatry who diagnosed the young woman with body dysmorphic disorder (BDD).

Phillips, director of the Body Dysmorphic Disorder and Body Image Program at Butler Hospital, is one of the nation's foremost experts of BDD, in which sufferers are obsessed with perceived flaws in their appearance to the extent that it disrupts their life, and at its extreme can lead to thoughts of suicide.

Jennifer purchased clothes through catalogs, went to the food store during the middle of the night, and rarely ventured out of her parents' home during the day because she believed her skin was pimpled and scarred, Phillips wrote in her book on the disorder, *The Broken Mirror.*

Once Jennifer tried to go to the store during the day, but got stuck in a traffic jam. Panicking that the other drivers were staring at her, she abandoned the car and ran to the seclusion of a telephone booth to call her mother.

"Their suffering can be so intense," said Phillips." It is clear that it is not under their control ... you just can't will yourself to stop." In Jennifer's words: "I try not to think about it, but I have to. I think about it for most of the day. It's the first thing I think of when I wake up."

Men as well as women are diagnosed with BDD, said Phillips. Most are in their 30s and worry about their appearance up to three hours a day. Their most common obsessions concern their skin, hair and nose.

Phillips began seeing patients with symptoms of BDD as a resident at the McLane Hospital in Belmont, Mass., but she had barely any knowledge on the disorder. There were never any lectures on BDD in either medical school or residency, she said. "I just listened to my patients. Some people came in and were extremely distraught," said Phillips. "I thought it was astounding, yet it was generally unknown ... somehow it had fallen through the cracks of our knowledge."

Once Phillips began researching the disorder, she discovered case descriptions from well-known psychiatrists going back 100 years that were remarkably consistent with the patients she was treating.

An estimated 2 percent of the population is afflicted with BDD, and Phillips said she has seen some 300 patients with the disorder. They include some as young as a 6-year-old boy who believed his teeth were yellow, his stomach was "fat," and his hair looked wrong. None of his "defects" were discernible to others. He would brush his hair for nearly an hour each morning, and if he could not get it to look "right" he would dunk his head in water and restart his grooming routine, often causing him to be late for school, according to Phillips.

When the boy first arrived in a psychiatrist's office at Butler, he crouched to look at his reflection in the chrome on the chair, she said. That boy, as well as some other patients, have responded well to treatment with a number of antidepressants, said Phillips. Cognitive behavioral therapy also has been a successful treatment, she said.

However, cautioned Phillips, "It is new territory—we are still very early in the research on BDD." BDD sufferers may eventually find relief through treatment that makes Phillips' research crucial, said former colleague David Guevremont.

"It's extremely valuable," said Guevremont, of the Blackstone Valley Psychological Institute in North Smithfield. "It's clear that people who have this disorder suffer greatly and may be reluctant to seek help." As word about the disorder spreads, the potential to identify and treat patients with the symptoms increases, said Guevremont.

Phillips is applying for a grant from the National Institute of Mental Health (NIMH) to study the effectiveness of treating adolescents' BDD with the antidepressant Prozac. Another NIMH grant already funds the same study on an adult population, a project that began in April 1995.

Doctors are also now showing increasing interest in BDD, as evidenced by the growing number of published reports on the disorder in psychiatric literature over the past few years, said Phillips.

Numerous people claiming to have BDD have contacted Phillips since her book was first published in 1996 and word of her research spread. Letters pile up on her office desk and the telephone rings with callers from as far away as England and India, relaying experiences and asking for help.

Phillips hopes that her research will ultimately "give a message of hope" to people like Jennifer, who had seen at least 15 dermatologists—most of whom had refused her treatment—before turning to Phillips.

"There are a lot of people out there suffering with this," said Phillips. "I'm sitting on mountains of data, and I want to write it up and get it out."

Chapter 10

# Laxative Abuse

Self-medication with laxatives is common in the U.S., as it is in many other countries. The use of laxatives is an effective short-term treatment for constipation. However, laxative use can become chronic, and lead to misuse and abuse.

Suspected chronic laxative users must be informed of the dangers associated with this practice, and pharmacists are in a prime position to facilitate this education. Pharmacists often have the most frequent face-to-face contact with patients, and the opportunity to ask questions and offer counseling when warranted. In addition, since most laxatives are available over-the-counter, pharmacists are often the only health care professionals who may observe signs of laxative misuse or abuse.

Misuse is often unintentional, and may be based on a lack of understanding of normal bowel function. Education on when laxative use may be appropriate can help to minimize misuse of these agents. However, people who are cognizant of their laxative abuse, like many drug abusers, may try to avoid recognition. Still, pharmacists are in a position to witness frequent laxative purchases, and may be the only health care professional able to identify the abuse. In some instances, a laxative abuser may seek advice from, and even confide in, the pharmacist if concerned about adverse effects.

Among the elderly, there is a common misperception concerning the need to "be regular." Many older people mistakenly believe that they need to have a daily bowel movement to remain healthy. This can result in a reliance on laxatives and eventual habitual use.

The elderly may experience constipation because of diet, medication use, or inadequate fluid intake. Such patients will likely benefit more from dietary counseling or advice to increase fluid intake. Dehydration is a common problem among the elderly, which can not only cause constipation but which can be exacerbated by laxative use that further depletes the body of fluid.

In recent years a much younger segment of the population has developed a problem with laxative use. Laxatives are being misused—or abused—most typically by young women, either seeking to lose weight or who have eating disorders.

Laxatives are popularly believed to help lower caloric absorption and, thus, prevent weight gain. Individuals who have the greatest potential to abuse purgatives for weight control are young women, commonly teenagers, and persons who have eating disorders, such as anorexia or bulimia nervosa. Many other weight-loss methods are popular as well, such as amphetamines, fad diets, diuretics and emetics, particularly among young to college-age women. This population often meets the diagnostic criteria for anorexia nervosa or bulimia nervosa.

In a recent survey of several hundred people in a college community, 13% showed the key symptoms for bulimia (Table 10.1). Of these, 87% were women and 13% were men. At least 10% of the students studied showed purging behavior such as self-induced vomiting and frequent laxative use.

## Definition and Classification of Laxatives

Overall, the term laxative includes all things that "clean out" the bowel, including purgatives, cathartics and evacuants. Examples of some classic purgative or laxative agents include honey, psyllium, aloe,

**Table 10.1.** Signs Suggestive of Bulimia

| | |
|---|---|
| • frequent eating binges | • self-destructive attitude |
| • bizarre food preferences | • diminished sexual interest |
| • common purging behavior | • excessive exercise |
| • social isolation | • depression |

senna and rhubarb. Many of these ingredients are still used in over-the-counter (OTC) and prescription laxatives. Senokot granules (Purdue Frederick) and Fletcher's Castoria (Mentholatum), for example, contain senna extracts. Psyllium is the major active agent in Metamucil (Procter & Gamble) and Serutan (Menley & James).

The five major classes of laxatives, which are grouped according to site and mechanism of action, include: bulk-forming; osmotic; surfactant and emollient; lubricant; and stimulant laxatives. In all cases, laxation ultimately involves the alteration of intestinal fluid and electrolyte levels.

For the most part, studies have not focused specifically on the abuse and dangers associated with long-term laxative use. In recent literature, however, various disorders related to laxative abuse have been reported (Table 10.2). These reports emphasize the need for continued education related to safe weight-control measures. Adequate labeling on laxative-type products and foods should be an integral part of this. Some common foods with laxative effects are listed in Table 10.4. When conducting patient assessments, pharmacists must include questions about use of these foods.

In addition to standard OTC laxative products available in pharmacies, many products are promoted for similar uses in health food stores. They are marketed as colon- or bowel-cleansing agents, or

**Table 10.2.** Various Disorders Related to Laxative Abuse

Laxative-induced diarrhea

Osteomalacia and arthropathy

Finger clubbing and aspartylglucosamine excretion; cytoplasmic inclusions in phagocytic cells

Hypertrophic osteoarthropathy

Dental erosion, parotid and submandibular gland enlargement, oral and perioral trauma, pharyngeal and esophageal inflammation, aspiration and esophageal-gastric tears, cathartic colon and melanosis coli, dehydration and electrolyte disturbances

Coma and neuropathy related to an herbal laxative containing podophyllin

Hepatitis after chronic abuse of senna

Low serum albumin in older persons

"regulating" agents that guarantee "smooth movements." Ingredients commonly found in these products are listed in Table 10.3. Some are standardized formulations that contain usual laxative dosages of common agents (for example, aloe vera, cascara sagrada, psyllium seed,

**Table 10.3.** Select Herbal Agents with Laxative Effects

*Laxatives*

    Aloe species
    Castor Oil/Seed—Ricinus Communis

*Purgatives (Bulk purgatives, lubricant purgatives, irritant purgatives)*

    Plantago psyllium
    Oenanthe sarmentosa (water parsley)
    Podophyllum peltatum (mayapple)
    Sambucus glauca (blue elderberry)
    Garcinia species (resinous bark exudates)
    Ipomaea (exogonium)
    purge (root resin)
    Cornus pubescens (dogwood)
    Bryonia species
    Citrulis colocynthis (bitter gourd)
    Ecballium elaterium (wild cucumber)
    Croton species (croton oil)
    Japtropha curcas (purging nut)
    Mallotus philippinensis (kalama powder)
    Ricinus communis (castor bean)
    Cassia species (senna)
    Tamarindus indica (tamarind)
    Iris florentina
    Aloe barbadensis and related species
    Linum usitatissimum (flaxseed)
    Pimenta officinalis
    Olea europaea (olive oil)
    Pobgonum species
    Rheum species (rhubarb)
    Rumex crispus (curled dock)
    Rhamnus species (buckthorn)
    Veronicastrum virginicum (Culver's root)

guar gum and senna) either singly or as combination products. While some products containing these ingredients are promoted specifically for weight control, these products can be dangerous if overused, and many do not contain labeling on the hazards of misuse. Pharmacists can be instrumental in informing individuals about the risks of laxative dependence that can occur with prolonged misuse, much like other addictions, such as caffeine and nicotine.

## Adverse Effects

Among the most common early symptoms of laxative misuse or abuse are dehydration, abdominal cramping, constipation, diarrhea, nausea, vomiting and bloating. Generally, once laxative misuse or abuse is curtailed, the symptoms abate over time. When a patient reports these symptoms, health care professionals should consider the possibility of laxative abuse.

Regular use of laxatives tends to weaken the muscles in the intestine, making them less able to function properly. A change in laxative use (including discontinuation) can lead to constipation that is worse than it was initially. Excessive use can lead to lazy bowel syndrome, producing diarrhea or real constipation. Laxatives also can interfere with the effectiveness of other medications.

More serious effects include: dehydration; nutrient loss and imbalance; fluid and electrolyte loss resulting in metabolic changes; cathartic colon; gastrointestinal (GI) bleeding; allergic reactions; and melanosis coli. Long-term laxative use can result in reflex constipation that can worsen if cathartic abuse persists. As colonic binding may occur during cathartic withdrawal, this may hinder discontinuation of laxative abuse.

**Dehydration:** The conservative use of any category of laxatives can lead to life-threatening levels of dehydration, especially when other medical complications exist or if laxative treatment is combined

**Table 10.4.** Common Foods with Laxative Effects (* in large doses)

| | |
|---|---|
| Figs* | Tamarind* |
| Dates* | Cinnamon |
| Prunes | Cloves |
| Lemon juice | Dandelion roots |

with a low-salt diet. Monitoring the proper use of laxatives is essential. Overuse and abuse of laxatives clearly present a very serious risk of complications related to dehydration.

**Cathartic colon:** Cathartic colon generally is severe and possibly irreversible. Changes include inflammation of the mucosa, as well as alterations in the muscular layers of the colon. Symptoms associated with cathartic colon include abdominal pain, constipation and a bloating sensation. For the most part, this type of condition is related to the chronic abuse of stimulant cathartics. Care must be taken to differentiate these symptoms from ulcerative colitis and regional enteritis, thus, physician referral may be warranted.

**Nutrient loss:** Rapid bowel transit, which may result from the use of any laxative, can lower the absorption potential for many nutrients, including potassium, calcium and magnesium. As a result, long-term misuse may result in tetany, paralysis and muscle weakness. Since lessened absorption of other medications absorbed in the lower GI tract can also occur with long-term use, patients must be made aware of the implications.

**Fluid and electrolyte loss:** Fluid and electrolyte loss, which can result from excessive use of any type of laxative, includes the following characteristic symptoms: light-headedness, dizziness, dehydration, weakness and cardiac arrhythmias. Untreated potassium loss (hypokalemia) may result in nephropathy and concomitant chronic renal failure as well as rhabdomyolysis. Electrolyte and fluid imbalances also can lead to edema. Edema can occur with both laxative withdrawal and abuse. Diarrhea itself can produce a loss of bicarbonate in the stool, with subsequent metabolic acidosis.

**GI bleeding:** GI bleeding, a possible reaction to abuse of any laxative, can be observed directly or via testing stool samples for occult blood. Persistent bleeding can result in anemia.

**Allergic reactions:** Allergic reactions have been well documented with the phenolphthalein stimulant laxatives. Skin rashes that resemble erythema multi-forma may occur. Often, extreme and severe burning and itching accompany the rash. If present, the phenolphthalein-containing laxative should be immediately discontinued, and a physician should be contacted. Excessive phenolphthalein use also has been related to osteomalacia.

**Melanosis coli:** Melanosis coli, prolonged use of the anthracene-containing laxatives, such as Modane (Adria ), Colace (Mead Johnson) and cascara (various), may produce a brownish-black discoloration of the mucous membrane of the lower colon and rectum (visible on endoscopy). This unusual and characteristic discoloration is considered a benign pigmentation disorder that may be diagnostic of chronic cathartic misuse. It takes four to 12 months of abuse for this to occur. Fortunately, melanosis reverses over several months after discontinuing use of these products.

## Laxative Misuse

Traditional ideas about monitoring ones own health have included being sure to have "regular" bowel movements. "Regular" is often thought, especially among the elderly, to mean daily. In fact, "healthy" regularity differs from person to person, and with each person rhythms may vary with changes in daily diet and life. Three bowel movements a week is a common "regularity" rate for many, for others once a day is "regular."

To determine whether or not a problem exists, less focus should be placed on "regularity" while a stronger emphasis should be placed on symptoms of constipation. The passage of hard stools less frequently than three times a week, abdominal bloating and discomfort are signs of constipation.

## Diagnosis and Intervention

Constipation can be caused by various problems, from serious medical conditions, to eating habits and diet, or even medication reactions. Ironically, laxatives themselves, when overused, can cause constipation, among other adverse reactions. Therefore, it is essential to identify the problem. For a simple problem of constipation, laxatives often are not the best solution.

The Mayo Clinic offers some helpful advice on alternatives to laxatives in its "Family Health Book." Their suggestions may be particularly helpful in counseling elderly patients with constipation problems. Some of their suggestions are:

- The patient should try to drink at least six to eight glasses of water or other liquids daily. If the patient has problems with having to use the bathroom frequently, remind him or her that a laxative could have an even greater effect on frequency.

- Suggest that the patient increase the fiber content of his or her diet by eating more fresh fruits and vegetables. Adding a fiber or bran supplement to the diet should be considered, such as having a high-fiber cereal for breakfast every morning. The patient's diet could also include a bulk former with the vegetable fiber psyllium.

- Patients should be told not to resist the urge to move their bowels, and perhaps to set aside a specific time every day for trying to have a bowel movement.

- A daily regimen of regular physical exercise should be planned.

- If the patient finds that constipation continues, it then may be reasonable to suggest use of a nonstimulating laxative, such as milk of magnesia or mineral oil, occasionally at bedtime, although regular use should be avoided.

- Explain that enemas should be avoided. A thorough "cleansing" of the colon, by either an enema or a laxative, actually contributes to the problem of constipation.

- If after following the above suggestions the constipation is still not improved, a physician should be consulted.

Pharmacists will need to follow up and help patients who have been overusing laxatives. Withdrawal symptoms may be confusing, uncomfortable and even dangerous. It may be advisable to work with the patient's physician. Serious, long-term, habitual users of laxatives may even need hospitalization.

## Laxative Abuse in Weight Control

Intermittent use of most laxatives is generally safe. Abuse is characterized by using laxatives at much higher-than-recommended doses.

For the most part, laxative abuse stems from misuse of these agents for the relief of constipation (real or perceived), and attempts to reduce weight gain and to prevent fluid retention. Recent studies have shown that laxatives cannot prevent caloric absorption and weight gain. Specifically, purging via a stimulant laxative causes colonic water secretion and evacuation of feces (acute weight loss), but has little effect on the small intestine (the primary site of caloric absorption). Through this mechanism, many experience an immediate but transient weight loss due to fluid loss rather than body mass. This water depletion often creates a false sense of weight control. The resultant effect on mood strengthens an individual's psychological dependence on these agents.

Stimulant laxatives appear to be favored by individuals who have eating disorders because they act quickly and produce loose, watery stools. Generally, the public also misuses stimulant laxatives for the purported "body cleansing" attributes of these agents, and because these agents are inexpensive, palatable and easily purchased. While hazards are associated with abuse of all laxative agents, the greatest incidence of medical complications (such as physical dependence, and fluid and electrolyte imbalances) is seen in persons using stimulant cathartics.

## Diagnosis and Intervention

Because individuals can be very sensitive and secretive about weight issues, laxative abuse is difficult to ascertain. Any knowledge of a weight-control problem or eating disorder in a patient should evoke suspicion of laxative abuse. Pharmacists should recognize that young women are the most common abusers of laxatives. Anxiety is often associated with laxative abuse in bulimic patients, thus, pharmacists should consider the individual's actions when assessing the patient. If a patient profile is available to assist in making a clinical assessment, then diet, psychological profile, concomitant diseases and drug therapy should be considered.

Pharmacists are often the health professional with the highest likelihood of identifying a laxative abuse problem. While it must be recognized that individuals who abuse laxatives and/or other medications may try to avoid recognition, some practical guidelines in discussing pertinent issues with a suspected laxative abuser are:

- Determine extent and type of laxative abuse (for example, frequency, type of agent used, duration of abuse).

- Assess the patient's beliefs about laxatives

- Emphasize that laxatives do not promote weight loss. Provide supportive counseling and education about healthful and non-hazardous weight-control methods (such as, regular exercise, behavior modification, altered eating habits and food choices, including increased vegetable and fiber intake and decreased fat intake from fried foods and red meat).

- Discuss the short- and long-term physical effects of laxative abuse and agree on a schedule and plan to wean the patient from laxative use.

- Assure patients that bloating, constipation, weight gain, edema and discomfort are temporary symptoms after discontinuing chronic laxative use. It is important that the patient knows to monitor withdrawal and that he or she is prepared to work with the pharmacist or physician.

- Encourage maintenance of adequate fluid intake, moderate exercise and increased dietary fiber intake, especially during laxative withdrawal.

- Maintain adequate and close follow-up (e.g., every two weeks) to monitor patient progress.

- If constipation occurs and persists, recommend a short course of a mild nonstimulant laxative.

It must be recognized that hospitalization may be necessary for assessment and treatment of severely dependent patients. Group or individual psychotherapy may be beneficial if personality and mood disorders are involved. All abusers should be encouraged to participate in education and prevention programs. Pharmacists should be aware of local organizations and prevention and treatment programs.

When possible, to determine the extent and effects of laxative abuse with laxative abusers who are more forthcoming about their problem and with suspected abusers, pharmacists should try to work with other health professionals and the patient to get a reliable diagnosis and create a treatment plan.

While a reliable diagnosis can only be reached through use of a chemical analysis, a number of items should be included in the diagnostic work-up. Some of these items are as follows:

1. Complete history and physical exam to rule out medical complications of laxative abuse

2. History of diet, exercise, eating habits, body image and weight control

3. Questions about anxieties related to food intake, self-esteem and depression

4. Physical warning signals, such as parotid gland enlargement, dental erosion, knuckle abrasion and dehydration

5. Use of a standard questionnaire (such as the Eating Disorder Inventory)

6. Laboratory tests (for example, hemoglobin test for anemia; depletion of protein, potassium, magnesium, calcium and chloride; test for occult blood in stool samples; toxicological screens for laxatives containing phenol and anthraquinone)

7. Barium enema and endoscopic evaluations

## Conclusion

Pharmacists are in a position to take a leading role in educating patients about the adverse effects of laxatives and how, when and whether they should be used. Pharmacists can inform individuals of abuse dangers; clarify misperceptions about laxatives and weight control; help to ensure proper patient assessment; refer patients to physicians; and develop preventive community education programs.

Chapter 11

# Night-Eating Syndrome

Night-eating syndrome has not yet been formally defined as an eating disorder. Underlying causes are being identified, and treatment plans are still being developed. It seems likely that both biological/ genetic and emotional factors contribute to the problem.

If you are seeking help for night-eating syndrome, you would be wise to schedule a complete physical exam with your physician and also an evaluation with a counselor trained in the field of eating disorders. In addition, a dietitian can help develop meal plans that distribute intake more evenly throughout the day so that you are not so vulnerable to caloric loading in the evening.

## Signs and Symptoms

- The person has little or no appetite for breakfast. Delays first meal for several hours after waking up. Is not hungry or is upset about how much was eaten the night before.

- Eats more food after dinner than during that meal.

- Eats more than half of daily food after dinner hour.

- This pattern has persisted for at least two months.

- Person feels tense, anxious, upset, or guilty while eating.

- Has trouble falling asleep or staying asleep.

- Behavior is not like binge eating which is done in relatively short episodes. Night-eating syndrome involves continual eating throughout evening hours.

- This eating produces guilt and shame, not enjoyment.

## *How Many People Have Night-Eating Syndrome?*

Perhaps only one to two percent (1-2%) of adults in the general population have this problem, but one study suggests that more than a quarter (27%) of people who are overweight by at least 100 pounds eat this way.

Chapter 12

# Lesser-Known Eating Disorders

Because of publicity and media attention, the words "eating disorders" usually bring to mind anorexia nervosa, bulimia nervosa, and binge eating disorder. There are, however, several other less well-known disorders that fall in this category. Some have existed for decades and are considered formal diagnoses. Others have come to the attention of clinicians and researchers more recently. They have not yet been accepted as legitimate diagnoses, but work continues, and they may gain that status in the future.

They include:

- Muscle dysmorphia (bigarexia)
- Nocturnal sleep-related eating disorder
- Pica
- Gourmand syndrome
- Prader-Willi syndrome
- Cyclic vomiting syndrome
- Obesity

## Muscle Dysmorphia (Bigarexia)

### What Is Muscle Dysmorphia?

Sometimes called bigarexia, muscle dysmorphia is the opposite of anorexia nervosa. People with this disorder obsess about being small and undeveloped. They worry that they are too little and too frail. Even if they have good muscle mass, they believe their muscles are inadequate. In efforts to fix their perceived smallness, people with muscle dysmorphia lift weights, do resistance training, and exercise compulsively. They may take steroids or other muscle-building drugs, a practice with potentially lethal consequences.

## Who Gets Muscle Dysmorphia?

Both men and women. So far there are no statistics available, but researchers suspect the disorder is more common in males since the culturally defined ideal male is big and strong while the ideal female is small and thin.

## Consequences of Muscle Dysmorphia

The constant preoccupation with perceived smallness interferes with school and career accomplishments. It robs friendships and romantic relationships of spontaneity and enjoyment. Since the person is exceedingly self-conscious at all times, s/he cannot relax and enjoy life without worrying about how other people may be seeing, and criticizing, the perceived smallness. In almost all cases, people with muscle dysmorphia are not small at all. Many have well-developed musculature, and some even compete in body building competitions.

Muscle dysmorphia may be one kind of obsessive-compulsive disorder. People with this problem cannot or will not stop their excessive exercise even when they are injured. They will not give up their unhealthy steroid use even when they fully understand the risks involved.

## Treatment of Muscle Dysmorphia

Many people with this problem resist getting treatment stating that they are content with the way they are. Some admit they are afraid that if they give up the drugs and exercise, they will wither away to frailty.

Family members and concerned friends may be able to persuade the person to at least get an evaluation by focusing on the problems caused by the behaviors, such as job loss, relationship failure, and physical harm.

Nonetheless, about half of people with this problem are so convinced of their perceived smallness that they refuse help and continue their excessive exercise and steroid use.

For those who enter treatment, cognitive-behavioral therapy combined with medication holds promise. The best place to start is an evaluation by a physician trained in sports medicine. Ask for a referral to a mental health counselor who also works with athletes. After both professionals have completed their evaluations, consider their recommendations and choose a course of action that is in your own best interests. Best wishes.

# Nocturnal Sleep-Related Eating Disorder

When I woke up this morning, there were candy bar wrappers all over the kitchen, and I had a stomach ache. I had chocolate on my face and hands. My husband says I was up eating last night, but I have no memories of doing so. Could he be playing a joke on me?

Maybe not. You might have nocturnal sleep-related eating disorder, a relatively unknown condition that is just beginning to be investigated.

## What Is Nocturnal Sleep-Related Eating Disorder (NS-RED)?

In spite of its name, NS-RED is not, strictly speaking, an eating disorder. It is thought to be a type of sleep disorder in which people eat while seeming to be sound asleep. They may eat in bed or roam through the house and prowl the kitchen.

These people are not conscious during episodes of NS-RED. They are not aware they are eating. They have no memories of having done so when then wake, or they have only fragmentary memories. Episodes probably occur in a state somewhere between wakefulness and sleep.

When people with NS-RED awake and discover the evidence of their nighttime forays, they are embarrassed, ashamed, and afraid they may be losing their minds. Some, when confronted with the evidence by family members, deny that they were the perpetrators. They truly do not believe they could have done such a thing and cannot admit to such dramatic loss of control.

Food consumed during NS-RED episodes tends to be high-fat, high-sugar comfort food that people restrain themselves from eating while awake. Sometimes these folks eat bizarre combinations of food (hotdogs dipped in peanut butter, raw bacon smeared with mayonnaise, etc.) or non-food items like soap they have sliced like they would slice cheese.

## Who Gets NS-RED?

One to three percent of the general population seems to be subject to this disorder, and ten to fifteen percent of people with eating disorders are affected. The problem may be chronic or appear once or twice and then disappear. Many of these people are severely stressed, anxious individuals who are dismayed and angry at themselves for their nocturnal loss of control.

Many of these individuals diet during the day, which may leave them hungry and vulnerable to binge eating at night when their control is weakened by sleep.

People with NS-RED sometimes have histories of alcoholism, drug abuse, and sleep disorders other than NS-RED like sleep walking, restless legs, and sleep apnea. Their sleep is fragmented, and they are often tired when they wake.

Sleep disorders, including NS-RED, seem to run in families. They may have a genetic component.

### How Can People Eat and Not Remember Doing So? Are They Lying?

No, they are not lying. It seems that parts of their brains are truly asleep, and, at the same time, other parts are awake. The parts that regulate waking consciousness are asleep, so the next day there are no memories of eating the night before.

### Is There Any Treatment for NS-RED? If There Is, What Is It?

Yes, there is treatment. It begins with a clinical interview and a night or two at a sleep-disorders center where brain activity is monitored. Sometimes medication is helpful, but sleeping pills should be avoided. They can make matters worse by increasing confusion and clumsiness that can lead to injury. Regular use of sleeping pills can also lead to dependency and rebound wakefulness on withdrawal.

Also helpful are interventions that reduce stress and anxiety; for example, stress management classes, assertiveness training, counseling, and reducing intake of alcohol, street drugs, and caffeine.

If you think you may have NS-RED, talk to your physician and ask for a referral to a sleep-disorders treatment center. Help is available. Take advantage of it.

## Pica

Pica is a craving for non-food items. The most frequent are:

- Dirt, clay
- Paint chips, plaster, chalk
- Cornstarch, laundry starch, baking soda

- Coffee grounds
- Cigarette ashes, burnt match heads
- Rust
- Other items that are not usually considered food

Pica is usually found in:

- Pregnant women
- People whose diets are deficient in minerals contained in the consumed substances
- People who have psychiatric disturbances such as hysteria
- People whose family or ethnic customs include eating certain non-food substances
- People who diet, become hungry, and then try to ease hunger and cravings with low-calorie, non-food substances.

Some pica is harmless, but if the craved substance is toxic or contaminated, or if it blocks the intestines, it can lead to medical emergency and death. Medical evaluation is essential.

## Pica: *Facts and Theories*

- The person must regularly eat these craved substances for a month or more before a diagnosis is given.
- The name "pica" comes from the Latin word for magpie, a bird that is famous for eating anything and everything.
- Perhaps ten to twenty percent of children have pica at some time before adulthood.
- Depending on the population, zero percent to sixty-eight percent of pregnant women have pica. Those in lower socioeconomic groups seem to have more problems with these cravings.
- In some cases, pica is related not to dietary deficiencies but to folk traditions passed on in families or ethnic groups.
- Some people treat clay or dirt eating as a part of daily routine, somewhat like smoking.
- Others believe that eating dirt will help them incorporate magical spirits from the Earth into their bodies.

- Still others believe that certain kinds of clay will suppress morning sickness when eaten.

- Some children with pica may be imitating a pet dog or cat.

- Stress may be a precipitating factor, especially the stress of dieting when the person tries to relieve hunger and cravings with non-food substances.

- There is evidence to support the hypothesis that at least some pica is a response to dietary deficiency. Pregnant women, for example, have given up pica after they were treated for iron-deficiency anemia.

- But other cases of pica can cause dietary deficiencies because the consumed substances block absorption of necessary minerals in the intestines.

- If pica is a lifestyle choice that does not harm the individual, and if it is not part of an underlying eating disorder, it can go untreated, but care should be taken to protect against toxic substances (such as lead in paint and plaster chips). The person must be alert for symptoms (pain, lack of bowel movements, abdominal bloat and distention) that suggest the substance has formed an indigestible mass that has blocked the intestines. If such is the case, immediate medical attention is necessary.

## *Gourmand Syndrome*

The following behaviors are representative of Gourmand Syndrome:

- Person is preoccupied with fine food, including its purchase, preparation, presentation, and consumption.

- Person is less engaged than previously with friends, family, job, and other activities.

- Thought to be caused by injury to the right side of the brain: tumor, concussion, stroke, etc.

- Very rare. Only 34 reported cases in medical literature.

- Some symptoms overlap with obsessive-compulsive and addictive disorders.

- In spite of their "lusting after food" and enthusiastic consumption of it, people with gourmand syndrome do not seem to become fat.

- Nor do they vomit, abuse laxatives, or engage in other pathological weight-loss behaviors.

- They had normal relationships with food before the brain injury.

- Cognitive, behavioral, and motor impairments are common, probably also related to the brain injury.

- People are not particularly troubled by their new consuming interest.

- Treatment should begin with a neurologist or possibly a psychiatrist.

## Prader-Willi Syndrome

*We have just learned that our son has Prader-Willi syndrome. Sometimes he acts bulimic. What's the difference?*

Prader-Willi syndrome is a congenital problem that affects one in every ten to fifteen thousand children. It includes the following characteristics:

- Mental retardation

- Behavior problems, some of them severe

- Speech problems

- Muscle weakness

- Abnormal growth

- In some children, unpredictable rage attacks

- Constant hunger and an implacable drive to eat

People who have Prader-Willi syndrome will lie, cheat, and steal to get food. If their access to food is not controlled, they will gorge until they become so obese that they die. They do not vomit or purge in other ways as bulimics do.

Paradoxically, Prader-Willi babies are usually thin and weak. They eat very poorly. When they do begin to eat, however, they do not stop.

Sometimes Prader-Willi is mistakenly thought to be bulimia. Bulimia is a psychosomatic disorder. The person wants to solve problems and improve self-esteem by losing weight. The unhealthy weight loss behaviors hurt the body. Prader-Willi, on the other hand, is the result of a genetic defect. The person shows little concern about body image and gorges because the physiological brakes that control appetite and hunger are missing.

Researchers have not yet discovered what causes the genetic defect that leads to Prader-Willi. It does not seem to run in families. It involves some sort of malfunctioning in the hypothalamus, a major control center in the brain.

Prader-Willi syndrome is difficult to manage in the home. Prozac and other psychiatric medications can help, but there is no cure.

## Cyclic Vomiting Syndrome

### What Is Cyclic Vomiting Syndrome?

Cyclic vomiting syndrome is usually found in children between 2 and 16, although some adults have received the diagnosis as well. CVS is not very common, and so far researchers have no definite explanations.

Symptoms include recurrent episodes of stomach pain, nausea, vomiting, and headaches. During an episode the person can do little else but be miserable. Often s/he is bothered by bright light.

Vomiting occurs frequently, up to 10 or more times per hour. Episodes last from a few hours up to several days. People afflicted with CVS are usually well and normal between episodes.

### What Causes Cyclic Vomiting Syndrome?

Researchers are not sure. Because migraine headache sufferers report the same cluster of symptoms (nausea, vomiting, abdominal pain, and light sensitivity), the two problems may share common mechanisms.

### What Is the treatment for Cyclic Vomiting Syndrome?

CVS is currently treated with amitriptyline or cyproheptadine.

Both these medications are also used to prevent migraine headaches, and so far they seem to work for CVS as well.

## Obesity: Is It an Eating Disorder?

Like most things, obesity is a complex phenomenon about which it is dangerous to generalize. What is true for one person is not necessarily true for the next. Nevertheless, we shall try to make sense out of conflicting theories and give answers to people who struggle to maintain self-esteem in a world that seems to be obsessed with youth, thinness, and the perfect body—whatever that may be.

## What Is Obesity?

A person with anorexia nervosa may define obesity as a weight gain of five pounds, from 89 to 94. A grandmother past menopause may call herself obese because she carries 165 pounds on her large-boned, muscular body. A modeling agency may talk about obesity when one of the women on the payroll puts 135 pounds on her 5'10" body.

None of these women is clinically obese. The anorexic and the model are underweight.

Men are split in their personal definitions of obesity. Many are just as concerned about overweight as women are, while others, frankly rotund, believe they are just fine, perfectly healthy, and universally attractive to potential romantic partners.

Many physicians consider a person to obese only if s/he weighs more than 20% above expected weight for age, height, and body build. Morbid or malignant obesity is usually considered to be any weight in excess of 100 pounds above that expected for age, height, and build.

In recent years, the definition of expected, or healthy, weight has expanded to include more pounds per height in view of research that links reduced mortality (longer lives) with more weight than is currently considered fashionable.

## How Many Americans Are Obese?

Over half of American adults weigh more than they should. As many as 40 million Americans are overweight to the point of obesity, about one-third of all adults. The prevalence is increasing in all major socioeconomic and ethnic groups, including younger adults between 25 and 44.

## What Are the Causes of Obesity?

- Consumption of more calories than are burned through work, exercise, and other activities.

- Inexpensive, tasty, plentiful food and a combination of leisure time, sedentary lifestyle, TV, and other "activities" that require little or no physical activity.

111

- Attempts to medicate or escape emotional pain and distress. For various emotional reasons, including loneliness and depression, some people eat when their bodies do not need food.

- Diets and prolonged caloric restriction. When people try to make the body thinner than it is genetically programmed to be, it retaliates by becoming ravenous and vulnerable to binge eating. Ninety-eight percent of dieters regain all the weight they manage to lose, plus about 10 extra pounds, within five years. Yo-yo dieting repeats the cycle of weight loss followed by ever-increasing weight gain when hunger ultimately wins.

- Some individuals are obese because of specific biological problems such as malfunctioning thyroid or pituitary glands. Others may have physical problems or disabilities that severely limit or prohibit entirely exercise, strenuous work, and other physical activity.

- Researchers believe that in most cases obesity represents a complex relationship between genetic, psychological, physiological, metabolic, socioeconomic, and cultural factors.

The children of heavy parents are more likely to be heavy than the children of thin parents. If friends and family members offer comfort in the form of food, people will learn to deal with painful feelings by eating instead of using more effective strategies. Poor folks tend to be fatter than the affluent. People living in groups that frequently celebrate and socialize at get-togethers featuring tempting food tend to be fatter than those who do not. Some individuals eat great quantities of food, exercise moderately or not at all, and never seem to gain weight. Others walk past a bakery and gain ten pounds. No two people are the same, and no two obesity profiles are identical.

### Health Risks Associated with Obesity

- *Hypertension* (high blood pressure, a contributor to stroke and heart disease). Overweight young people (20-45) have a six times higher incidence of hypertension than do peers who are normal weight. Older obese folks seem to be at even greater risk.

- *Diabetes.* Even moderate obesity, especially when the extra fat is carried in the stomach and abdomen (instead of hips and thighs), increases the risk of non-insulin dependent diabetes mellitus (NIDDM) ten-fold.

- *Cardiovascular disease.* Both the degree of obesity and the location of fat deposits contribute to the potential for heart and blood vessel disease. The fatter the person, the higher the risk. People who carry extra weight in the trunk area (stomach and abdomen) are at higher risk than folks who store fat in hip and thigh deposits.

- *Cancer.* Obese men are at elevated risk of developing cancer of the colon, rectum, and prostate. Obese women are at elevated risk of developing cancer of the breast, cervix, uterus, and ovaries.

- *Endocrine problems.* Irregular menstrual cycles; other menstrual problems; and pregnancy complications, especially toxemia and hypertension. Hormone imbalances of various kinds may contribute to, or be the result of, obesity.

- *Gall bladder disease.* Obese women 20-30 years old are at six times greater risk of gall bladder disease than their normal-weight peers. By age 60 almost one-third of obese women will have developed gall bladder disease.

- *Lung and breathing problems.* Obesity can impede the muscles that inflate and ventilate the lungs. Obese individuals may have to work hard to get enough air and over time may not be able to take in the oxygen needed by all body cells.

- *Arthritis.* Obese individuals are at increased risk of developing gouty arthritis, a distressingly painful disorder. Excess weight stresses vulnerable joints, in particular the back and knee, which may develop osteoarthritis, a mechanical rather than metabolic problem.

- *Premature death.* Research indicates that obese people die sooner than their normal weight peers.

### Other Problems Associated with Obesity

- Sleep disturbances including sleep apnea (breathing stops for several seconds; then the person rouses, gasps, and struggles to catch breath; episodes may continue through the night)

- Inability to fully participate in recreational activities

- Inability to compete effectively in sports and athletics; being picked last, or not at all, for team sports

- Inability to perform some jobs; reduced job opportunities

- Prejudice and discrimination in school and the workplace
- Restricted social opportunities
- Restricted opportunities for romantic relationships
- Low self-esteem and body-image problems, related at least in part to prejudice and discrimination encountered in school, at work, and in social settings.

## One Important Piece of Good News

Obese people do not seem to have any more psychological problems, or more serious psychological problems, than folks of normal weight. The problems they do have are more likely a consequence of prejudice and discrimination than a cause of overweight. In fact, several studies have suggested that the obese are significantly less anxious and depressed than normal-weight peers.

## What Can Be done about Obesity?

The simplistic answer: eat less and exercise more. The realistic answer:

- Work with a physician to identify and correct any underlying medical, biological, or physiological problems contributing to excess weight.
- Check with a counselor to see if you are using food for a purpose food cannot fulfill: love, comfort, escape, an antidote to boredom, and so forth. If you are self-medicating with food, work with the therapist to come up with better ways of managing stress, painful emotions, and problems.
- Don't ever diet or restrict calories when you are legitimately hungry. If you do, you will set yourself up to binge later.
- Eat normal, reasonable, moderate amounts of healthy foods. Emphasize fruits, vegetables, and whole grains. Don't cut out sweets and fats completely. If you do, you will crave and sneak them. Besides, your body needs the nutrients found in fats and carbohydrates. Just don't overdo it.
- Most important: Exercise consistently. Get regular amounts of moderate, self-loving exercise. Start with a few minutes of walking and slowly extend the time until you can do 30-60 minutes a

day, 3-5 days a week. If you haven't exercised in a while, be sure to check with your doctor first.

- Find a support system. Friends are great; so are support groups. There are both online and in-person opportunities.

- Be gentle and realistic with yourself. If everyone in your family is round and sturdy, chances are you will never be a super model—but you can be happy and healthy. Also remember that healthy, realistic weight loss takes time. Losing one-half to one pound a week isn't very glamorous, but if you go any faster, you will make yourself hungry, and hunger will inevitably make you overeat.

## How about Diet Pills and Other Weight-Loss Products? Surgery?

*Over-the-counter products*. There are many items in drugstores and health food stores that claim to help people lose weight. None seem to be both safe and effective. The ones that are effective are only minimally so, and they have significant side effects and health risks. The ones that are safe don't seem to be very effective in helping folks lose weight and keep it off. Think about it: if there really were a safe and effective weight loss product available over the counter, everyone in the United States would be thin. Our best advice: save your money.

*Prescription medications*. In spite of a tremendous amount of research, there still is no magic pill that melts pounds away effortlessly. Obese people and their physicians had great hope for fen-phen, a combination stimulant and antidepressant, but those hopes were dashed when some of the people taking it developed potentially fatal heart problems. New medications are available, and more are in the pipeline. Talk to your doctor about their pros and cons.

*Surgery*. For some obese people, gastric bypass (stomach stapling) may be a lifesaving measure. The procedure is major surgery and is associated with risk of significant side effects and complications. For this reason it should be considered a treatment of last resort. Also, to be successful, the patient must cooperate with an entirely new way of eating and managing food. If nothing else has worked for you, and if your medical situation warrants such a drastic approach, talk to your physician to see if you might be a candidate for this procedure.

# Part Three

# Causes and Adverse Affects

# Chapter 13

# What Causes Eating Disorders?

There are many theories and no one simple answer that covers everyone. For any particular person, some or all of the following factors will be woven together to produce starving, stuffing, and purging.

## Biological Factors

Temperament seems to be, at least in part, genetically determined. Some personality types (obsessive-compulsive and sensitive-avoidant, for example) are more vulnerable to eating disorders than others. New research suggests that abnormal levels of brain chemicals predispose some people to anxiety, perfectionism, and obsessive-compulsive thoughts and behaviors. These people seem to have more than their share of eating disorders.

Also, once a person begins to starve, stuff, or purge, those behaviors in and of themselves can alter brain chemistry and prolong the disorder. For example, both undereating and overeating can activate brain chemicals that produce feelings of peace and euphoria, thus temporarily dispelling anxiety and depression. In fact some researchers believe that eating disordered folks may be using food to self-medicate painful feelings and distressing moods.

---

## Psychological Factors

People with eating disorders tend to be perfectionistic. They may have unrealistic expectations of themselves and others. In spite of their many achievements, they feel inadequate, defective, and worthless. In addition, they see the world as black and white, no shades of gray. Everything is either good or bad, a success or a failure, fat or thin. If fat is bad and thin is good, then thinner is better, and thinnest is best—even if thinnest is sixty-eight pounds in a hospital bed on life support.

Some people with eating disorders use the behaviors to avoid sexuality. Others use them to try to take control of themselves and their lives. They are strong, usually winning the power struggles they find themselves in, but inside they feel weak, powerless, victimized, defeated, and resentful.

People with eating disorders often lack a sense of identity. They try to define themselves by manufacturing a socially approved and admired exterior. They have answered the existential question, "Who am I?" by symbolically saying "I am, or I am trying to be, thin. Therefore, I matter."

People with eating disorders often are legitimately angry, but because they seek approval and fear criticism, they do not know how to express their anger in healthy ways. They turn it against themselves by starving or stuffing.

## Family Factors

Some people with eating disorders say they feel smothered in their families. Others feel abandoned, misunderstood, and alone. Parents who overvalue physical appearance can unwittingly contribute to an eating disorder. So can those who make critical comments, even in jest, about their children's bodies.

These families tend to be overprotective, rigid, and ineffective at solving conflict. Sometimes they are emotionally cold. There are often high expectations of achievement and success. The children learn not to disclose doubts, fears, anxieties, and imperfections. Instead they try to resolve their problems by manipulating weight and food.

In addition, research suggests that daughters of mothers with histories of eating disorders may be at higher risk of eating disorders themselves than are children of mothers with few food and weight issues.

According to a report published in the April 1999 issue of the *International Journal of Eating Disorders*, mothers who have anorexia,

120

bulimia, or binge eating disorder handle food issues and weight concerns differently than mothers who have never had eating disorders. Patterns are observable even in infancy. They include odd feeding schedules, using food for rewards, punishments, comfort, or other non-nutritive purposes, and concerns about their daughters' weight.

Still to be determined is whether or not daughters of mothers with eating disorders will themselves become eating disordered when they reach adolescence.

## Social Factors

TV, movies, and magazines are three examples of media that flood people with messages about the "advantages" of being thin. Impressionable readers and viewers are told, sometimes directly, sometimes indirectly by the actors and models that are chosen for display, that goodness, success, power, approval, popularity, admiration, intelligence, friends, and romantic relationships all require physical beauty in general and thinness in particular.

The corollary is also promoted: People who are not thin and beautiful are represented as failures: bad, morally lax, weak, out of control, stupid, laughable, lonely, disapproved of, and rejected.

Girls and women are disproportionally affected by eating disorders and cultural demands for thinness. Never before in recorded history have females been exhorted to be as thin as is currently fashionable.

Men, by contrast, are encouraged to be strong and powerful. As they work to develop their power in the gym and workplace, they equate "thin" with "skinny" and "weak." Even though today's female models often look frail, wounded, and vulnerable (characteristics men abhor in themselves), female thinness is not rejected as "skinny." Instead it is coveted and defined as glamorous, sexy, and evidence of the with-it woman. Perhaps this explains, at least in part, why only five to ten percent of people with eating disorders are male.

## Triggers

If people are vulnerable to eating disorders, sometimes all it takes to put the ball in motion is a trigger event that they do not know how to handle. A trigger could be something as seemingly innocuous as teasing or as devastating as rape or incest.

Triggers often involve the breakup of a valued relationship with its loss of personal connection and resulting loneliness.

Triggers often happen at times of transition where increased demands are made on people who already are unsure of their ability to meet expectations. Such triggers include starting a new school, beginning a new job, death, divorce, marriage, family problems, graduation into a chaotic, competitive world, and so forth.

Perhaps the most common trigger of disordered eating is dieting. It is a bit simplistic, but nonetheless true, to say that if there were no dieting, there would be no anorexia nervosa. Neither would there be the bulimia that people create when they diet, make themselves hungry, overeat in response to that hunger, and then, panicky about weight gain, vomit or otherwise purge to get rid of the calories.

Feeling guilty and perhaps horrified at what they have done, they swear to "be good." That usually means more dieting, which leads to more hunger, and so the cycle repeats again and again. It is axiomatic in eating disorders treatment programs that the best way to avoid a binge is to never, never allow oneself to become hungry.

Chapter 14

# Who Is at Risk?

### Who gets eating disorders?

These disorders usually appear in bright, attractive young women between twelve and twenty-five, although there are both older and younger exceptions. At least five to ten percent (5-10%) are male, possibly more. Researchers and statisticians are just now beginning to determine how widespread eating disorders are in men and boys.

### What kinds of things trigger eating disorders?

Problems often begin when a person is dealing with a difficult transition, shock, or loss: puberty, marriage, divorce, family problems, death, new job, new school, breakup of an important relationship, sexual or physical abuse, critical comments from a respected authority figure, and so forth. These situations sometimes overwhelm a person's ability to handle them. S/he feels helpless and out of control.

People vulnerable to eating disorders also, in most cases, are experiencing relationship problems, loneliness in particular. Some may be withdrawn with only superficial or conflicted connections to other people. Others may seem to be living exciting lives filled with friends and social activities, but later they will confess that they did not feel they really fit in, that no one seemed to really understand them, and that they had no true friends or confidants with whom they could share their innermost thoughts, feelings, doubts, insecurities, fears, hopes, ambitions, and so forth. Often they desperately want healthy connections to others but fear criticism and rejection if their perceived flaws and shortcomings become known.

Wanting to take control and fix things, but not really knowing how, and under the influence of a culture that equates success and happiness with thinness, the person tackles her/his body instead of the problem at hand. Dieting, bingeing, purging, exercising, and other strange behaviors are not random craziness. They are heroic, but misguided and ineffective, attempts to take charge in a world that seems overwhelming.

Note: dieting and the resulting hungers, both physical and emotional, caused by deprivation are two of the strongest triggers of binge eating we know of. It is a bit simplistic, but nonetheless true, that if no one dieted, there would be no anorexia nervosa. Neither would there be the bulimia that results from prolonged restricted eating, the hunger that follows, and the overwhelming cravings for lots of calorie-laden food that naturally accompany strict self-denial. About 50% of people who have starved themselves into anorexia become bulimic when they lose control of urges to make up for lost time, and calories, by eating lots of food very rapidly.

## What are people with anorexia like?

People who become anorexic often were good children: conscientious, hard working, and good students. They may be people pleasers who seek approval and avoid conflict. They may take care of other people and strive for perfection, but underneath they feel defective and inadequate. They want to be special, to stand out from the mediocre masses. They try to achieve that goal by losing weight and being thin.

## What are people with bulimia like?

People who become bulimic often have problems with anxiety, depression, and impulsivity (shoplifting, casual sexual activity, binge shopping, alcohol and drug abuse, and so forth). They may be dependent on their families even though they fiercely profess independence. Many have problems trusting other people. They have few or no truly satisfying friendships or romantic relationships.

## Are some people at special risk?

Because of intense demands for thinness, some people are at high risk for eating disorders: wrestlers, jockeys, cheerleaders, sorority members, socialites, dancers, gymnasts, runners, models, actresses, entertainers, and male homosexuals.

## Eating Disorders and Physical or Sexual Abuse

Some clinicians find that a high percentage of their clients with eating disorders also have histories of physical or sexual abuse. Research, however, suggests that people who have been abused have about the same incidence of eating disorders as those who have not been mistreated. Nevertheless, the subject arises often enough to warrant discussion here.

People who have survived abuse often do not know what to do with the strong feelings and overwhelming memories that remain, sometimes even many years later. Some try to escape those feelings and memories by numbing themselves with binge food or through starvation. Some try to symbolically cleanse themselves by vomiting or abusing laxatives. Some starve themselves because they believe they feel they are "bad" and do not deserve the comfort of food and the nurture it represents.

As with all eating disorders, the starving and stuffing that follow abuse are coping behaviors. The key to recovery is finding out what the person is trying to achieve, or avoid, with the behaviors. S/he then needs to find, and use, healthier and more effective behaviors to feel better and make life happier. Almost always professional counseling is necessary to complete the process.

Chapter 15

# Males with Eating Disorders

### What Eating Disorders Do Men and Boys Get?

Just like girls and women, males get anorexia nervosa and bulimia nervosa. Many males describe themselves as compulsive eaters, and they may have binge eating disorder.

### How Many Males Have These Disorders?

Perhaps as many as one in six cases of anorexia nervosa occur in males. Binge eating disorder seems to occur almost equally in males and females, although males are not as likely to feel guilty or anxious after a binge as women are sure to do.

It is difficult to know exactly how many males have bulimia. Some researchers believe the figure is 10-15 percent of all cases of this disorder, but others suggest it is higher. Clinics and counselors see many more females than males, but that may be because males are reluctant to confess what has become known as a "teenage girls' problem." Also, health professionals do not expect to see eating disorders in males and may therefore under diagnose them.

### Are the Risk Factors Any Different for Males Than They Are for Females?

Risk factors for males include the following:

- They were fat or overweight as children.

- They have been dieting. Dieting is one of the most powerful eating disorder triggers for both males and females.

- They participate in a sport that demands thinness. Runners and jockeys are at higher risk than football players and weight lifters. Wrestlers who try to shed pounds quickly before a match so they can compete in a lower weight category seem to be at special risk. Body builders are at risk if they deplete body fat and fluid reserves to achieve high definition.

- They have a job or profession that demands thinness. Male models, actors, and entertainers seem to be at higher risk than the general population.

- Some, but by no means all, males with eating disorders are members of the gay community where men are judged on their physical attractiveness in much the same way as women are judged in the heterosexual community.

Compare and contrast males and females who have eating disorders:

- Males often begin an eating disorder at older ages than females do, and they more often have a history of obesity or overweight.

- Heterosexual males are not exposed to the same intense cultural pressures to be thin that women and girls endure. A casual review of popular magazines and TV shows reveals that women are encouraged to diet and be thin so they can feel good about themselves, be successful at school and at work, and attract friends and romantic partners. Men, on the other hand, are exhorted to be strong and powerful, to build their bodies and make them large so they can compete successfully, amass power and wealth, and defend and protect their skinny female companions.

- It's interesting to note that when women are asked what they would do with one magic wish, they almost always want to lose weight. Men asked the same question want money, power, sex, and the accessories of a rich and successful lifestyle. They usually think their bodies are fine the way they are. If they do have body concerns, they often want to bulk up and become larger and more muscular, not tiny like women do. Males usually equate thinness with weakness and frailty, things they desperately want to avoid.

## Treatment of Eating Disorders in Males

Because eating disorders have been described as female problems, males are often exceedingly reluctant to admit they are in trouble and need help. In addition, most treatment programs and support groups have been designed for females and are populated exclusively by females. Males report feeling uncomfortable and out of place in discussions of lost menstrual periods, women's socio-cultural issues, female-oriented advertising, and similar topics.

Nevertheless, like females, males usually need professional help to recover. The research is clear that males who complete treatment given by competent professionals have good outcomes. Being male has no adverse affect on recovery once the person commits to an effective, well-run program.

The wisest first step is two evaluations: one by a physician to identify any physical problems that are contributing to, or resulting from, the eating disorder; and a second by a mental health therapist to identify psychological issues underlying food behaviors.

When the two evaluations are complete, treatment recommendations can be made that address the individual's specific circumstances.

It is important to remember that eating disorders in males, as well as in females, can be treated, and people of both genders do recover. Almost always, however, professional help is required. If you are concerned about yourself or your child, find a physician and mental health therapist who will be sympathetic to the male perspective. The sooner treatment is begun, the sooner the person can turn the problem around and begin building a happy, satisfying life. The longer symptoms are ignored or denied, the harder that work will be when it is finally undertaken.

Chapter 16

# The Male Athlete and Eating Disorders

A high school baseball star is hospitalized six times, once with his pulse and blood pressure dangerously low. A college cross-country runner is emotionally frazzled, lashing out at friends and teammates, and suffers from anemia and mononucleosis. A wrestler smiles too quickly and his dry, taut skin cracks. He frequently spits saliva into a can.

These are some of the many faces of disordered eating. But none of these faces belong to women. For years, eating disorders have been considered a women's disease. Now it is becoming clear they afflict men, and particularly, male athletes.

As is the case with women, eating disorders are increasing among men. Of the more than 8 million eating disorder victims in the United States, "about a million and climbing are men," according to the National Association of Anorexia Nervosa and Associated Disorders.

Disordered eating, a more expansive term that includes clinical diagnoses of anorexia nervosa and bulimia nervosa as well as cases of chronic poor nutrition and obsessive exercising, is even more widespread.

Concerns about what male athletes eat and the methods some employ to lose weight have surged in recent weeks with the deaths of three college wrestlers. Each collapsed during vigorous workouts, and all three deaths were attributed to intense attempts to shed

"Losing Weight, Losing Lives," by Michael Dobie, ©1999 SIRS Mandarin, Inc., from *Newsday* (Long Island, NY), Dec. 28, 1997, Page A4+; reprinted with permission.

131

weight quickly. As shocking as those events were, however, experts are increasingly concerned about thousands of other male athletes whose eating and weight-loss habits put them at risk for a variety of medical problems.

Those concerns, experts say, are exacerbated by two facts: Estimates of males with eating disorders are rising; and male athletes, as with their female counterparts, are more at risk for disordered eating than their non-athletic peers.

"Originally, eating disorders in all males were under-diagnosed and I think now we're more likely to look for certain kinds of characteristics that might be related to males with eating disorders. Athletics is one of them," said Janet David, a board member of the Center for the Study of Anorexia and Bulimia in Manhattan and a psychologist who specializes in eating disorders. "Male athletes and—especially if you include dancers and models—performers, males who have a high investment in appearance, in weight, are more at risk than other males."

East Northport therapist Cynthia Pizzulli said she is treating three Long Island high school football players who have bulimia, two of whom are captains of their teams. "I tend to have a lot of males in my practice," said Pizzulli, director of the Renfrew Center of Long Island's Intensive Outpatient Treatment Program for Eating Disorders. Among Pizzulli's male patients have been wrestlers and basketball players, virtually all of whom are of high school or college age.

Many men are reluctant, however, to admit they have a problem. Rob, a junior and a distance runner on full scholarship at a prominent Midwestern university, endured both anorexia and bulimia. After years of training hard and watching what he ate, Rob began monitoring his diet even more intently as a college freshman. He cut back on his eating so much that besides losing weight he also found himself perpetually tired, extremely irritable and prone to frequent illness. And when he reacted angrily with episodes of binge eating to compensate for slowly starving himself, Rob would force himself to vomit afterward.

After months of fighting the identification, Rob finally admitted he had an eating disorder. "People who have an eating disorder are perceived maybe as psychological cases or weak-willed or maybe just generally very troubled people. I guess I'm scared of being viewed like that," said Rob, who requested anonymity. "I felt like I had control but I knew that there was something wrong, that I shouldn't be thinking of food all the time, that all that stuff I was doing is not normal."

Statistically and anecdotally, the sports in which male athletes are most at risk for eating disorders include wrestling, gymnastics, crew, cross country and track, football, bodybuilding and horse racing. "Some sports for men are associated with weight loss, others with the opposite—bulking up," said Arnold Andersen, professor of psychiatry at the University of Iowa College of Medicine.

Disordered eating can have severe health consequences. The most stark examples were the deaths of the three college wrestlers—from Campbell University in North Carolina, University of Wisconsin-La Crosse and University of Michigan—all of which occurred in the fall of 1999 within a six-week period. An eating disorder can cause heart failure due to the loss of minerals and electrolyte imbalance. Other problems include dehydration, kidney failure, erosion of tooth enamel and inflammation of the esophagus from regular vomiting, as well as sensitivity to cold, tiredness, mood swings and lack of concentration. New research also suggests that men with eating disorders share with female victims a similar risk for premature osteopenia, a weakening of the bones that is a half-step from full-blown osteoporosis. And, like women, a low percentage of body fat appears to play a role in the process.

"Our research, and we have yet to publish the findings so I won't say too much about it, indicates they have the same vulnerability to osteopenia as women," said Andersen, one of the nation's preeminent experts on male eating disorders.

And men with eating disorders find recovery just as difficult and arduous. "My eating disorder was a wonderful way to just destroy myself," said Gary Grahl, a baseball-football-basketball star in a small Wisconsin town whose battle with anorexia and compulsive exercise led to six hospitalizations. When he was admitted the second time, Grahl said a doctor gave him sobering news.

"He said, 'Right now, your pulse is so low and your blood pressure is so low that if you keep up this routine I won't give you more than a month, and probably less than that, and you'll die,'" Grahl said. "I was so addicted nothing was going to stop me."

## Out from the Shadows

One of sports medicine's most confounding problems, eating disorders are little understood by the public. The stigma surrounding the disease, combined with the secrecy and denial practiced by its victims has long stifled public conversation. Research and education on the topic has increased in recent years, but the majority of that attention has been devoted to women, with the consequence that male eating disorders remain a problem largely cloaked in shadows.

Some researchers have attempted to quantify the issue. Craig Johnson, a psychologist who runs the eating disorders program at the Laureate Psychiatric Clinic and Hospital in Tulsa, Okla., recently surveyed more than 1,400 college athletes. He found that 38 percent of the males were at risk for what he called "disturbed eating behaviors." Wrestling, at 93.8 percent, had the highest figure for any sport, including women's sports.

Another study of college athletes in 15 sports found that one in seven male athletes satisfied strict diagnostic criteria for bulimia, compared with less than 1 percent of young men in general. (Bulimia, with its cycle of binge-eating and purging, is far more common among men than anorexia. But anorexia still is far more prevalent among male athletes than men in general.)

In a third study, nearly one in five male college athletes in Ohio reported suffering from an eating disorder in the past; one in eight said they currently were suffering from one.

Sport-specific studies have produced similar results. Researchers in Wisconsin, for example, found that 45 percent of the state's high school wrestlers exhibited at least two criteria for bulimia. One study of marathon runners found that a majority were anorexic or showed significant anorexic-like characteristics. And a recent study of lightweight football players at Cornell University in Ithaca found that 42 percent engaged in "dysfunctional eating" while one in 10 showed binge-purge behavior that suggested an eating disorder.

Many horse racing jockeys, who usually begin their careers as teenagers, routinely binge and purge. It's known as "flipping" in the industry. Use of laxatives, diuretics such as Lasix, diet pills, saunas and rubber suits to maintain low body weight also are common. A study of jockeys in Great Britain found that a majority abused laxatives and diuretics. Former or current jockeys who reportedly admitted either flipping or using pills include Laffit Pincay, Jose Santos, George Martens, Randy Romero and Braulio Baeza. "Everybody does what they have to do," veteran jockey Eddie Maple said. "I've done just about everything there is to do in my 30 years. But the last 15, besides watching what I eat, I've done the rest of it in the sweat room."

"You might go to the laxative and maybe Lasix or some kind of diuretic, but it tends to do too much harm to your muscles and reflexes. I would say there are still some flippers, yes, but I would say the younger guys are relying more on the diet."

The use of Lasix was at the center of a controversy in Illinois, which last year passed legislation making it illegal to supply child athletes with drugs to help them gain or lose weight quickly. The legislation was prompted by a scandal in which the athletic director of a youth football league admitted giving Lasix to players as young as 10 years old to help them stay under maximum weight limits. The governing body of New York State high school athletics bans the use of any diuretic.

Experts who hoped education would help eliminate incidents such as the one in Illinois are dismayed the trend has not abated. "Eating disorders are still continuing to increase even though there's been a lot of education, especially of people like coaches and dance teachers and teachers in general who work with people of that age," David, the psychologist, said.

The recent spate of publicity has helped, however, in focusing attention on the role of parents in monitoring the eating behaviors of their sons. "We rely on our teachers to teach our kids but we get involved to make sure they did their homework," said Rich Langsam, whose son Mitchell wrestles and runs track at Massapequa High School where he is a sophomore. "It's the same thing with any sport. We rely on the coaches but we ultimately have to be the last resort for our children to make sure the coaches are pushing our kids in the right direction. I don't want to say I should rely solely on the coach because he knows the sport 1,000 times better than I do. This is my son. I think I should take a role."

## Wrestling with Problems

Much of the research on eating disorders among male athletes has focused on wrestling, with its frequent demands on participants to cut large amounts of weight in short periods of time and then quickly add that weight back. The cycle is more extreme for wrestlers who begin the school year playing football, for which they often are expected to bulk up.

One study of Massachusetts high school wrestlers found that 27 percent had binged and 8 percent had vomited. The study of Ohio college athletes determined that two of three wrestlers binged regularly and one in three purged. In a survey of high school wrestling coaches in New York State published earlier this year by West Islip sports nutritionist Karen Sossin and others, 20 percent reported a suspicion that at least one of their wrestlers had an eating disorder.

"It's widespread in that I'd say it exists in almost every school, but I'd say it's not widespread on every team," said Ray Nelson, director of athletic training at Long Island Sports Rehabilitation and a consultant on wrestling policies to the state athletic association. Nelson, a former wrestler at Bellmore JFK High School, comes from a family of wrestlers.

"A lot of wrestlers are sick in season. They have skin problems—a lot of dryness, a lot of cracking, eczema, dry and scaly skin," Nelson said. "A lot of wrestlers don't smile in wrestling season because if they smile rapidly their skin will crack. Their resistance is down because good nutrition is one of the ways we fight off illness."

"Yo-yo dieting" is a term describing the way wrestlers shed weight quickly to reach a certain weight class, then eat and drink heartily after weigh-in to put pounds back on prior to the actual competition several hours later. Nelson said the process is especially dangerous because it puts added stress on the heart. "That yo-yo-ing back and forth is not good. Rapid weight loss dumps a lot of broken-down fat into the bloodstream, which then has to be detoxified," Nelson said. "The systems of the body have to do double-time...If you're asking your body to do twice as much work, it can fail twice as fast."

Often, wrestlers exercise obsessively (for example, running in a hot shower or working out in multiple sweat suits in a heated room) to lose weight quickly. But most of this loss is water weight, which can lead to dehydration. Dehydration can result in electrolyte imbalance, which can lead to heart problems. Other side effects include damage to the heart, kidneys and liver, and a depletion of lean muscle tissue.

Some wrestlers chew gum to curb their appetites, then spit out the saliva in an attempt to keep their weight down. Nelson said wrestlers calculate the weight they lose while sleeping (a practice called "drifting"), count the number of swallows they take at a water fountain and spit into a can they carry around as a match approaches. "They're definitely practicing pathogenic weight-control behaviors," Hofstra trainer Rick Zappala said. "I've seen everything. I've seen people taking Lasix to get down to weight. I've seen rubber suits...When I see some of the stuff they're doing, it is kind of scary to me. I question it, too."

Zappala recalled working with one wrestler at the 1991 Olympic Festival in Los Angeles. The wrestler cut weight from 154 to 128 pounds in a matter of days and "almost died." After collapsing in the locker room and being hospitalized, he was fed intravenously and resumed normal eating. Within 24 hours, he gained 20 pounds, Zappala said.

The three college wrestlers who died were not as lucky. Two of the victims—Jeff Reese of the University of Michigan and Joe LaRosa of the University of Wisconsin-La Crosse—reportedly were wearing rubber suits when they collapsed. All three, including Campbell University freshman Billy Jack Saylor, were exercising vigorously in an attempt to lose weight to compete in a lower weight class in an upcoming meet.

But reaction to those incidents indicates the difficulty health professionals experience in convincing some in the wrestling community to change their ways. One Long Island wrestling coach with a reputation for caring about his athletes said of the deaths of the collegians, "I guarantee you it was not just from cutting weight. I cut weight my whole life, it never was a problem."

Autopsy reports, however, did blame methods used by the wrestlers to lose weight. "The problem is coaches don't understand these practices are unhealthy," Penn State physician Margot Putukian said. "They figure, 'I did that. They'll be fine.'" Zappala said traditional ways of thinking can be altered. "There certainly is a mentality among the wrestling world that, 'Hey, I did it, he can do it,' although that is slowly starting to change," Zappala said.

In 1991, Wisconsin passed regulations barring from competition any high school wrestler whose body fat falls below 7 percent. This year, New York became the fifth state to enact such rules when it instituted guidelines on weight loss and body composition. Officials said the high school governing bodies of 20 other states are considering similar measures.

Tom Howard, athletic director at Farmingdale High School, has had two sons wrestle at St. Anthony's High School. The first, Trevor, cut weight from 141 to 112 pounds as a senior in the early 1990s. "Trevor has done some crazy things," Howard said. "The day before the match he'd be 4 pounds over, he'd come home and he wouldn't be able to eat or drink. He was a 96 average student; he wouldn't be studying or doing homework. At that time he was nasty, he had an attitude.

"It was almost like I'd seen other kids do it, so I knew my son could do it. I knew he would be stronger at the lower weight. Meanwhile, I knew in the back of my mind all he was doing was fighting the scale. The more I watched it, I realized he shouldn't be doing it, but I did it to my own kid. And I'm not doing it to my second kid, so I guess I've learned a little along the way."

Sossin's research on the state's high school wrestling coaches produced mixed results. On the one hand, the research team concluded that the coaches "were ill-prepared to advise on safe and effective methods for weight reduction." On the other hand, Sossin said, "The vast majority are very concerned about nutrition, disapprove of binge eating, understand the importance of exercise, believe their wrestlers need specific nutritional information and believe wrestlers have the potential to develop eating disorders." Sossin has developed a nutrition education component to complement the new wrestling guidelines being implemented by the state. "We need to get away from sucking weight," Sossin said. "Maybe people will begin to look at wrestling as a healthy sport. Maybe this will take the stigma away." And maybe, Nelson said, the new programs will help eliminate problems, such as stunted growth, that can afflict wrestlers and other male athletes years after their competition days are over. One study of Harvard students 10 years after graduation, for example, found that eating disorders had dropped in half among the women but had doubled among the men. "I know a lot of wrestlers have weight problems post-wrestling career because they learn to be in control of their weight. Later in life, when their metabolism starts to slow down, they resort to those odd tactics," Nelson said. "I know guys up to 30 years old who these days are still bulimic, who still throw up after Thanksgiving."

## Men and Women

Male athletes who develop eating disorders often share with female victims such traits as being high achievers and obsessive-compulsive perfectionists. But the sexes differ in significant ways as well.

Where many women of average weight "feel" overweight before they begin the kind of dieting that leads to more serious problems, most male victims actually are medically overweight at the onset of an eating disorder.

"They were chubby as children...They were called fat and slobby and all these other things," Pizzulli said. "Usually, they start by dieting and the diet works and someone says, 'You look great.' That's positive reinforcement. Now they've gotten all this attention. One day they slip and have a piece of cake and they say, 'Oh my God, I can't go back to the way I was,' and that's when it happens."

Pizzulli said many male athletes become victims in the wake of an injury. No longer active and fearful of gaining weight while recovering, a male athlete begins to diet. At some point, he loses control. "It's like getting into a canoe headed for Niagara Falls," Andersen said. "You get into the canoe voluntarily, but by the time you reach the falls you're no longer in control."

Improvement in sports performance is one goal men typically adopt when they begin the kinds of diets that lead to an eating disorder. There are three other possible goals, according to Andersen—a desire not to be teased for being overweight, a desire to avoid weight-related medical diseases experienced by their fathers or a desire to please a gay lover.

138

The key, Andersen said, is that male athletes, like men in general, view weight loss as a means to an end—getting better in their sport. "As I got into high school, the competition got tougher. That, I think, was the impetus," Grahl said. "I started to feel the pressure more. All of a sudden, I started to diet...I got into it so much I found it was a way to relieve pressure and tension and it just snowballed."

Most experts agree that once an eating disorder develops, a man might be even more likely to keep it secret than a woman. Pizzulli said that is due partly to the myth that a man with an eating disorder must be gay, an outgrowth of its identification as a women's disease.

What is viewed as an added pejorative frightens many male athletes. "That's certainly another aspect of why I don't feel like I want to make this public," said Rob, the Midwestern runner. "It would be difficult with some of the comments from guys on the team...I think if I got help and people found out, I would never be perceived the same again."

People close to a male victim of an eating disorder often fail to recognize the symptoms, partly because they are not looking for them and partly because men are adept at hiding their behavior. "I didn't want anyone to know," Grahl said. "I was a popular guy and I was good in sports, good grades. I was the last guy people thought would have something like this."

Compounding the problem of identification is the lack of telltale physical sign for men that corresponds to an interrupted or missing menstrual cycle for women. The absence of such a warning means the eating disorder also goes undetected by a trainer or doctor; often, the disorder is more serious and more deeply entrenched by the time a male athlete seeks help. Rob, for example, exhibited a number of symptoms of disordered eating during the most serious phase of his illness, when he cut back to 1,200 calories per day while running 70 to 90 miles per week. Even though he dropped below 120 pounds on his 5- foot-9-inch frame, Rob said no one knows he has an eating disorder.

"When I'm having a lot of problems with the eating, emotionally I'm stressed out and grouchy and I'll snap at people easily," Rob said. "Physically, you're tired all the time, you get up and get the big head rushes. A lot of days I feel like I'm just walking to class in a haze, very, very fatigued."

Rob, like many male athletes who are victims, suffered from elements of both anorexia and bulimia. "When I was cutting down that much, there was a cycle involved," he said. "Eventually, I got so hungry that I would mess up a little bit and eat more than I would want to and you go crazy and lose control and, yeah, I would throw up." Rob said he used his fingers to induce vomiting and, at times, laxatives to purge. One of Pizzulli's patients takes as many as 45 laxatives a day. Andersen said Rob's pattern of behavior is common for eating-disordered male athletes.

"As they try to push their weight down, their body says, 'Nuts,' and they binge. A binge initially is appetite breaking through," Andersen said. "The purging becomes a way to undo the binge they didn't want in the first place. Anorexia and bulimia are really two sides of the same coin, not two separate disorders."

When his behavior was at its most severe, Rob suffered from mononucleosis and anemia, both of which he attributes to his eating disorder. He is not sure what to make of his two stress fractures, but Andersen said an increase in fracture risk seems to be as true for men as it is for women.

For eating-disordered women, amenorrhea—the loss of the menstrual cycle—is an indication of an estrogen deficiency. The lack of estrogen leads to a loss of bone density and, if amenorrhea continues long enough, osteoporosis. This process has become known as the Female Athlete Triad. Andersen said a similar process occurs in male athletes suffering from an eating disorder.

Lower body weight means the bones receive less stimulus from exercise, which weakens bones. Andersen said male eating disorder victims also have higher levels of cortisol, a hormone that leeches calcium from the bones. Men also experience a gradual decrease in the hormone testosterone as they lose weight, which has a negative effect on sexual drive and performance—and bones.

"The analogue to estrogen in women is that low testosterone in men leads to decreased mineralization or bone loss," Andersen said. "The whole body chemistry is changed by the process of starvation." The testosterone level in a man with an eating disorder can drop to as little as 10 percent to 20 percent of normal—about the same as an average woman, said Andersen, who recommends a bone density test for any "chronically ill eating-disordered" male.

Andersen, who also directs the Eating and Weight Disorders Clinic at Johns Hopkins University, stressed that his research is on-going and that such issues as the rate at which bone loss occurs have yet to be determined.

## Search for Understanding

Trying to determine what he might have achieved without his eating disorder is something Rob grapples with every day. In college, his performances have been inconsistent. He has noticed that a bad race tends to follow a week in which he has "struggled" with his eating disorder. Rob still has not sought treatment, nor does he feel he can confide in anyone close to him. He has been comforted only by his own research that has taught him that he is not alone.

"There needs to be an increased knowledge and an increased— I don't want to say acceptability—maybe, awareness. There needs to be more of an awareness of the characteristics of these diseases," Rob said. "And society, or the sporting community, has got to be able to be more understanding. "For a long time, I thought I had some kind of odd psychological screw-up. But the characteristics that I display are very similar to what a lot of other people are going through and that's sort of comforting."

## Definitions

**disordered eating:** An umbrella term that includes behavior ranging from poor nutrition and/or an inadequate intake of calories to the use of diet pills, laxatives or diuretics. Also included are severe, clinically diagnosed eating disorders such as anorexia nervosa or bulimia nervosa.

**anorexia:** An eating disorder characterized by a refusal to maintain a minimally normal body weight and an intense fear of gaining weight.

**bulimia:** An eating disorder characterized by binge-eating and purging through such behavior as vomiting, excessive exercise and the use of laxatives.

## Effects and Complications

*Disordered Eating*—Bulimia can cause severe dehydration, thirst and lightheadedness; gastrointestinal problems such as irritations and/or tears in the esophagus, stomach, salivary gland and throat; erosion of tooth enamel; depletion of blood potassium, sodium and chloride levels, which leads to muscle spasms, weakness, cardiac arrhythmia and kidney failure; substance abuse; depression; anxiety; calluses or scars on hands; chronic sore throat; difficulty swallowing; stomach cramps; anemia; and electrolyte imbalance.

*Anorexia*—Can cause muscle fatigue; deterioration of muscle tissues; decreased coordination and poor judgment; changes in physical features, including hair loss, gaunt and hollow facial features, dry skin, bruises, sharply protruding bones and a feeling of always being cold; mood changes; insomnia; constipation; kidney failure; bradycardia (abnormally low heart rate); low blood pressure; peripheral edema (fluid retention); severe hypotension; hypothermia; and cardiac arrhythmia.

New research also suggests that excessive weight loss among men can lead to osteopenia.

*Osteopenia*—A condition of low bone density that precedes osteoporosis, the so-called "brittle-bone" disease. Both involve an increased risk of fractures of the spine and hip, in particular, and curvature of the spine.

Chapter 17

# The Female Athlete and Eating Disorders

Since passage of Title IX legislation in 1972, there has been a dramatic increase in the number of girls and women participating in organized sports. For most of these individuals, sport participation is a positive experience, providing improved physical fitness and better health.[1] Yet, for some the desire for athletic success, combined with the pressure to achieve a prescribed body weight, may lead to development of a triad of medical disorders—eating disorders, amenorrhea, and osteoporosis—known collectively as the female athlete triad, or the "Triad."[1-3] Alone or in combination, the disorders of the Triad can negatively affect health and impair athletic performance. Consequently, school personnel should have a working knowledge of the Triad components, their relationships, risk factors, and be prepared to develop procedures for identification, prevention, and treatment.

## Triad Components

Pressure to achieve and maintain a particular body weight or body shape considered desirable in her chosen sport may place a female athlete at risk for developing disordered eating behaviors. The resulting energy restriction and pathogenic weight control behaviors predispose

"Understanding the Female Athlete Triad: Eating Disorders, Amenorrhea, and Osteoporosis," by Katherine A. Beals, Rebecca A. Brey, and Julianna B. Gonyou, © 1999 American School Health Association, Kent, Ohio, from *Journal of School Health*, Oct. 1999, Vol. 69, Issue 8, Page 337; reprinted with permission.

her to menstrual dysfunction, subsequent decreased bone mineral density, and premature osteoporosis.[1-9] Each individual disorder of the Triad poses a significant medical concern. When the three disorders of the Triad occur together, the potential health consequences become even more serious, and often life-threatening.[1,6]

## Disordered Eating

Disordered eating refers to the spectrum of abnormal and harmful eating patterns used in a misguided attempt to lose weight or maintain a lowered body weight.[2,10,11] Anorexia nervosa represents the extreme of restrictive eating behavior in which the individual feels terrified of gaining weight and views herself as overweight though she is significantly underweight (at least 15% below ideal body weight for age).[10] Bulimia nervosa is characterized by repeated cycles of uncontrolled bingeing and purging occurring a minimum of two times per week for at least three months.[10] Purging methods may include vomiting, excessive exercise, or use of laxatives, diuretics, or enemas. Individuals also may experience subclinical variations of anorexia and bulimia nervosa. These individuals do not meet diagnostic criteria of the clinical conditions,[10] yet they exhibit body image disturbances and pathogenic weight control behaviors that place them at risk for serious endocrine, metabolic, skeletal, and psychological disorders.[4,11]

Medical complications associated with disordered eating include, but are not limited to, depleted glycogen stores, decreased lean body mass, chronic fatigue, micronutrient deficiencies, dehydration, anemia, electrolyte and acid-base imbalances, gastrointestinal disorders, parotid gland enlargement, decreased bone density, and erosion of tooth enamel.[2,12-14] Psychological problems often accompany disordered eating, including decreased sell-esteem, anxiety, depression, and death owing to suicide.[4,11]

## Amenorrhea

Amenorrhea is usually defined as the absence of three or more consecutive menstrual cycles.[2,9] Primary amenorrhea or delayed menarche is the absence of menstruation by age 16 in a girl with secondary sex characteristics.[2,15] Secondary amenorrhea is the absence of three or more consecutive menstrual cycles after menarche.[2,15] As with disordered eating, a continuum of menstrual dysfunction occurs in the female athlete, with complete cessation of menstruation at the extreme and periods of oligomenorrhea (menstrual cycles lasting longer than 36 days) falling at an intermediate point along the continuum.[1,15] Once considered a relatively benign and "normal" response to physical training, professionals now recognize menstrual dysfunction as a serious medical condition.[2,15] The primary medical concern from menstrual dysfunction includes decreased bone density and premature osteoporosis.[8,17,18]

## *Osteoporosis*

Osteoporosis in young female athletes refers to premature bone loss and inadequate bone formation resulting in low bone mineral density, microarchitectural deterioration, increased skeletal fragility, and increased risk of stress fractures to the extremities, hips, and spine.[1,3,7,19] Studies suggest that the bone mineral density lost as a result of amenorrhea may be completely or, at least partly, irreversible even with calcium supplementation, resumption of menses, and estrogen replacement therapy.[18,20]

## *Triad Risk Factors*

The American College of Sports Medicine considers all physically active females at risk for developing one or more of the components of the Triad.[2] However, the biological changes, peer pressure, societal drive for thinness, and body image preoccupation that occur during puberty may render adolescent girls the most vulnerable.[2]

Factors implicated in contributing to the development of disordered eating include societal pressures to be thin; chronic dieting; low self-esteem; family dysfunction; physical or sexual abuse; participation in sports that emphasize a low body weight or particular body shape such as figure skating, gymnastics, distance running, swimming, diving, tennis, volleyball and cheerleading; participation in individual sports versus team sports; elite or highly competitive versus recreational athlete; and traumatic life events such as personal or family illness or injury, a change of coach, or relationship problems.[2,21,22]

Risk factors implicated in the development of amenorrhea include disordered eating, low energy availability or chronic negative energy balance, and significant and abrupt increases in training volume or intensity.[5,10,23] The primary risk factor for the osteoporosis that occurs as part of the Triad is amenorrhea (and, perhaps, oligomenorrhea) and the resulting hypoestrogenemia.[8,18]

While female athletes represent the group most susceptible to developing the disorders of the Triad, physically active girls not competing in a specific sport, and even female nonathletes can be at risk.[2] In addition, male athletes, particularly those participating in sports with weight classifications such as wrestling, rowing, horse racing, weight lifting, and body building are at risk for developing disordered eating.[24,25]

## Prevention and Treatment

Prevention and treatment of athletes with eating disorders can be organized into three broad categories including primary, secondary, and tertiary prevention.[25] Primary prevention involves educational programs designed to prevent development of an eating disorder. Secondary prevention focuses on early identification and subsequent intervention. Tertiary prevention involves treating those who developed an eating disorder.[25] These same prevention categories can be readily adapted to include all the disorders of the Triad.

### Primary Prevention

For school health personnel, primary prevention may be viewed as a more manageable task to tackle versus treatment, due to the high failure rate of treatment and the irreversible nature of some of the disorders.[25] The goal of primary prevention is to inoculate athletes against the factors that may predispose them to developing these disorders.[25] Thus, primary prevention should focus on dispelling myths and misconceptions surrounding nutrition, dieting, body weight, and body composition and their effect on athletic performance, while stressing the role of sound nutrition in promoting health and optimal performance.

Effective prevention demands close cooperation among all school health personnel. Health educators can advance primary prevention efforts by including a nutrition unit in their curriculum. School counselors and school nurses can contribute to primary prevention by promoting acceptance of diverse body shapes and sizes and encouraging a healthful attitude about competition and performance. School food service staff can play an important role in primary prevention by providing a variety of healthy and appetizing food choices.

Primary prevention strategies also should be aimed at the athletic environment with the goal of changing prevailing attitudes and practices regarding body weight and performance that too often form an accepted part of sport. In certain sports, pathogenic weight loss measures and menstrual dysfunction have almost become an accepted part of the sport.[25] The athletic staff can play an important role in changing these attitudes and behaviors by being clear and direct about the acceptability of weight loss practices and training techniques. In addition, athletic support staff, especially males, need to understand that body weight, menstrual cycles, and eating habits can be sensitive issues for young women, and they should address these issues accordingly. While the athlete's behaviors need to be monitored, methods such as group weigh-ins or "constructive criticism" regarding body weight, size, and shape are counterproductive and potentially harmful, and they should be avoided.[25]

## Secondary Prevention

Secondary prevention involves early identification of athletes at risk for developing the disorders of the Triad with the goal of limiting the progression and shortening the duration of the disorders. To be successful, school health personnel should be familiar with the warning signs and symptoms of the Triad. The National Collegiate Athletic Association (NCAA) published a list of warning signs for eating disorders. In addition, the American College of Sports Medicine developed a set of Triad educational materials available for purchase.[2]

Screening athletes for disorders of the Triad represents an effective method for early identification. The preparticipation physical exam provides the best opportunity to screen.[29] During the exam, clinicians should ask specific questions regarding menstrual irregularities, eating behaviors, weight loss attempts, and history of musculoskeletal injury.[1,2,30] Other issues such as life stressors, depressive symptoms, dissatisfaction with weight and body shape, training frequency and intensity, and other lifestyle behaviors may also be addressed at this time.[1,15,30,31] Johnson[30] and Tanner[31] provide a detailed description of components in the preparticipation exam.

## Tertiary Prevention

Treating the disorders of the Triad usually involves a treatment "team," including the athlete's physician, a psychologist or psychiatrist, a dietitian, and the athlete's parents. The decision regarding the most appropriate treatment is based on the severity of the disorder and the presence of medical complications or additional diagnoses such as substance abuse. Health professionals recommend that treatment programs include psychological counseling (behavioral, psychoeducational, psychodynamic group, and family therapy), medical and nutritional support, and in certain cases, medication.[25,32]

Depending on resources available to school districts, tertiary prevention may not be appropriate in the school setting. Consequently, school health personnel should maintain a list of local practitioners specializing in disorders of the Triad. Many national organizations provide information and resources that identify therapists, physicians, treatment programs, and hospitals specializing in treatment for disorders of the Triad.

## Conclusion

Because of the serious, potentially life-threatening health consequences associated with disorders of the Triad, prevention and early identification are paramount. School health personnel must possess a working knowledge of the Triad components, be familiar with risk factors and warning signs of disordered eating and menstrual dysfunction, and maintain a list of referral sources for treatment. Likewise, athletes participating in school-sponsored sports programs should be required to undergo a pre-participation physical exam that includes screening for disorders of the Triad. Only through involvement and cooperation of all school health personnel can disorders of the Triad be detected early and prevented.

## References

1. Nattiv A, Agostini R, Drinkwater BL, Yeager KK. The female athlete triad: the inter-relatedness of disordered eating, amenorrhea, and osteoporosis. *Clin Sports Med.* 1994:13(2):405-418.

2. American College of Sports Medicine Position Stand. The female athlete triad: disordered eating, amenorrhea, and osteoporosis. *Med Sci Sports Exerc.* 1997;29:i-ix.

3. Yeager KK, Agostini R, Nattiv A, Drinkwater BL. The female athlete triad: disordered eating, amenorrhea, osteoporosis commentary. *Med Sci Sports Exer.* 1993:25:775-777.

4. Beals KA, Manore MM. Prevalence and consequences of subclinical eating disorders in female athletes. *Int J Sport Nutr.* 1994;4:175-195.

5. Benson JE, Englebert-Fenton K, Eisenman PA. Nutritional aspects of amenorrhea in the female athlete triad. *Int J Sport Nutr.* 1996;6:134-145.

6. Constantini NW. Clinical consequences of athletic amenorrhea. *Sports Med.* 1994;17:213-223.

7. Lewis RD, Modlesky CM. Nutrition, physical activity, and bone health in women. *Int J Sport Nutr.* 1998;8:250-284.

8. Nattiv A, Armsey TD. Stress injury to bone in the female athlete. *Clin Sports Med.* 1997:16(2): 197-224.

9. Warren MP. Eating, body weight, and menstrual function. In: Brownell KD, Rodin J, Wilmore JH, eds. *Eating, Body Weight, and Performance: Disorders of Modern Society.* Philadelphia, Pa: Lea & Febiger; 1992:222-234.

10. American Psychiatric Association. *Diagnostic and Statistical Manual of Mental Disorders. 4th ed.* Washington, DC: American Psychological Association. 1994;539-550.

11. Beals KA, Manore MM. Subclinical eating disorders in physically active women. *Topics Clin Nutr.* 1999; 14:14-29.

12. Bachrach LK, Guido D, Katzman D, Marcus R. Decreased bone density in adolescent girls with anorexia nervosa. *Pediatrics.* 1990;86:440-447.

13. Brownell KD, Steen SN. Weight cycling in athletes; effects on behavior, physiology, and health. In Brownell KD, Rodin J, Wilmore JH, eds. *Eating, Body Weight, and Performance in Athletes: Disorders of Modern Society.* Philadelphia, Pa: Lea and Febiger; 1992:159-171.

14. Pomeroy C, Mitchell JE. Medical issues in the eating disorders. In Brownell KD, Rodin J, Wilmore JH, eds. *Eating, Body Weight, and Performance in Athletes: Disorders of Modern Society.* Philadelphia, Pa: Lea & Febiger; 1992:202-221.

15. Otis CL. Exercise associated amenorrhea. *Clin Sports Med.* 1992;11 (2):351-362.

16. Shangold M, Rebar RW, Wentz AC, Schiff I. Evaluation and management of menstrual dysfunction in athletes. *JAMA.* 1990;263:1665-1669.

17. Drinkwater BL, Nilson K, Chestnut CH III, Bremer WJ, Shainholtz S, Southworth MB. Bone mineral content of amenorrheic and eumenorrheic athletes. *N Engl J Med.* 1984;311:227-281.

18. Drinkwater BL. Amenorrhea, body weight, and osteoporosis. In Brownell KD, Rodin J, Wilmore JH, eds. *Eating, Body Weight, and Performance in Athletes: Disorders of Modern Society.* Philadelphia, Pa: Lea and Febiger; 1992:235-247.

19. Myburgh K, Jutchins J, Fataar AB, Low bone density is an etiological factor for stress fractures in athletes. *Ann Int Med.* 1990; 113:754-759.

20. Drinkwater BL, Nilson K, Orr S, Chestnut CH III. Bone mineral density after resumption of menses in amenorrheic athletes. *JAMA.* 1986;256:380-382.

21. Sundgot-Borgen J. Risk and trigger factors for the development of eating disorders in female elite athletes. *Med Sci Sports Exert.* 1994;26:414-419.

22. Wilson GT, Eldredge KL. Pathology and development of eating disorders: implications for athletes. In Brownell KD, Rodin J, Wilmore JH, eds. *Eating, Body Weight, and Performance: Disorders of Modern Society.* Philadelphia, Pa: Lea & Febiger: 1992:115-127.

23. Dueck CA, Manore MM, Matt KS. Role of energy balance in athletic menstrual dysfunction. *Int J Sport Nutr.* 1996:6:165-190.

24. Andersen AE. Eating disorders in males: A special case? In Brownell KD, Rodin J, Wilmore JH, eds. *Eating, Body Weight, and Performance in Athletes: Disorders of Modern Society.* Philadelphia, Pa: Lea and Febiger: 1992:172-190.

25. Thompson RA, Sherman RT. *Helping Athletes with Eating Disorders.* Champaign, Ill: Human Kinetics Publishers: 1993.

26. Allensworth D, Kolbe LJ. The comprehensive school health program: exploring an expanded concept. *J Sch Health.* 1987;57(10):409-412.

27. Marx E, Wooley SE, eds, with Northrop D. *Health is Academic: A Guide to Coordinated School Health Programs.* New York, NY: Teachers College Press, Columbia University; 1998.

28. Neumark-Sztainier D. School-based programs for preventing eating disturbances. *J Sch Health.* 1996;66(2):64-71.

29. Nattiv A, Lynch L. The female athlete triad: managing an acute risk to long-term health. *Phys Sportsmed.* 1994;22(1): 60-68.

30. Johnson MD. Tailoring the preparticipation exam to the female athletes. *Phys Sportsmed.* 1992;20(7):61-72.

31. Tanner SM. Preparticipation examination targeted for the female athlete. *Clin Sports Med.* 1994;13(2):330-353.

32. Johnson C, Tobin D. The diagnosis and treatment of anorexia nervosa and bulimia among athletes. *JNATA.* 1991;26:119-128.

Chapter 18

# Males and Females and Obligatory Exercise

Lay people know it as compulsive exercising. The person seems addicted to his or her sport, which is often running. Researchers are calling it obligatory exercise. The person feels obliged to pursue an excessive regimen in spite of injuries, damaged relationships, and too much time taken off work in service of the activity.

## Exercise Used As a Drug

At some point the overexerciser begins to look like a drug addict. S/he reports that the activity is no longer an enjoyable part of life. It has taken over life and become the top priority under which everything else is subordinate. Exercising is no longer a free choice; it is now necessary and essential. It provides temporary feelings of well being and even euphoria. The person believes s/he must do the activity, and more and more of it. If s/he does not, s/he feels overwhelming guilt and anxiety, which are sometimes described as withdrawal.

Eventually the obligatory exerciser becomes obsessive in thought and compulsive in deed. S/he may keep detailed records, scrupulously observe a rigid diet, and constantly focus on improving his or her personal best.

Researchers say that prolonged, strenuous exercise stimulates the body to produce substances similar to the opiate morphine. Debate continues whether or not compulsive exercisers become physiologically addicted to these substances. If they do, then obligatory exercise is a vicious circle where the biochemical products of activity lead to a self-induced high, which in turn demands more activity to generate more biochemical products.

## The Social Context of Exercise Addiction

Sociologists say we live in an age of narcissism, or self-absorption in ourselves and our bodies. Both men and women are expected to achieve perfect or near-perfect bodies: slim, toned, strong, agile, and aesthetically appealing. The closer people get to the cultural ideal, the more they notice the flaws that remain.

A preoccupation with appearance may grow out of a preoccupation with health and unrealistic expectations. We want to live to a hundred, never be sick, keep all our hair, have unlined faces and flat bellies, be attractive forever to romantic partners, and be strong, quick, and admirably competent. Paradoxically, in the United States, as increasing affluence and improving health care following World War II enabled more and more people to be better nourished and healthier, our satisfaction with our health and appearance has decreased.

## Recognizing the Obligatory Exerciser

Recognition is relatively easy. These people talk of nothing but their sport, their training schedules, and their injuries. When injured, they will not take time off to heal unless immobilized. Obligatory runners with stress fractures, torn ligaments, and joint injuries have been known to work out in their walking casts.

Exercise addicts misuse their athletic achievements. Instead of enjoying their abilities as one part of a multidimensional life, they make exercising their whole life. They try to boost self-esteem, meet deep needs, and solve complex problems through performance excellence. Or they hide from emotional pain in workout schedules. It doesn't work, but instead of trying more effective behaviors, they raise their goals and standards, hoping that the increased effort will get the job done. It doesn't.

Many obligatory exercisers repress anger, have low self-esteem, and struggle with depression in spite of significant victories and achievements.

## Are You in Danger of Becoming an Exercise Addict?

There are two warning signs. First, is your sport or workout schedule something fun? If so, you are probably OK. Watch out, though,

154

when the activity ceases being fun and becomes a duty, a chore, an obligation that is definitely not fun, but that you must do—or else suffer strong guilt or anxiety.

The second danger sign is hearing repeated comments from family members, friends, co-workers, boss, and especially your physician to the effect that you are hurting yourself and losing perspective. The person who still has control heeds these warnings and backs off. The person who has lost control to exercise addiction will ignore sound advice and continue the compulsive behavior.

Elite athletes may be at special risk in this regard. They believe their single-minded discipline and ability to endure pain and injury set them apart and mark them as special people, even heros, in a world gone comfortable and soft. Elite athletes who have become addicted to exercise, and to the lifestyle that is admired in their sports milieu, cannot see that they have fallen far from the goal of a healthy mind in a healthy body. They have become obsessive, compulsive, and vulnerable to permanent physical damage from minor injuries that they do not allow to heal by resting.

## How Much Is Too Much Exercise?

Cardiovascular health requires that 2,000 to 3,500 calories be burned each week in aerobic exercise: running, jogging, dancing, brisk walking, and so forth. That can be accomplished by thirty minutes of exercising a day for six days a week, or less strenuous efforts (gardening, tennis, etc.) for an hour a day five days a week. After 3,500 hundred calories are burned per week, the health benefits decrease, and the risk of injury increases.

Building and maintaining muscle and bone mass requires weight-bearing exercise. Individual requirements vary depending on age and level of fitness. We recommend you follow the advice of a competent trainer. Overdoing weight-bearing exercise can tear down muscle tissue instead of building it, and also damage bones, joints, cartilage, tendons, and ligaments.

## What Are the Consequences of Obligatory Exercising?

Obsessive thoughts, compulsive behaviors, self-worth measured only in terms of performance, abandoned relationships, damaged careers, lower grades in school, stress fractures, damaged bones, joints, and soft tissues; and depression, guilt, and anxiety when exercise is impossible.

If the exercise addict abuses steroid drugs in an effort to increase muscle mass, s/he faces additional risks: blurred vision, hallucinations, rages and tantrums, depression, acne, other skin problems, increased blood pressure, muscle cramps, joint pain, loss of sex drive, and mood swings.

For most of us, exercise is a good thing. It relaxes us and dissipates stress. It recharges our batteries so we can be more productive on the job and more attentive in relationships. In some cases exercise will lengthen our lives and make our sexual relationships more enjoyable.

For some people, however, those benefits are neutralized when exercise pushes everything else to the periphery of life. The well balanced person enjoys home, career, hobbies, friends, physical activity, interests, spiritual disciplines, and intellectual and cultural pursuits. Such a life is rich and satisfying. When one of these elements, however, dominates the rest, the person becomes unbalanced. If you are concerned about yourself, talk to a coach, trainer, physician, or counselor about how you can regain a healthier perspective.

Chapter 19

# Eating Disorders
# and Pregnancy

*I have an eating disorder, but I want to have a family
someday. Will I be able to have babies?*

You may have trouble conceiving a baby and carrying it to term.
The closer to normal your weight is, and the healthier your diet, the
better your chances of a successful pregnancy. If you are underweight
or overweight, and if you do not eat a wide variety of healthy foods,
you and your baby may have problems.

*If I do manage to get pregnant before I'm recovered, could
I hurt my baby by being eating disordered?*

You might. Women with eating disorders have higher rates of mis-
carriage than do healthy, normal women. Also, your baby might be born
prematurely, meaning that it would not weigh as much, or be as well
developed, as babies who are born full term. Low birth weight babies
are at risk of many medical problems, some of them life threatening.

*I know this sounds selfish, but could I hurt myself by try-
ing to have a baby before I am recovered?*

You are wise to think ahead. If you become pregnant now, you could
seriously deplete your own body. The baby will take nourishment from
you, and if you don't replenish your own reserves, you could find yourself

struggling with the depression and exhaustion associated with malnutrition. You would also have to deal with the physical and emotional demands of pregnancy. You might find yourself overwhelmed and feeling out of control.

### *Are there any specific medical problems I might have trouble with?*

Your teeth and bones might become weak and fragile because the baby's need for calcium takes priority over yours. If you don't replenish calcium with dairy products and other sources, you could find yourself with stress fractures and broken bones in later years. Once calcium is gone from your bones, it is difficult, if not impossible, to replace it.

Pregnancy can exacerbate other problems related to the eating disorder such as potentially fatal liver, kidney and cardiac damage. A woman who is eating disordered, pregnant, and diabetic is at high risk for serious problems. All pregnant women should receive prenatal care. Those who have one or more of the above complicating factors should consult with a physician as soon as they think they might be pregnant. To increase their own, and the baby's, chances of life and health, they should follow recommendations scrupulously.

### *That's pretty scary, but I'm more concerned about my baby than I am about myself. Assuming it was born healthy, would it be OK from then on?*

Maybe. There is evidence suggesting that babies born to eating disordered mothers may be retarded or slow to develop. Physically they may be smaller, weaker, and slower growing than other children their age. Intellectually they may lag behind peers and classmates. Emotionally they may remain infantile and dependent. They also may not develop effective social skills and successful relationships with other people.

At this point no one knows how many of the child's developmental difficulties are due to the medical consequences of an eating disorder and how many are the result of being parented by someone who is emotionally troubled and overconcerned about food and weight.

### *This is scary stuff. I wish I had never started this stupid eating disorder. I may as well have all the bad news. What else could go wrong if I try to have a baby?*

You could become depressed and frantic because of weight gain during pregnancy. You might feel so out of control of your life and body that you would try to hurt yourself or the unborn baby. You might worry and feel guilty about the damage you could be causing the baby. You might underfeed your child to make her thin, or, you might over-feed her to show the world that you are a nurturing parent. Power struggles over food and eating often plague families where someone has an eating disorder. You could continue that pattern with your child.

*This gets worse and worse, but I have a lot of love in my heart. I think I would be a good mother. The eating disorder wouldn't be that important if I had a child.*

Motherhood is stressful. If you are not strong in your recovery, you will be tempted to fall back on the starving and stuffing coping be-haviors that are so familiar to you. Ideally, as you begin raising a fam-ily, you will already have learned, and will have had practice using, other more healthy and effective behaviors when you feel over-whelmed.

Also, eating disordered women make poor role models. Your influ-ence could lead your daughters to their own eating disorders and your sons to believe that the most important thing about women is their weight.

*I really want a baby, and I think having one would give me the motivation I need to recover. I think I would enjoy being pregnant even though handling the weight gain would be scary. What can I do to give myself and my child the best possible chance of success?*

Some women with eating disorders welcome pregnancy as a vaca-tion from weight worries. They believe they are doing something im-portant by having a baby and are able to set aside their fear of fat in service to the health of the child. Others fall into black depression and intolerable anxiety when their bellies begin to swell. Most fall some-where between these two extremes.

If you think you are pregnant, or if you want to become pregnant, tell your physician as soon as possible. Cooperate with prenatal care to increase the chances that your baby will be born healthy. Also, this would be a good time to check with a counselor who can help you manage your doubts, fears, and worries as you proceed through preg-nancy. A couple of classes on pregnancy, childbirth, and child devel-opment after birth can give you reassuring information about what to expect. You can learn parenting skills, but role modeling comes from your sense of yourself. Acquire the former and improve the latter.

Chapter 20

# Eating Disorders
# and Diabetes

Most of us savor the aromas, textures, and tastes of food. We consider a well-prepared meal one of the great pleasures of life. But for over 8 million Americans, food is an obsession, laden with lifelong feelings of guilt and shame. They are so preoccupied with food, weight, and body image that they are unable to eat normally. And they are so embarrassed by their abnormal eating habits that they go to great lengths to hide them. They have an eating disorder.

That is serious in itself, but when someone with an eating disorder also has either type I or type II diabetes, the consequences can be devastating.

## Dovetailing with Diabetes

Although no one is sure whether eating disorders are more common in people with diabetes, it seems highly probable. That's because diabetes can be a natural jumping off place for an eating disorder, and a perfect mask for the disorder once it starts. Many of the causes, symptoms, and consequences of both are similar.

First, diabetes can create a preoccupation, even an obsession, with food. That obsession can develop into an eating disorder. When that occurs, a person may then claim that his or her rigidly controlled eating habits are a result of the diabetes regimen.

Reprinted with permission from *Diabetes Forecast*. Copyright 1997, American Diabetes Association. For information on joining ADA and receiving *Diabetes Forecast*, call 1-800-806-7801.

Second, diabetes can lead someone to see food as dangerous, something to avoid rather than to consume in a reasonable manner, a mindset that can also lead to an eating disorder.

Third, some people with diabetes feel their lives are out of control, that they have lost power over their world. Excessive control of food to the point of an eating disorder helps alleviate that feeling.

Fourth, teens with diabetes sometimes feel their families are overly involved in their lives. They want to rebel and become independent at almost any cost. That rebellion can take the form of unhealthy control over food and weight.

Finally, the weight loss that comes from the eating disorder may be passed off as the result of careful diabetes control. Family members and others may even compliment a young woman on the weight loss, telling her they are pleased she is taking such good care of her diabetes. Actually, they are inadvertently reinforcing the hidden eating disorder. No wonder an eating disorder in someone with diabetes can go undetected for years.

## The Insulin Factor

An eating disorder and diabetes dovetail in yet another way. Anyone taking insulin has a unique method of losing weight readily at hand: lowering or skipping an insulin dose.

For example: A teenager happily notices that, even though she isn't feeling well, she is losing weight. That pleases her. Then she is diagnosed with type I diabetes and put on insulin. Now the weight comes back. In fact, since insulin itself causes some weight gain, she may wind up heavier than before. That doesn't please her. But by now she has learned a dangerous lesson: Insulin can affect weight.

If she decides to use that lesson and cut back on her insulin, the weight may, indeed, begin to come off again, but at great cost; soaring blood sugars may begin to destroy her eyes, kidneys, and nerves.

## Danger: Eating Disorders And Diabetes

While eating disorders harm everyone, they are particularly dangerous for people with either type I or type II diabetes.

Hypoglycemia (low blood glucose) is a risk when food is restricted, meals are skipped, or food is purged.

Hyperglycemia (high blood glucose), severe enough to bring on ketoacidosis, which can lead to death, may come on quickly after a period of binge eating.

And the person who eats and purges—even if she takes her insulin—does not know how much food has been absorbed before the purging, so she can't judge whether she has enough—or too much—insulin to cover the food that has been absorbed.

Because people with diabetes and an eating disorder have unhealthy blood glucose levels over a long period of time, they are at great risk for diabetic complications that can affect every system of the body.

Whenever an eating disorder and diabetes are both involved, the result can be death. Anyone who denies themselves needed insulin is actually retreating to the days before insulin was discovered. And, as they knew back then, lack of insulin, like lack of food, leads to death.

## The Story of a "Bad" Girl

I thought I was bad.

I had been diagnosed with diabetes when I was 9, and as a teen I ate what I liked and ran my blood sugars high on purpose so I wouldn't gain weight.

I would do things like wait till my mom left the room, then eat everything in sight. Then I'd lie and say I didn't eat a thing.

Of course, every day I would decide to be "good," to eat nothing but vegetables and maybe an apple. And when I slipped—which I did almost every day—I felt terrible, worthless, "bad."

Now I'm 32. I'm starting to have complications in my eyes and kidneys. And now, believe me, I'm really trying to be "good." I listen to my doctor, test my blood sugar four to six times a day, and take enough insulin to cover what I eat. And I keep telling myself that gaining weight is not worse than going blind or losing my kidneys. (I didn't think much about that when I was a teen.)

I know now that you are not a "bad" person if you want to eat a candy bar—or many candy bars. You are a human person.

I also know that if you are struggling with diabetes, food, and negative feelings about your body, you deserve a round of applause just for trying. You also deserve love—from yourself as well as from others. So praise yourself when you succeed; forgive yourself when you fail.

Don't ask for perfection from yourself. And please believe that the way you treat your body now will affect your health and happiness in the future. I know.

Please believe, too, that you—yes you—are a good person who deserves to be happy and healthy. So take care of yourself. Now.

*—Miriam E. Tucker has been a medical writer in Rockville, Md., for 10 years and has had type I diabetes for 23 years.*

## *Prevention*

Healthy diabetes control calls for healthy eating. However, an extremely rigorous meal plan can start some people on the road to an eating disorder. To keep your meal plan reasonable and satisfying:

• Don't get involved in a lot of food restrictions. They can make you obsess about food and feel deprived.

• Make sure that at least some portions of the foods you like are included in your food plan, even high-sugar and high-fat foods.

• Learn how to be flexible with your meal plan. When a slice of apple pie looks delicious, be able to substitute that slice of pie for other carbohydrates.

• Avoid an "all or nothing" attitude. If you've eaten something inappropriate, don't decide that the day is no longer perfect so you might as well eat anything you want.

• Consider seeing a registered dietitian familiar with diabetes to help you draw up a reasonable, tasty food plan.

• Don't expect perfection from yourself, especially in your diet.

Chapter 21

# Psychological Effects of Starvation

A review of the literature and research on food restriction indicates that inhibiting food intake has consequences that may not have been anticipated by those attempting such restriction. Starvation and self-imposed dieting appear to result in eating binges once food is available and in psychological manifestations such as preoccupation with food and eating, increased emotional responsiveness and dysphoria, and distractibility. The negative consequences of restricting eating and diet to lose weight, may outweigh the benefits of restraining one's eating. Instead, healthful, balanced eating without specific food restrictions should be recommended as a long-term strategy to avoid the perils of restrictive dieting.

The decision to restrict one's eating, or diet, is usually made in the context of an attempt at self-improvement. For several decades, the North American cultural ethos has been that most of us are too fat (whether this is objectively true or not), and the solution was for the majority of people, especially women, to restrain their eating and follow weight-loss diets. People dieted in the expectation that this would help them achieve enhanced health, appearance, and feelings of well-being. It has become clear, however, that this "solution" did not solve the problem. In fact, given the increase in obesity in the Western world since the 1970s, when the dieting ethic began to dominate societal consciousness, it could be argued that the emphasis on dieting may

Excerpted from "Psychological Consequences of Food Restriction," © 1996 American Dietetic Association. Reprinted by permission from *Journal of the American Dietetic Association*, June 1996, Vol. 96, No. 6, Pg. 589(6).

have contributed to the increase in overweight. Arguments about the efficacy of dieting aside, however, what are the psychological ramifications of dieting or food restriction?

## Studies of Effects of Food Restriction

The classic psychological study of food restriction, the World War II study of conscientious objectors by Keys et al,[1] provides the most compelling data. Normal-weight (presumably nondieting) men were asked to restrict their eating for 6 months to lose 25% of their initial body weight, so that the effects of starvation could be studied.

The men were fed only 75% of their normal intake, and when they stopped losing weight while consuming that intake, their food was further restricted until they achieved a weight loss to approximately 76% of initial body weight.

Careful observations were made of these subjects over several months, and some interesting psychological reactions were noted. One change was that subjects became increasingly focused on food; they collected recipes, hung pinup pictures of food, and changed career plans to food-related activities such as becoming a chef. They also grew increasingly upset and irritable, fighting with each other and their girlfriends. The men appeared apathetic and lethargic and seemed to lose interest in sex (replacing pictures of women with their food pinups!) In some respects, the most striking change occurred during the semistarvation period and after weight was restored to normal and the study had ended: When the men were subsequently allowed to eat as much as they wanted, these previously normal, healthy eaters began to gorge themselves when attractive foods were available.[2,3] Moreover, they reported feeling out of control of their eating and obsessed with food; some even stole food or gum. Food restriction actually appeared to produce binge eating in previously normal eaters.

A similar tendency to overeat after food deprivation has been observed in human beings and animals. Canadian soldiers captured and held prisoner by the Germans after the abortive raid on Dieppe, France, during World War II were questioned 50 years later about their postwar feelings and behaviors.[4] While prisoners of war, these men had been starved and lost substantial amounts of weight. Not surprisingly, they reported more negative emotions (anxiety and post-traumatic stress reactions) than did soldiers who were not taken prisoner. They also reported, however, that they had had episodes of binge eating after they were released and returned home to Canada (and after their normal weight was restored).

166

A similar reaction in soldiers kept on short rations during a prolonged military campaign was reported as long ago as in ancient Greece. Xenophon described "boulimos" or "a ravenous hunger" (distinguished from a normal hunger) in these deprived soldiers.[5] Likewise, a study of female rats deprived of food, then allowed to refeed back to their normal weight,[6] indicated that the rats overate palatable food presented to them ad libitum after their return to a normal diet (and weight). Finally, patients with anorexia nervosa who starve themselves into emaciation frequently become bulimic; thus, they alternate between uncontrollable eating binges and starvation, and often purge themselves.[7] Prior deprivation thus appears to produce a tendency to overeat and even binge, despite the restoration of both food availability and weight to their initial levels.[8]

## Cognitive and Emotional Effects of Restrained Eating

The participants in the study by Keys et al[1] and others undergoing semistarvation exhibited cognitive and emotional changes or differences when their food intake was restricted. Restrained college students who are presumably limiting their eating to some extent at least some of the time, show similar differences from nondeprived, unrestrained students. Patients with anorexia and bulimia nervosa, another group of food-deprived persons, exhibit similar differences from nondeprived normal persons. For example, like food-deprived subjects, restrained eaters and patients with anorexia nervosa and bulimia nervosa are more focused on food and weight than are normal, unrestrained eaters. When presented with information about a fictitious person, restrained eaters and patients with anorexia nervosa remembered more food and weight-related information about the person and less of other types of information than did unrestrained controls.[32] Similarly, studies indicate that the performance of patients with eating disorders,[33-36] fasting/hungry normal persons[37], and restrained eaters,[38,40] is disrupted by food and/or weight-related words, particularly after a high-energy preload, which indicates that these subjects are all more cognitively concerned with food and weight.

The starving men in the study by Keys et al[1] reported difficulty concentrating on a task. Chronic dieters are also more distractible than are nondieters. Given a boring task such as proofreading, restrained eaters actually focus well on the task and perform better than do unrestrained eaters, as long as they are in a quiet, nondistracting environment. If, however, distracting audiotapes are played while subjects are performing, restrained subjects' performance deteriorates markedly, and it is significantly worse than that of their unrestrained counterparts.[41]

Irritability and negative emotionality were observed in the starving subjects studied by Keys et al and appear to characterize patients with eating disorders. Restrained eaters have also been found to exhibit heightened affective responsiveness, responding more strongly than unrestrained eaters to emotion-eliciting slides,[9] audiotapes,[41] and fear-inducing situations.[23] Moreover, restrained eaters score as more emotionally labile or neurotic than unrestrained eaters on personality measures such as anxiety measures,[23] self-esteem scales,[42] narcissism scales,[43] and more general measures such as the California Personality Inventory.[44]

Physiologic differences are also brought about by food deprivation. Taste perception has been shown to differ from normal in starving, weight-reduced normal persons, patients with anorexia nervosa, and dieters. All these groups show negative alliesthesia, which is a failure to reject sweet tastes after consuming a high-energy intensely sweet preload. In addition, salivary changes in response to palatable food have been reported in dieters.[45] Moreover, patients with anorexia nervosa show a variety of hormonal changes, and even normal dieters have been found to have elevated levels of free fatty acids in their blood.[14]

## Conclusions and Implications for Dietitians

The consequences of food deprivation are extraordinarily similar in animals and in human beings. This appears to be true whether the food restriction for human beings is involuntary, that is, controlled by external forces, or a voluntary choice to restrain one's eating, either for the benefit of science (as in the starvation study by Keys et al[1]) or for personal goals (e.g., those of dieters or patients with eating disorders). Both display a tendency toward excessive eating or even bingeing when restrictions are lifted, heightened emotional responsiveness, and cognitive disruptions, including distractibility and a focus on food and eating. This is true despite the fact that most human dieters do not appear to be particularly successful at depriving themselves—at least not successful enough to reduce their weight on any long-term basis.[10-12] In fact, persons whose weights fluctuate over time (self-defined "yo-yo" dieters) appear to have lower general well-being and eating self-efficacy and higher stress levels than nonfluctuators.[46]

These negative changes thus seem to reflect the effects of either repeated episodes of short-term deprivation, psychological deprivation (refraining from eating one's preferred but fattening foods except when the diet is broken), or the stress of not being able to eat enough or what one desires. Persons who are food deprived for whatever reason suffer more than simply not getting sufficient or preferred food; they exhibit a variety of cognitive, emotional, and behavioral changes as reviewed here. These consequences cannot be prevented in those whose food deprivation is the involuntary result of insufficient supplies of comestibles. However, we can certainly warn those about to subject themselves to voluntary restrictions through ill-advised dieting that there are a variety of consequences of food restriction, and weight loss is among the least likely of these.

What then can we do to help restrained eaters? The first thing is to recognize which dieters should be advised to give up their energy restrictions and learn to eat a balanced, healthful diet. Those whose weights are within the normal range and who are already eating in a reasonably healthful manner are unlikely to experience medical problems related to weight and should be so advised. These persons need to be helped to establish a healthful lifestyle that incorporates moderate exercise, balanced diet, and no restrictions on any particular food (except to maintain total fat intake under 30% daily). Those whose weights are even lower than normal should be educated more vigorously about the hazards of dieting, as well as being encouraged to eat and exercise in a healthful manner.

For those persons whose weights fall into the obese range, and in particular for those who show some signs of developing health problems associated with weight, some restriction of intake may be necessary, Even with obese patients, however, the dangers of psychological deprivation leading to overindulgence must be remembered. These people should be taught to incorporate their favorite foods into more moderate levels of intake, as well as increasing their energy expenditure through gradual increments in physical activity. The goal for all should be a healthful lifestyle that can be maintained indefinitely, rather than a short-term "diet" that will most likely be abandoned and produce more overweight and psychological discomfort. A reduction in counterproductive "restraint" seems likely to produce both physical and psychological well-being.

## References

1.  Keys A, Brozek J, Henschel A, Mickelson O, Taylor HL. *The Biology of Human Starvation*. 2 vols. Minneapolis, Minn: University of Minnesota Press; 1950.

2. Franklin JS, Schieie BC, Brozek J, Keys A. Observations on human behavior in experimental starvation and rehabilitation. *J Clin Psychol.* 1948; 4:28-45.

3. Schiele BC, Brozek J. "Experimental neurosis" resulting from semistarvation in man. *Psychosom Med.* 1948; 10:31-50.

4. Polivy J, Zeitlin SB, Herman CP, Beal AL. Food restriction and binge eating: a study of former prisoners of war. *J Abnorm Psychol.* 1994; 103:409-411.

5. Stunkard AJ. A history of binge eating. In: Fairburn CG, Wilson GT, eds. *Binge Eating: Nature, Assessment and Treatment.* New York, NY: Guilford Press; 1993:15-34.

6. Coscina DV, Dixon LM. Body weight regulation in anorexia nervosa: insights from an animal model. In: Darby PL, Garfinkel PE, Garner DM, Coscina DV, eds. *Anorexia Nervosa: Recent Developments.* New York, NY: Allan R. Liss; 1983:207-220.

7. Garfinkel PE, Moldofsky H, Garner DM. The heterogeneity of anorexia nervosa. *Arch Gen Psychiatry.* 1980; 37:1036-1040.

8. Polivy J, Herman CP. Dieting and binging: a causal analysis. *Am Psychol.* 1985; 40:193-201.

9. Polivy J, Herman CP, Warsh S. Internal and external components of emotionality in restrained and unrestrained eaters. *J Abnorm Psychol.* 1978; 87:497-504.

10. Heatherton TF, Polivy J, Herman CP. Restraint, weight loss and variability of body weight. *J Abnorm Psychol.* 1991; 100:78-83.

11. Klesges RC, Isbell TR, Klesges LM. Relationship between dietary restraint, energy intake, physical activity, and body weight: a prospective analysis. *J Abnorm Psychol.* 1992; 101:668-674.

12. Tiggemann M. Dietary restraint as a predictor of reported weight loss and affect. *Psychol Rep.* 1994; 75:1679-1682.

13. Herman CP, Polivy J. Restrained eating. In: Stunkard AJ, ed. *Obesity.* Philadelphia, Pa: WB Saunders; 1980: 208-225.

14. Herman CP, Polivy J. Studies of eating in normal dieters. In: Walsh BT, ed. *Eating Behavior in Eating Disorders, Washington, DC*: American Psychiatric Association Press; 1988: 95-112.

15. Herman CP, Polivy J, Esses VM. The illusion of counter-regulation. *Appetite.* 1987; 9:161-169.

16. Knight L, Boland F. Restrained eating: an experimental disentanglement of the disinhibiting variables of calories and food type. *J Abnorm Psychol.* 1989; 98:412-420.

17. Polivy J. Perception of calories and regulation of intake in restrained and unrestrained subjects. *Addict Behav.* 1976; 1:237-244.

18. Spencer JA, Fremouw WJ. Binge eating as a function of restraint and weight classification. *J Abnorm Psychol.* 1979; 88:262-267.

19. Polivy J, Herman CP. The effects of alcohol on eating behavior: disinhibition or sedation. *Addict Behav.* 1976; 1:121-125.

20. Polivy J, Herman CP. Effects of alcohol on eating behavior: influences of mood and perceived intoxication. *J Abnorm Psychol.* 1976; 85:601-606.

21. Heatherton TF, Herman CP, Polivy J. Effects of physical threat and ego threat on eating behavior. *J Pers Soc Psychol.* 1991; 60:138-143.

22. Heatherton TF, Polivy J, Herman CP, Baumeister R. Self-awareness, task failure and disinhibition: how attentional focus affects eating. *J Pers.* 1993: 61:49-61.

23. Herman CP, Polivy J. Anxiety, restraint, and eating behavior. *J Abnorm Psychol.* 1975; 84:666-672.

24. Herman CP, Polivy J, Lank C, Heatherton TF. Anxiety, hunger and eating. *J Abnorm Psychol.* 1987; 96:264-269.

25. Polivy J, Herman CP, McFarlane T. Effects of anxiety on eating: Does palatability moderate distress-induced overeating? *J Abnorm Psychol.* 1994; 103:505-510.

26. Ruderman AJ. Obesity, anxiety, and food consumption. *Addict Behav.* 1983; 8:235-242.

27. Ruderman A. Dysphoric mood and overeating. *J Abnorm Psychol.* 1985; 94:78-85.

28. Cools J, Schotte DE, McNally R. Emotional arousal and overeating in restrained eaters. *J Abnorm Psychol.* 1992; 101:348-351.

29. Herman CP, Polivy J. Excess and restraint in bulimia. In: Pirke K, Vandereycken W, Ploog D, eds. *The Psychobiology of Bulimia.* Munich, Germany: Springer Verlag; 1988:33-41.

30. Polivy J, Herman CP. The diagnosis and treatment of normal eating. *J Consult Clin PSychol.* 1987; 55:635-644.

31. Polivy J, Herman CP. Etiology of binge eating: psychological mechanisms. In: Fairburn CG, Wilson GT, eds. *Binge Eating: Nature, Assessment and Treatment. New York, NY:* Guilford Press; 1993:173-205.

32. King G, Polivy J, Herman CP. Cognitive aspects of dietary restraint: effects on person memory. *Int J Eat Dis.* 1991; 10:313-322.

33. Ben-Tovim DI, Walker MK, Fok D, Yap E. An adaptation of the Stroop test for measuring shape and food concerns in eating disorders: a quantitative measure of psychopathology? *Int J Eat Disord.* 1989; 8:681-687.

34. Cooper MJ, Anastasiades P, Fairburn CG. Selective processing of eating, shape, and weight-related words in persons with bulimia nervosa. *J Abnorm Psychol.* 1992; 101:352-355.

35. Fairburn CG, Cooper PJ, Cooper MJ, McKenna FP, Anastasiades P. Selective Information processing in bulimia nervosa. *Int J Eat Disord.* 1991; 10:415-422.

36. Walker MK, Ben-Tovim DJ, Paddick S, McNamarra J. Pictorial adaptation of Stroop measures of body-related concerns in eating disorders. *Int J Eat Disord.* 1995; 17:309-311.

37. Channon S, Hayward A. The effect of short-term fasting on processing of food cues in normal subjects. *Int J Eat Disord.* 1990; 9:447-452.

38. Mahamedi F, Heatherton TF. Effects of high calorie preloads on selective processing of food and body shape stimuli among dieters and nondieters. *Int J Eat Disord.* 1993; 13:305-314.

39. Ogden J, Greville L. Cognitive changes to preloading in restrained and unrestrained eaters as measured by the Stroop task. *Int J Eat Disord.* 1993; 14:185-195.

40. Perpina C, Hemsley D, Treasure J, De Silva P. Is the selective information processing of food and body words specific to patients with eating disorders? *Int J Eat Disord.* 1993; 14:359-366.

41. Herman CP, Polivy J, Pliner P, Munic D, Threlkeld J. Distractibility in dieters and nondieters: an alternative view of "externality." *J Pers Soc Psychol.* 1978; 36:536-548.

42. Polivy J, Heatherton TF, Herman CP. Self-esteem, restraint, and eating behavior. *J Abnorm Psychol.* 1988; 97:354-356.

43. Ruderman AJ, Grace PS. Restraint, bulimia, and psychopathology. *Addict Behav.* 1987; 12:249-255.

44. Edwards FE, Nagelberg DB. Personality characteristics of restrained/binge eaters versus unrestrained/nonbinge eaters. *Addict Behav.* 1986; 11:207-211.

45. Pliner P, Herman CP, Polivy J. Palatability as a determinant of eating: finickiness as a function of taste, hunger, and the prospect of good food. In: Capaldi ED, Powley TD, eds. *Taste, Experience, and Feeding.* Washington, DC: American Psychological Association; 1990: 210-226.

46. Foreyt JP, Brunner RL, Goodrick GK, Cutter G, Brownell KD, St Jeor ST. Psychological correlates of weight fluctuation. *Int J Eat Disord.* 1995; 17:263-275.

47. Ernsburger P, Haskew P. Health implications of obesity: an alternative view. *J Obes Weight Regul.* 1987; 6:1-81.

49. Ernsburger P, Koletsky RJ, Baskin JS, Foley M. Refeeding hypertension in obese spontaneously hypertensive rats. *Hypertension.* 1994; 24:699-705.

# Part Four


# Treatment and Prevention

Chapter 22

# Treating Eating Disorders

## Is Recovery Possible?

Eating disorders are treatable, and people do recover from them. Recovery is a difficult process that can take several months or even years. Some people do better than others. The folks who do best, work with physicians and counselors who help them resolve medical and psychological issues that contribute to, or result from, disordered eating.

## What Is Recovery?

Recovery is much more than the abandonment of starving and stuffing. At minimum it includes the following:

* Maintenance of normal or near-normal weight

* In women, regular menstrual periods (not triggered by medication)

* A varied diet of normal foods (not just low-cal, non-fat, non-sugar items)

* Elimination or major reduction of irrational food fears

* Age appropriate relationships with family members

* Awareness of unreasonable cultural demands for thinness

* One or more mutually satisfying friendships with appropriate people

© 1998 ANRED, Anorexia Nervosa and Related Eating Disorders, Inc.; reprinted with permission.

177

- Age-appropriate interest/participation in romantic relationships
- Strong repertoire of problem-solving skills
- Fun activities that have nothing to do with food, weight, or appearance
- Understanding of the process of choices and consequences
- Person has a sense of self and goals and a realistic plan for achieving them.

## What Is the Best Treatment for an Eating Disorder?

Because many factors contribute to the development of an eating disorder, and since every person's situation is different, the "best treatment" must be custom tailored for each individual. The process begins with evaluation by a physician or counselor. Recommendations include any or all of the following. In general, the more components included in the treatment plan, the faster the person makes progress.

- Hospitalization to prevent death, suicide, and medical crisis
- Medication to relieve depression and anxiety
- Dental work to repair damage and minimize future problems
- Individual counseling to develop healthy ways of taking control
- Group counseling to learn how to manage relationships effectively
- Family counseling to change old patterns and create healthier new ones
- Nutrition counseling to debunk food myths and design healthy meals
- Support groups to break down isolation and alienation

Please note: Support groups by themselves are not sufficient treatment for an eating disorder. To be effective, they must be integrated into a comprehensive treatment plan.

## Where to Find Help

If you are in crisis, go to a hospital emergency room or call a crisis hotline. Find the number in the yellow pages under "Crisis Intervention."

If you are not in crisis, ask your family doctor for an evaluation and referral. Don't let embarrassment stop you from telling the physician all the details. Doctors, nurses, and counselors have heard the eating disorder story many times before. You can also ask people you trust, and who have been in your situation, for the names of physicians and counselors they found helpful.

If you are a student, check with the school counseling center. Services may be low cost or free. If your income is limited, or if your insurance will not cover treatment for eating disorders, look for community service agencies in the "Counselors" section of the yellow pages. The organizations listed there may not provide formal eating disorders programs, but they do offer basic assistance to people who have few other options.

## Binge Prevention Tips

Never ever let yourself get so hungry that the urge to binge is overwhelming. People who recover from bulimia say that they eat regularly. Because they are never ravenous, they have no physical reason to binge eat.

Hunger is probably the most powerful binge trigger we know of. It is a recognized fact that the longer one has dieted, and the more severely calories are restricted, the higher the risk of binge eating.

Never ever deprive yourself of good-tasting food, even if it has more fat and calories than you are used to eating. If you refuse to eat appealing foods that you really want, you will feel deprived and crave them. Then you are vulnerable to bingeing.

Remember Adam and Eve in the Garden of Eden? The one food they were not supposed to eat was the one they could not stay away from. Don't deprive yourself of other satisfying experiences either. If you make yourself feel needy, you will be tempted to look for comfort in the refrigerator. Make sure that every day you spend time with friends. In person is best, but phone calls and e-mail are better than nothing.

Also every day spend time doing things you are good at, things you can take pride in, things that demonstrate your competency and abilities. Allow yourself to enjoy your accomplishments and refuse to listen to the nagging inner voice that insists you could do better if only you tried harder.

Last, but by no means least, every day do something that's fun and pleasurable. Watch comedy videos and laugh out loud at the outrageous jokes. Play something—a board game, a computer game, tapes or CDs. Go outside and enjoy the birds, trees, flowers, and fresh air. If you live in the middle of a big city, go to a park. Figure out how to give yourself a fun break from the daily routine, and then do it.

Keep tabs on your feelings. Several times during the day, especially in the first stages of recovery, take time out and ask yourself how you feel. If you notice rising stress, anger, fear, sadness, and sometimes even strong joy, be alert to the possibility that you may try to dull these strong emotions by turning to food. Find a better way of dealing with your feelings such as talking them over with a trusted friend.

The 12-step folks have a handy formula. When they feel on the verge of falling into old behaviors, they say HALT! Then they ask, "Am I too Hungry, too Angry, too Lonely, or too Tired?" All of those states are strong binge triggers. Additional triggers for people with eating disorders seem to be Boredom and Unstructured time. If you find yourself in any of these states, figure out a healthier and more effective way of dealing with the situation than binge eating.

Until you have achieved some balance and perspective, stay away from temptation. Don't go to all-you-can-eat salad bars. If ice cream is a binge trigger, don't keep it in your freezer.

When you want potato salad, for example, or rocky road ice cream, go to a sit-down restaurant and order a single portion, ideally as part of a balanced meal. By doing so, you accomplish three things. You avoid depriving yourself. You avoid the urges to binge created by deprivation, and you also learn how to integrate normal food into a reasonable and healthy meal plan.

When you do feel powerful urges to binge, postpone the act for thirty minutes. Surely you can wait half an hour. During that time think about what is going on in your life. What stresses are you facing? What is missing right now from your life that you need in order to be happy and avoid the looming binge? Make a list of things you could you do instead of binge eating to deal with your situation. If you are truly committed to recovery, at least some of the time you will choose one of these healthier behaviors instead of binge food.

Take charge of your life. Stop using words like, "I wish," "I want," "I hope," and "I can't." They are weak victim words. Say instead things like, "I choose," even if you are choosing to binge. Say, "I will," even if the thing you will do is vomit. These are words that express responsibility, power, and control. If you can choose to binge, then by implication at some future time you can choose NOT to binge. If you will vomit, then next week or next month or next year you can choose to say, "I WON'T vomit."

Chapter 23

# An Eating Disorders
# Prevention Program

Research on developing, implementing and evaluating a school
personnel eating disorders prevention training program examined
effects of the training with 117 high school staff persons, 85 in the
experimental group and 32 in the control group. The two groups
showed significant differences in knowledge after the training. Those
in the experimental group were more likely to identify students at
risk. Training holds promise.

Eating disorders are chronic syndromes affecting more than 8 million people in the United States (ANAD, 1994). Eighty-six percent of
those suffering from an eating disorder develop the disease before
21 years of age. In its National Health Promotion and Disease Prevention Objectives for Adolescents (1990), the United States Department of Health and Human Services identified sound nutrition
as one of the major goals for Healthy Youth 2000. However, no state
has an adequate program to combat eating disorders. Very few schools
or colleges have programs with the goal of preventing eating disorders.

Every state and thousands of schools have extensive programs
seeking to prevent drug and alcohol abuse (ANAD, 1994). The value
of education programs for substance abuse has been documented
(Eigen & Rowden, 1993; Meers, Werch, Hedrick, & Lepper, 1995). The

Excerpted from "An eating disorders prevention program," by Pamela S.
Chally, © 1998 Nursecom, Inc., from *Journal of Child and Adolescent Psychiatric Nursing*, April-June 1998, Vol.11, No. 2, Pg. 51(10); reprinted with permission.

number of victims, seriousness of health consequences, chronicity of the illness, and cost of treatment make it imperative that educational programs be developed and implemented to prevent eating disorders.

School personnel—including teachers, school nurses, counselors, psychologists, and athletic coaches—who spend large amounts of time with our youth must meet the challenge of an ever-intensifying struggle to save adolescents from eating disorders. They must be knowledgeable about such disorders and recognize both young people at risk and signs and symptoms of eating disorders. The Florida Minimum Essential Teaching Competencies (I.S. Baker, personal communication, June 22, 1989) discussed the importance of promoting physical development as well as the necessity of recognizing overt signs of emotional distress in students. Yet elementary teachers are required to take only 3 semester hours of college course work in health, and secondary teachers have no health requirement (J. Frazier, personal communication, April 6, 1994). It seems accurate to assume that the majority of Florida's teachers have been given no special training to recognize youths at risk for eating disorders or to identify signs and symptoms in students they interact with daily. These facts served as the basis for the development of an eating disorders prevention program for school personnel.

Studies indicate that knowledge can be improved by students' participation in educational programs on eating disorders. Despite the fact that signs and symptoms of eating disorders do occur in both junior and senior high school students, no program has been found effective in preventing eating disorders. The present research was built on the findings of the literature review, particularly the Killen et al. (1993) and Paxton (1993) studies. It was decided to offer training to school personnel so they would be more likely to identify students at risk for eating disorders and intervene early in the disease cycle. Early intervention is believed to be important in the effectiveness of treatment (Levine, 1995).

The purpose of this research was to develop, implement, and evaluate a school personnel training program on eating disorders. Research questions were:

1.  How do attitudes and knowledge differ in school personnel who have been trained on eating disorders versus non-trained personnel?

2.  How does the number of eating disordered students identified by trained versus non-trained school personnel differ?

It was determined that school personnel who attended the training were more likely to identify students at risk for an eating disorder. This finding was statistically significant despite the fact that one person in the control group was very concerned about eating disorders and identified more students at risk in the third smallest high school than any one else. Only 34 school personnel in both groups together returned their tally sheets at the end of the 3-month period, however. The number was small even with follow-up and reminders from both the researcher and school administrators.

The presentation to school personnel holds promise as an approach to the prevention of eating disorders, rather than all students participating in a curriculum. Killen et al. (1993) reported that their curriculum designed to modify attitudes toward eating and unhealthy weight regulation practices had no long-term success in preventing eating problems. Conducting research in the school setting has given this researcher an even greater understanding of the tremendous amount of material teachers must include in the curriculum, as well as the multiple demands made on their time by students' individual and group needs. It is also known that deviant eating disorder behaviors are sometimes learned in discussions on the topic despite the fact that the goal is to identify and prevent the disorder, not to increase symptoms (Murray, Touyz, & Beumont, 1990; Watts & Ellis, 1992). For these reasons it seems unjustifiable to ask that all students be exposed to a lengthy curricular discussion on eating disorders. Instead, giving teachers the tools to identify those at risk for developing an eating disorder and assisting the identified students to get help with the problem seems to be a solution holding much promise.

This is not to suggest that students should not have the benefit of school curricula addressing concepts of nutrition, links between food and emotions and biologic, psychological and social components of adolescence. It is important that basic nutritional facts and normal aspects of adolescent growth and development be discussed with students. Such information is basic to their overall general knowledge.

## Implications

Based on the findings of this study, it seems appropriate that school personnel be given training in the identification of students at risk for eating disorders, skills on how to approach identified students, and treatment resources for referring students for additional help. The material can be presented to teachers in approximately an hour, although longer time periods would allow more content to be presented and give time for discussion.

Additional time appears necessary to alter attitudes toward eating disorders, which may increase an individual's commitment to prevention. It seems appropriate that all school personnel have some background in understanding eating disorders. Those more likely to deal with such problems include counselors, school nurses, coaches, and social science, physical education, health, and home economics teachers. In reality, however, anyone a student feels comfortable enough to confide in may be the first to identify that eating problems are present. The problem may come to the teacher's attention in a written assignment, formal conference, observation of behavior, or simply by a passing comment. The researcher was surprised at the number of English teachers who indicated that students had discussed multiple emotional concerns including eating disorders in written essays.

One limitation of this study was that it was conducted in the high school setting. Replicating the study in junior high schools is needed because it is known that symptoms of eating disorders are apparent in many students before high school (Killen et al., 1993). Prevention may be even more effective if it is begun earlier than high school.

Nurses are in a position to initiate a program to train school personnel to identify students at risk for eating disorders. With an appropriate background the nurse may do the presentation or find an expert in the subject to do so. Additionally nurses should be very familiar with signs and symptoms of anorexia and bulimia so that they readily identify those at risk and appropriately refer students as soon as help is needed.

Research is needed to determine if identification and referral of students by teachers trained in eating disorders will have long-term positive results in the prevention of these disorders. This study was limited in that school personnel counted students they had identified at risk for only 3 months. No long-term follow-up was initiated, but ideally students would be followed over a number of years to determine if an eating disorder developed or became more of a concern.

It is important to identify with specificity and sensitivity those students who actually are at risk for an eating disorder. In the eating-disorder presentation described in this article, a detailed discussion of signs and symptoms of eating disorders occurred. School personnel identified students as being at risk based on this discussion and their own knowledge of the disorders. It is desirable that a reliable and valid screening tool be developed to determine more accurately which students are indeed at risk. A short questionnaire and/or interview, as suggested by the National Eating Disorders Screening Program, may be an appropriate screening technique. Additional work is needed in this area.

Additional research is warranted to determine if the documented successes in substance abuse prevention are applicable to prevention programs for eating disorders. Preventing alcohol tobacco, and drug use among children and adolescents has received significant funding during the past two decades and successful results have been documented (Eigen & Rowden, 1993). Those working to prevent eating disorders should learn from the positive outcomes of prevention research in related areas.

## Conclusions

The findings of this research study indicated that after a training session, school personnel increased their knowledge concerning eating disorders and were more likely to identify students at risk for developing an eating disorder. Training school personnel to identify students at risk for eating disorders holds promise as a strategy for dealing with this disease. All students at risk for eating disorders should be further evaluated and additional treatment initiated as needed.

## References

ANAD. (1994, March). *Newsletter of the National Association of Anorexia Nervosa and Associated Disorders*. (Available from ANAD, Box 7, Highland Park, IL 60036).

Eigen, L.D., and Rowden, D.W. (1993). Prevention works: A discussion paper on preventing alcohol, tobacco, and other drug problems. (DHHS Publication No. SMA 93-2046). Washington, DC: U.S. Department of Health and Human Services.

Killen, J.D., Taylor, C.B., Hammer, L.D., Litt, I., Wilson, D.M., Rich, T., Hayword, C., Simmonds, B., Kraemer, H., and Varady, A. (1993). An attempt to modify unhealthful eating attitudes and weight regulation practices of young adolescent girls. *International Journal of Eating Disorders, 13,* 369-384.

Levine, P. (1995). Connections in primary prevention. *The Renfrew Perspective,* 1 (3), 4-5.

Murray, S., Touyz, S., & Beumont, P. (1990). Knowledge about eating disorders in the community. *International Journal of Eating Disorders*, 9(1), 87-93.

Paxton, S.J. (1993). A prevention program for disturbed eating and body dissatisfaction in adolescent girls: A 1-year follow-up. *Health Education Research*, 8(1), 43-51.

Chapter 24

# How to Make
# Peace with Your Body

In this world of super-hunks and airbrushed beauties, finding fault with normal bodies has become a national pastime. Here's how to hold your head high and think the best of yourself—whatever your body's shape.

Many teens suffer from what the experts call "negative body image"—they don't like their bodies. And they're letting their thoughts about their bodies shatter their self-esteem, their sense of how valuable they are as people.

"I find it impossible to ever be satisfied with my body," says Sarah, a high school senior from San Diego, California. "After each pound slips away, I still feel the need to be thinner." Her friend Stephanie understands Sarah's dilemma. "All I see are models in magazines who look so perfect, and that's how I want to be," she says. Sarah and Stephanie are not alone.

Nearly two of every five teens who replied to a nationwide survey that appeared in *USA Weekend* last year said they would feel better about themselves if they lost weight or (among boys) bulked up. The survey, published in May 1998, discovered that nearly seven out of 10 respondents said they felt either "somewhat satisfied" or "not at all satisfied" with their looks.

Tony, 14, probably would agree. "I feel sad because everyone calls me fat," he says. "I exercise and do push-ups to help me lose weight. The kids call me 'Fat Boy,' 'Fatso,' and stuff—and it makes me mad."

Sarah, Stephanie, and Tony take part in a weekly body image group held for adolescents at Mesa Vista Hospital in San Diego. They asked to be identified by first name only. The group began when teens expressed a need to discuss their feelings and perceptions about their bodies in a supportive forum.

In this media-driven age, it seems most people are dissatisfied with their bodies. Recent studies show that kids as early as third grade are concerned about their weight. But, with body shapes rapidly changing, teens are the most vulnerable. During teen years, there is a lot of pressure to fit in.

How do you feel about your body? When you look in the mirror, are you proud of what you see, or do you think, "I'm too short," "I'm too fat," or "If only I were thinner or more muscular"? Answer the following questions to determine how you view yourself. If you answered "Yes" to three or more questions, you may have a negative body image. Read on to learn how to change your perception to a more positive one.

## How Do You See Yourself?

1. Have you avoided sports or working out because you didn't want to be seen in gym clothes?

2. Does eating even a small amount of food make you feel fat?

3. Do you worry or obsess about your body not being small, thin, or good enough?

4. Are you concerned your body is not muscular or strong enough?

5. Do you avoid wearing certain clothes because they make you feel fat?

6. Have you ever disliked your body?

7. Do you feel bad about yourself because you don't like your body?

8. Do you want to change something about your body?

9. Do you compare yourself to others and "come up short"?

## Mirror, Mirror

Girls, in general, tend to be overly concerned about weight and body shape, say psychologists. Many strive for the "perfect" body and judge themselves by their looks, clothes, and ability to stay cover-girl thin. But boys don't escape, either. Today's culture celebrates tough, muscular, and well-sculpted males. So naturally, boys are concerned with the size and strength of their body. They think they have to be "real" men. Yet many admit being confused as to what's expected of them. This confusion can make it harder than ever to feel good about themselves. It's not surprising that sports such as wrestling, boxing, and gymnastics—which demand top conditioning—an contribute to a negative body image. The need to make weight for a sport often leads to eating problems.

But boys like Jon Maxwell, 15, say sports make them feel better about themselves. "Guys are in competition, especially in the weight room," Jon says. "One will say, 'I can bench 215 pounds,' and the other guy says, 'Well, I can bench 230 pounds.' If you're stronger, you're better." Daniel Schaufler, age 16, agrees. "Guys are into having the perfect body," he says." And if you feel good about your body, you automatically feel good about yourself."

## Mission Impossible

Most of our cues about what we should look like come from the media, parents, and peers. This constant obsession with weight, the size of our body, and longing for a different shape or size can be painful.

Most teens watch an average of 22 hours of TV a week and are deluged with images of fat-free bodies in the pages of health, fashion, and teen magazines, according to Eva Pomice in her book, *When Kids Hate Their Bodies*. The result: Many try to achieve this "look," which is an impossible goal. A female should look like and have the same proportions as Barbie or Kate Moss, and a male should look like Arnold Schwarzenegger? As a result, many teens intensely dislike their bodies.

Take a look at the most popular magazines on the newsstands. Psychologist David M. Garner says in a recent *Psychology Today* article: "The media show an image of the perfect woman that is unattainable for somewhere between 98 and 99 percent of the female population." Remember: It's a career for these women; they're pros. Many have had major body makeovers and have full-time personal trainers. Photos in ads can be airbrushed or changed by computer. Body and facial imperfections, such as pimples, can be erased or changed at will.

The images of men and women in ads today have the power to make us feel bad about, and lose touch with, ourselves. Ads aren't intended to promote self-esteem or positive self-image. They're intended to sell products—and they do. In the United States, consumers spend billions of dollars to pursue the perfect body. The message "thin is in" is blasted at us thousands of times a day through TV, movies, magazines, billboards, newspapers, and songs. In a 1997 Body Image Survey, published by *Psychology Today*, teenagers reported that viewing very thin or muscular models made them feel insecure about themselves.

Parents can give mixed messages, Too—especially if they're constantly dieting or have body or food issues of their own. How young people perceive and internalize these childhood messages about their bodies determines their ability to be confident about their appearance.

## *Slimming Down, Bulking Up*

America's preoccupation with dieting has made the diet business a multibillion-dollar industry. And it put questionable diet drugs, such as fen-phen, on the market. Fenfluramine (Pondimin and Redux) diet pills were taken off the market last year [1997] because of their link to heart damage.

Just as bad, some student athletes who want to build strength are using dangerous anabolic steroids or other hormones. These chemicals have serious side effects, and they can stunt growth and cause liver damage, cancer, and high blood pressure.

This intense focus on food, fat, and body building also can lead to abnormal eating habits—such as yo-yo dieting and compulsive eating—that can turn into eating disorders. Eating disorders, such as anorexia and bulimia, aren't new. More than 100 years ago, the first case of anorexia nervosa, or self-induced starvation, was documented. The incidence of eating disorders, including compulsive overeating and dieting, continues to increase. The American Psychiatric Association (APA) estimates that at any given time 500,000 Americans are battling eating disorders.

These disorders hit males and females in every area of society. More people became aware of them in 1995 when Princess Di began talking openly about her struggles with bulimia.

Christy Henrich, a high-ranked gymnast, paid the highest price. At the time of her death, she was 22 years old and weighed barely 50 pounds. Actress Tracey Gold still struggles with her eating disorder.

## *Body Image, Body Love*

Psychologists and counselors recognize that a negative body image has a powerful impact on self-esteem, our assessment of our value

190

as individuals. When we think about body image, generally we think about aspects of our physical appearance. But body image is much more. It is our mental picture of our bodies as well as of our thoughts, feelings, judgments, sensations, awareness, and behavior. It's part of our mental picture of our total selves—the picture that shapes the way we think about our value as people.

Feel bad about your body, in other words, and in time you're likely to feel bad about other aspects of yourself. It's not uncommon for people who think poorly of their bodies to have problems in other areas of their lives—including relationships and careers. That's why it's so important, experts say, to avoid letting your body affect your self-esteem.

Positive self-esteem, says the National Mental Health Association (NMHA), "means you really like yourself a lot, both inside and out—how you look as well as what you believe in."

Iris, age 18, who is currently at Montecatini, a residential treatment center for anorexia in La Costa, California, is working to raise her self-esteem. "I must work hard to keep my chin up, establish eye contact, and have the courage, honesty, and trust to say what I am feeling," she says. "I have a right to be heard and to give my opinion. That is one way I will accomplish self-respect and gain the same respect from others."

But you don't have to have an eating disorder to find achieving a healthy self-image a challenge. Here are some tips from the NMHA and elsewhere on how teens who are unhappy with their bodies can start feeling better about themselves.

## Accepting Your Body

How can you learn to feel good and accept yourself no matter what your size or shape?

*First step:* When you look in the mirror, make sure you find at least one good point for every demerit you give yourself. Become aware of your positives. Here are some other steps you can take to build a better body image—and more positive self-esteem:

- Accept the fact that your body's changing. In the teen years, your body is a work in progress. Don't let every new inch or curve throw you off the deep end.

- Decide which of the cultural pressures—glamour, fitness, thinness, media, peer group—prevent you from feeling good about yourself. Then do something to counteract this. How about not buying magazines that promote unrealistic body images?

191

- Exercise. When you want to feel good about the way you look, exercise. It helps improve your appearance, health, and mood.

- Emphasize your assets. You have many. Give yourself credit for positive qualities. If there are some things you want to change, remember: Self-discovery is a lifelong process.

- Make friends with the person you see in the mirror. Say "I like what I see. I like me." Do it until you believe it.

- Question ads. Instead of saying "What's wrong with me?" say "What's wrong with this ad?" Write the company. Set your own standards instead of letting the media set them for you.

- Ditch dieting and the scale. These are two great ways to develop a healthy relationship with your body and weight.

- Challenge size bigotry and fight size discrimination whenever you can. Don't speak of yourself or others with phrases like "fat slob" or "thunder thighs."

- Be an example to others by taking people seriously for what they say, feel, and do rather than how they look.

Accepting yourself is the starting point. Monique, age 18, in treatment for an eating disorder in La Costa, California, says she has learned to feel better about her body and herself. She has become more appreciative of those "inner qualities that make up who I am, such as my creativity, my intuition, and my self-motivation." At the same time, she has learned to block out "the negative thoughts based on my distorted body image, such as being too fat, never good enough for anyone, including myself."

You can't exchange your body for a new one. The best you can do is find peace with the one you have. Your body is where you're going to be living for the rest of your life. Isn't it about time you made it your home?

For more information:

National Mental Health Association
1021 Prince Street
Alexandria, VA 22314-2971
Tel: 1-800-969-NMHA; Website: www.nhma.org

Brochures: "TEEN: Eating Disorders," "TEEN Self-esteem: Feeling Good About Yourself," single copy of each free with self-addressed, stamped business-size envelope. Call or write.

Food and Drug Administration (FDA)
Communications Staff, HFI-40
5600 Fishers Lane
Rockville, MD 20857
Toll Free: 888-INFO-FDA
Website: www.fda.gov

Brochure: "On the Teen Scene: Eating Disorders Require Medical Attention," single copy free.

American Academy of Pediatrics
400 Hahn Road
Westminster, MD 21157
Website: www.aap.org/family

Brochure: Online AAP publications include brochures about eating disorders.

Book : *Eating Disorders*, by John Barnhill, M.D. and Nadine Taylor, M.S., R.D. 1998; paperback, $5.50 (Dell Publishing).

Chapter 25

# How to Help Someone You Care About

Your biggest problem will be convincing the person to get help. At first s/he will deny there is a problem. S/he will fear weight gain and resist it mightily. S/he will be ashamed and not want to admit what s/he is doing. S/he has used the eating disorder to protect, comfort, and empower her/himself. In the beginning, at least, s/he will not want to give it up. Here are some suggestions to help you talk to an unhappy, and defiant, person.

Changing the behavior of other people, especially when they do not want to change, or when they are too frightened to change, is not possible. Nevertheless, folks with eating disorders need help and should not be abandoned. In most cases, the best service you can render is to continue being a friend. Encourage the person to seek professional treatment, and then stand by and be supportive, through all the resistance and denial, as the person struggles to gather courage to do the right thing.

We have added more details to the end of this section to explain why it is so hard to reach people with eating disorders even though they are quite obviously endangering their health, spoiling relationships, and making themselves miserable with all their obsessing about food and weight.

Remember, if your friend had cancer, you would urge professional treatment. You would not try to fix the problem yourself. People with eating disorders have a kind of soul cancer. Their minds and hearts are crippled and destroyed by the growing tumors of body dissatisfaction, drive to perfection, and need for control. You cannot fix those things. That is a job for physicians, psychologists, and other mental health therapists who have been trained to work with these desperately needy, yet stubborn and defiant, people who are doing the best they know how to take control of their lives in a world they find scary, lonely, and confusing.

Respect these people and love them, but don't try to fix them. Unless you are a physician or trained therapist, you don't have the skills. Remember that eating disorders can be treated, and people do recover from them, but almost always professional help is necessary.

## *If Your Child Is Younger Than Eighteen*

Get professional help immediately. You have a legal and moral responsibility to get your child the care s/he needs. Don't let tears, tantrums, or promises to do better stop you. Begin with a physical exam and psychological evaluation.

If the physician recommends hospitalization, do it. People die from these disorders, and sometimes they need a structured time out to break entrenched patterns. If the counselor asks you to participate in family sessions, do so. Children spend only one or two hours a week with their counselors. The rest of the time they live with their families. You need as many tools as you can get to help your child learn new ways of coping with life.

## *If Your Friend Is Younger Than Eighteen*

Tell a trusted adult—parent, teacher, coach, pastor, etc.—about your concern. If you don't you may unwittingly help your friend avoid the treatment s/he needs to get better.

## *If Your Child or Friend Is Older Than Eighteen*

Legally the person is now an adult and can refuse treatment if s/he is not ready to change. Nevertheless, reach out. Tell her/him that you are concerned. Be gentle. Suggest that there has to be a better way to deal with life than starving and stuffing. Encourage professional help, but expect resistance and denial. You can lead a horse to water, but you can't make it drink—even if it is thirsty.

## *Some Things to Do*

- Realize that the person will not change until s/he wants to.

- Provide information.

196

- Be supportive and caring.
- Be a good listener.
- Continue to suggest professional help. Don't pester. Don't give up either.
- Ask if starving and stuffing are achieving what s/he really wants out of life?
- Talk about the advantages of recovery and a normal life.
- Agree that recovery is hard, but emphasize that many people have done it.
- If s/he is frightened to see a counselor, offer to go with her the first time.
- Realize that recovery is the person's responsibility, not yours.
- Resist guilt. Do the best you can and then be gentle with yourself.

## Some Things Not to Do

- Never nag, plead, beg, bribe, threaten, or manipulate. These things don't work.
- Avoid power struggles. You will lose.
- Never criticize or shame. These tactics are cruel, and the person will withdraw.
- Don't pry. Respect privacy.
- Don't play police officer. You will create resentment.
- Don't try to control. The person will withdraw and ultimately outwit you.
- Don't give advice unless asked.
- Don't expect the person to follow your advice even if s/he asked for it.
- Don't say, "You are too thin." This is what the person wants to hear.
- Don't say, "It's good you have gained weight." S/he will lose it.
- Don't let the person always decide when, what and where you will eat.

- Don't ignore stolen food and evidence of purging. Ask for responsibility.

- Don't overestimate what you can accomplish.

People with eating disorders aren't crazy, irrational, stupid, or dumb. Even if they can't, or won't, express themselves directly, they want to feel better about themselves. They also want to accomplish something, or get something, or avoid something, and because they don't know how to do so in forthright ways, or because they are too frightened or inexperienced to know how to attack their problems directly, they resort to working symbolically through food, weight, and eating. For example, if you ask the question, "If you get your body exactly the way you want it, what will you have then that you don't have now?" Most tell me that they will feel better about themselves. Some add that other people will like and respect them more. Those who have been abused may say that they want to disappear or make themselves unapproachable so that people will leave them alone.

So does this mean that you should grab your eating disordered friend and demand to know just what s/he hopes to accomplish by starving or stuffing? Absolutely not! Even though they want us to think they are strong and can handle anything, folks who use food and diets to try to work out other problems are emotionally fragile and easily hurt. Before you can have a meaningful dialogue about food behaviors, the person must see you as trustworthy and committed to her/his best interests. The more you nag and natter trying to make the person do things your way, even if you are right, the more you damage the trust necessary to support change.

Nagging also sets up a power struggle. You want the person to do things your way. S/he does not want to be manipulated or controlled. Even when you are right, your approach invites the person to rebel and stubbornly resist taking your good advice. As one person put it, "Even though I'm healthier now, I feel like I've lost and you've won. I hate it!"

Once you have the person's trust, gently ask questions like, "What would your life be like if you got to the weight you want to be?" and "What are the advantages of eating the way you do?" Listen carefully. The answers will give you a glimpse of the person's intent. Chances are, the intent is legitimate.

In addition, questions like these invite the person to think more effectively—to analyze, evaluate, and arrive at a sane, logical, and rational conclusion or course of action instead of relying on feelings of the moment. These questions, even though they are sometimes uncomfortable, encourage people to think more realistically. They gently nudge folks to abandon magical, simplistic thoughts such as, "If I lose weight, things will be better," in favor of a more reasoned approach to life and all its challenges.

Back to the questions: After you have some sense of what the person wants to accomplish through disordered eating, ask in as neutral a way as possible if starving or stuffing is working to obtain the desired goal. Is it getting the person the kind of life s/he wants, or is it hurting self-esteem, relationships, career, and chances of long-term happiness?

You, of course, know the answer. The point of this question is to get the person to think about the consequences of disordered eating. Don't expect a quick "Aha!" and immediate behavior change. The most you can hope to do is plant seeds that may sprout in the future, sooner rather than later, but there are no guarantees.

The last question, one that can trigger constructive thought and planning, is, "What can you do differently to increase the chances that you will get what you want?" Here is where defenses will go up and you are likely to hear a lot of "yes, but . . ."

Making changes, even minor ones, is hard, and giving up entrenched habits like starving, binge eating, and purging is overwhelming. That's why I always recommend a physician and mental health therapist be involved in the process. Friends and family members, as loving and filled with good intentions as they may be, don't have the training and experience to shepherd a person through the usually lengthy and always hard journey from eating disorder to health.

This does not mean that friends and family must stand by and do nothing. You can certainly contribute to a relationship of trust and understanding. You can invite the person to think rationally by asking key questions: "What do you want?" "Is the eating disorder working to get you what you want?" "What could you do that's healthier and more effective than starving and stuffing to increase the chances that you will get what you want?"

And because you care about the person, you will never ask these or any other questions in an accusatory, hostile, punishing, or shaming way. You will ask them gently and with patience. You will also listen respectfully to the answers.

You can continue to urge professional help. You can repeatedly suggest that there is a better way to solve problems than through manipulation of food and weight. And perhaps most important of all, you can be available for contact, support, and conversation—not about calories and diets, but about deeper concerns.

Don't forget to have fun. A movie, shopping trip, or a day at an amusement park can give the person a glimpse of some of the benefits of living and acting like normal people do. Don't spoil the event with lots of talk about food.

And lastly, be aware of your limits, and keep your expectations reasonable. You can be a friend, and you can be supportive. You can invite the person to think about what s/he is doing and come up with a better plan, but you cannot control her or make him change before he is ready. If you are concerned about the safety of your minor child, arrange for medical and psychological care immediately. If your friend is in trouble, tell the parents. If you keep secrets, you only help your friend avoid necessary help. If you are concerned about someone older than eighteen, realize that you can only suggest treatment. In this country, people are free to refuse even critically needed and lovingly suggested care.

In the end each of us must be responsible for the choices we make. We can support one another, encourage mature thinking, provide information, and offer advice, but eventually each individual must decide what to do and how to do it. To live with honor and integrity takes courage. Life does not run like a TV show where some compassionate parent/friend/lover/pastor/counselor/doctor says just the right thing so that the victim/sufferer sees the light and makes a 180 degree turn before the last commercial. Life is complicated and messy. We don't have maps or scripts to follow, but we do have multiple opportunities to choose wisdom and integrity over blind adherence to destructive patterns.

Chapter 26

# For Parents, Partners, and Other Family Members

Parents, spouses, siblings, and other people who love the person with an eating disorder are all too often that disorder's forgotten victims. They want desperately to help, but everything they say or do is met with anger, withdrawal, or stony-faced silence. Denial and stubborn refusal to change, sometimes in spite of promises to "do better," block meaningful dialog. Laughter and fun disappear from the home, which is overshadowed by guilt, anxiety, desperation, frustration, anger, and even panic.

Nothing works. In spite of your logic, pleading, bribes, threats, and carefully thought out reasoning, the person continues to lose weight, or food continues to disappear off the shelves. What can you do?

To change the disordered eating behaviors? Nothing. That is something the person her/himself must do after realizing that starving and stuffing have not, and never will, achieve self-confidence and a life that is truly satisfying.

Is there anything you can do to make life a bit brighter, to establish perspective and improve matters for all concerned? A great deal. Begin with the following:

- If your child shows signs of an eating disorder, avoid denial. Get him/her a thorough evaluation and treatment if it is indicated. The sooner treatment is begun, the sooner recovery can be achieved. Remember too that first symptoms are much easier to reverse than behaviors that have become entrenched.

- If your child's doctor or counselor recommends hospitalization, do it. It may be lifesaving. It also may interrupt deeply ingrained behavior patterns that no other intervention can touch.

- If family or couples counseling is recommended, do it. The purpose of such sessions is not to blame you for the eating disorder but rather to help everyone create and maintain satisfying ways of relating and negotiating conflicts. Family and couples counseling has another bonus: It shows your child or partner how reasonable people consult experts to solve overwhelming problems. It also gives you a safe place to deal with your painful feelings. You are hurting. You deserve relief.

- Model healthy, effective coping behavior for your loved ones. When you are stressed, avoid turning to alcohol, other drugs, anger, or other destructive habits. Teach your children, or your partner, by your example how to solve problems and meet needs by making, and following, logical action plans.

- Model healthy food and exercise behaviors too. Talk about the difference between dieting (does not work and can lead to binge eating) and healthy meal plans. Never criticize your own body. Never criticize anyone's body. If you do, you send a message to your loved ones that you accept nothing less than perfection. Follow an exercise plan that includes regular, moderate amounts of healthy activity, not compulsive, driven competition.

- Never engage in power struggles over food. You will lose. Don't play food police either. You will lose, and the person will withdraw from the relationship. Leave food, eating, and weight issues with the person and her/his therapist. A good therapist will insist on medical intervention if the person gets into danger.

- Eat together as a couple or a family at least once a day. As much as possible, keep mealtimes social, happy, and fun. Talk about things other than food, calories, and weight. Even if the person will not eat with you, or even if s/he eats only celery sticks, insist s/he be present to share in family life.

- Last, but by no means least, take care of yourself. You are under tremendous stress. One of you has already succumbed to the eating disorder. There's no sense in you falling into the pit as well.

Participate regularly in some sort of stress reduction program. Maybe tai chi, maybe bowling with friends, but something that relaxes your body, soothes your mind, and gives you something else to think about for a few hours.

Use family or couples counseling to find relief for your own distress. The person with the eating disorder is not the only one who hurts.

Take time out regularly from the eating disorder. Don't let it dominate your life. Now and then eat in a restaurant that you choose, not one deemed safe by your loved one. Make sure your child is safe, and then take a weekend trip just for fun with friends. Participate in satisfying activities that bring you pleasure. If your partner will not accompany you because s/he wants to stay close to the refrigerator and bathroom, go alone or with friends. The eating disorder has already crippled one life. Don't let it control yours as well.

In summary, you cannot control or change your loved one's eating behavior, but you can make family life a bit brighter. You can also arrange treatment for your child and encourage your partner to begin it. Formal treatment by a trained professional clinician is by far the most effective way of achieving recovery from an eating disorder. Do everything you can to make it happen.

Chapter 27

# Questionable Dieting Behaviors

Both young men and women, regardless of gender or student status, use questionable dieting behaviors. These include diet pills or powders, diets, vomiting and laxatives. Since dieting, particularly using such uncertain methods, can be harmful to one's health and can lead to eating disorders, nutrition practitioners should look out for these behaviors in young adults, whatever the gender or student status.

It has been reported that about 80% of young women and 30% of young men in this country are dieters.[1] Furthermore, young people who diet are more. likely to have symptoms associated with eating disorders, such as poor body image; binge eating; and the use of fasting, vomiting, or diet pills.[2-4] Although conclusive evidence of long-term health effects of repeated weight loss is unavailable,[5] frequent dieting may be associated with physiologic and psychological problems such as increased ratio of fat to lean, lower metabolic rate, decreased long-term weight maintenance, and depression.[6-10]

College women and adolescent girls are thought to be most at risk for adopting questionable dieting habits,[11-13] but because data are scant on young men and young adult women who are not college students, it is not known whether these groups are also at risk. This study examined the use of various dieting methods by a random sample of

Excerpted from "Questionable dieting behaviors are used by young adults regardless of sex or student status," by Paula K. Peters, Rosalie J. Amos, Sharon L. Hoerr, Wanda Koszewski, Yali Huang, and Nancy Betts, © 1996 American Dietetic Association. Reprinted by permission from *Journal of the American Dietetic Association*, July 1996, Vol. 6, No. 7, Pg. 709(3).

18- to 24-year-olds, including male and female students, college graduates, and non-students, to determine whether prevalence of questionable dieting habits differs by gender or student status.

## Results

More than half of the women and about one fourth of the men were dieters. College graduates of both sexes tended to have the highest percentages of dieters (26 of 42 women; 5 of 19 men). The mean age at which the dieters started dieting was 17 years in both genders.

More than one fourth of the women in each category used diet pills, diet powders, or diets. A lower percentage of men used these methods, but their rates of using vomiting or laxatives for weight control were not different from those of the women.

Although the women used each of the three weight loss methods more frequently, all groups except the male college graduates reported some use of diet pills, diet powders, or diets at least weekly. The percentage who used diet pills, diet powders, or diets did not differ among the groups of women, but a higher percentage of the nonstudent women tended to use this dieting method more frequently (daily and weekly).

The percentage of regular users of any of the three specific methods for weight loss was higher for women than for men. Regular use was associated with weight fluctuation in female nonstudents.

Female nonstudents had the highest percentage of weight fluctuation (60%), indicating that they had lost and regained 10 lb at least once during the past 2 years. However, weight fluctuation was high in all sex/student categories. Twenty-two percent of the females and 16% of the males indicated that they had lost and regained 10 lb four or more times in 2 years.

## Discussion

Data from this study of young adults provide evidence that dieting and questionable eating behaviors are not restricted to female college students. Respondents to our survey were young adults of both genders and included non-students and college graduates in addition to students. Although we did find the prevalence of dieting to be higher in women (55% to 62%) than in men (22% to 26%), as has been reported previously,[5,14] a unique finding from this study is the fact that the rate of dieting is as high in women and men who were non-students or college graduates as in their college student counterparts.

Questionable dieting methods were used by all groups. It is cause for concern that from 5% (male college graduates) to 31% (female students) used them regularly. The methods most frequently used were diet pills, diet powders, or diets; more than one fourth of the women in each category used them, which is comparable to use reported elsewhere by adolescent girls[15] and college women.[16]

One of the most notable findings from this study was the high percentage of subjects from each sex/student status group who had experienced at least one weight fluctuation of 10 lb or more within the past 2 years. Many of these young people had repeated periods of weight loss and regain. Other researchers have suggested that weight fluctuation makes future weight loss more difficult.[8,9] If this is true, are these young people setting themselves up for a lifetime of frustrating weight-loss attempts?

## Conclusions and Application

Questionable dieting behaviors were used by both men and women, regardless of student status. Dieting, especially by questionable methods, can have long-term negative effects on health and can lead to eating disorders. Nutrition professionals need to be watchful for these behaviors in both genders and in nonstudents as well as students. Focus should be on prevention and early intervention aimed at minimizing weight concern and emphasizing self-acceptance and healthful eating.

## References

1. Connor-Greene PA. Gender differences in body weight perception and weight-loss strategies of college students. *Women Health*. 1988; 14:27-42.

2. Moore DC. Body image and eating behavior in adolescent. girls. *Am J Dis Child*. 1988; 142: 1114-1118.

3. Story M, Rosenwinkel K, Himes JH, Resnick M, Harris LJ, Blum RW. Demographic and risk factors associated with chronic dieting in adolescents. *Am J Dis Child*. 1991; 145: 994-998.

4. Krahn DD, Demitrack MA, Kurth C, Drewnowski A, Jordan KA, Reame NE. Dieting and menstrual irregularity. *J Women Health*. 1992; 1:289-291.

5.  National Task Force on the Prevention and Treatment of Obesity. Weight Cycling. *JAMA*. 1994; 272:1196-1202.

6.  Pavlou KN, Steffe WP, Lerman RH, Burrows BA. Effects of dieting and exercise on lean body mass, oxygen uptake, and strength. *Med Sci Sports Exer*. 1985; 17:466-471.

7.  Leibel RL, Rosenbaum M, Hirsch J. Changes in energy expenditure resulting from altered body weight. *N Engl J Med*. 1995; 332:621-628.

8.  Blackburn GL, Wilson GT, Kanders BS, Stein LJ, Levin PT, Adler J, Brownell KD. Weight cycling: the experience of human dieters. *Am J Clin Nutr*. 1989; 49:1105-1109.

9.  Haus G, Hoerr S, Mavis B, Robison J. Key modifiable variables in weight maintenance: fat intake, exercise, and weight cycling. *J Am Diet Assoc*. 1994; 94:409-413.

10. Wooley SC, Garner DM. Obesity treatment: the high cost of false hope. *J Am Diet Assoc*. 1991; 91:1248-1251.

11. Crowther JH, Chernyk B. Bulimia and binge eating in adolescent females: a comparison. *Addict Behav*. 1986; 11:415-424.

12. Fabian LJ, Thompson JK. Body image and eating disturbance in young females. *Int J Eat Disord*. 1989; 8:63-74.

13. Drewnowski A, Yee DK, Krahn DD. Bulimia in college woman: incidence and recovery rates. *Am J Psychiatry*. 1988; 145:753-755.

14. Miller TB, Coffman JG, Linke RA. Survey on body image, weight, and diet of college students. *J Am Diet Assoc*. 1980; 77:561-566.

15. Emmons L. Dieting and purging behavior in black and white high school students. *J Am Diet Assoc*. 1992; 92:306-312.

16. Grunewald K. Weight control in young college women: who are the dieters? *J Am Diet Assoc*. 1985; 85:1445-1450.

Chapter 28

# The "Skinny" on Dieting

Dieting is close to a national pastime. An estimated 50 million Americans will go on diets this year, and while some will succeed in taking off weight, experts suggest that very few—perhaps five percent—will manage to keep all of it off in the long run.

Although some people try to exercise off their excess pounds or inches, dieting is the most common way to lose weight. Recent surveys indicate that many dieters—more than 80 percent of women and 75 percent of men—eat fewer calories in their efforts to shed a few pounds. Unfortunately, simply cutting calories doesn't work for long.

Meanwhile, every year, about 8 million Americans enroll in some kind of structured weight-loss program involving liquid diets, special diet regimens, or medical or other supervision. Yet weight loss experts caution against fad diets, which rarely have a permanent effect. And they recommend that very-low calorie diets be pursued only under medical supervision because of their risks. The FTC also advises consumers to be skeptical of plans or products that promote easy or effortless long-term weight loss. They just don't work, according to the agency, which oversees the advertising and marketing of foods, nonprescription drugs, medical devices and health care services.

How can you tell the sizzle from the substance when it comes to claims about weight-loss programs and products? The FTC suggests a healthy portion of skepticism. Here are some claims made by advertisers in recent years—and the facts.

---

Federal Trade Commission (FTC), March 1997.

209

## *"Lose Weight While You Sleep"*

*Fact:* Losing weight requires significant changes affecting what kind of food—and how much—you eat. Claims for diet products and programs that promise weight loss without sacrifice or effort are bogus.

## *"Lose Weight and Keep It Off for Good"*

*Fact:* Weight loss maintenance requires permanent changes in how you eat and how much you exercise. Be skeptical about products that claim you will keep off any weight permanently or for a long time.

## *"John Doe Lost 84 Pounds in Six Weeks"*

*Fact:* Someone else's claim of weight loss success may have little or no relevance to your own chances of success. Don't be misled.

## *"Lose All the Weight You Can for Just $99"*

*Fact:* There may be hidden costs. For example, some programs do not publicize the fact that you must buy prepackaged meals from them at costs that exceed program fees. Before you sign up for any weight loss program, ask for all the costs. Get them in writing.

## *"Lose 30 Pounds in Just 30 Days"*

*Fact:* As a rule, the faster you lose weight, the more likely you are to gain it back. In addition, fast weight loss may harm your health. Unless you have a medical reason, don't look for programs that promise quick weight loss.

## *"Scientific Breakthrough—Medical Miracle"*

*Fact:* To lose weight, you have to reduce your intake of calories and increase your physical activity. Be skeptical of extravagant claims.

The FTC agrees with many health experts who recommend a combination of diet modification and exercise as the most effective way to lose weight and keep it off—and a goal of losing about a pound a week. A modest reduction of 500 calories a day will achieve this goal, because a total reduction of 3,500 calories is necessary to lose one pound of fat.

If you want to lose the proverbial "few pounds," the FTC suggests revising what you eat, cutting your caloric intake, and adding exercise to your weekly routine. Merely reducing calories often makes dieters feel hungry because it cuts down on important vitamins and minerals. This can end up sabotaging your efforts. Revising the diet by replacing many of the calories from fats with calories from other food groups and exercising several times a week to increase the use of calories should keep most people feeling full, satisfied, and motivated to continue healthful eating habits. Many health experts recommend that adults limit their fat consumption to 25 percent of total caloric intake.

How can you lower your fat intake and cut your calories without feeling hungry, sacrificing important nutrients, or losing money? The FTC has the following suggestions:

- Before beginning any weight loss program, check with your doctor. Some diet plans have been associated with health complications. Make sure your diet is well balanced, and meets dietary guidelines set by experts in clinical nutrition. In cases where obesity results in life threatening complications, medical intervention may be necessary.

- Consider all the alternatives before deciding on a product or program, including non-profit support groups, counseling services, physician-supervised programs, and self-discipline. Choose the one that's best for your needs and your budget.

- Follow a nutritionally sound diet plan. These often are available from hospitals, clinics, national health organizations, insurance companies, and health maintenance organizations. Most libraries also stock a variety of books that include healthful meal plans and recipes.

- Remember that individual diet needs vary according to body size, health, and level of activity.

- Create a meal plan that incorporates your food preferences or modify an existing plan to fit your tastes. Be realistic: A low-fat diet doesn't mean swearing off fatty foods forever. It means eating them once in a while.

- Increase your physical activity gradually. Regular physical exercise can help reduce and control weight by burning up calories.

- Pill power cannot replace will power. Successful weight loss depends on a personal commitment to changing your eating habits and increasing your levels of physical exercise. There are no magic bullets.

If you have complaints about a weight loss program or product, contact your state Attorney General, local consumer protection office, or Better Business Bureau. Or you may file a complaint with the FTC. Write to:

Correspondence Branch, FTC
Washington, D.C. 20580

Although the FTC does not intervene in individual cases, the information you provide may indicate a pattern of possible law violations that require Commission actions.

The FTC publishes several brochures for consumers who are interested in weight loss programs and products. Write for:

Best Sellers, Public Reference Branch
Room 130, 6th and Pennsylvania Avenue, NW
Washington, D.C. 20580
Tel: (202) 326-2222
TDD: (202) 326-2502.

Chapter 29

# Weight Loss for Life

Who should lose weight? Health experts generally agree that adults can benefit from weight loss if they are moderately to severely overweight. Health experts also agree that adults who are overweight and have weight-related medical problems or a family history of such problems can benefit from weight loss. Some weight-related health problems include diabetes, heart disease, high blood pressure, high cholesterol levels, or high blood sugar levels. Even a small weight loss of 10 to 20 pounds can improve your health, for example by lowering your blood pressure and cholesterol levels.

## How We Lose Weight

Your body weight is controlled by the number of calories you eat and the number of calories you use each day. So, to lose weight you need to take in fewer calories than you use. You can do this by becoming more physically active or by eating less. Following a weight loss program that helps you to become more physically active and decrease the amount of calories that you eat is most likely to lead to successful weight loss. The weight loss program should also help you keep the weight off by making changes in your physical activity and eating habits that you will be able to follow for the rest of your life.

National Institute of Diabetes and Digestive and Kidney Diseases (NIDDK), Jan. 1998.

# Types of Weight Loss Programs

To lose weight and keep it off, you should be aware of the different types of programs available and the important parts of a good program. Knowing this information should help you select or design a weight loss program that will work for you. The three types of weight loss programs include: do-it-yourself programs, non-clinical programs, and clinical programs.

## Do-It-Yourself Programs

Any effort to lose weight by yourself or with a group of like-minded others through support groups, worksite or community-based programs fits in the "do-it yourself" category. Individuals using a do-it-yourself program rely on their own judgment, group support, and products such as diet books for advice (Note: Not all diet books are reliable sources of weight loss information).

## Non Clinical Programs

These programs may or may not be commercially operated, such as through a privately-owned, weight loss chain. They often use books and pamphlets that are prepared by health-care providers. These programs use counselors (who usually are not health-care providers and may or may not have training) to provide services to you. Some programs require participants to use the program's food or supplements.

## Clinical Programs

This type of program may or may not be commercially owned. Services are provided in a health-care setting, such as a hospital, by licensed health professionals, such as physicians, nurses, dietitians, and/or psychologists. In some clinical programs, a health professional works alone; in others, a group of health professionals works together to provide services to patients. Clinical programs may offer you services such as nutrition education, medical care, behavior change therapy, and physical activity.

Clinical programs may also use other weight loss methods, such as very low-calorie diets, prescription weight loss drugs, and surgery, to treat severely overweight patients. These treatments are described below:

- Very low-calorie diets (VLCDs) are commercially prepared formulas that provide no more than 800 calories per day and replace all usual food intake. VLCDs help individuals lose weight more quickly than is usually possible with low-calorie diets. Because VLCDs can cause side effects, obesity experts recommend that only people who are severely overweight use these diets, and only with proper medical care. A fact sheet on VLCDs is available from the Weight-control Information Network (WIN).

- Prescribed weight loss drugs should be used only if you are likely to have health problems caused by your weight. You should not use drugs to improve your appearance. Prescribed weight loss drugs, when combined with a healthy diet and regular physical activity, may help some obese adults lose weight. However, before these medications can be widely recommended, more research is needed to determine their long-term safety and effectiveness. Whatever the results, prescription weight loss drugs should be used only as part of an overall program that includes long-term changes in your eating and physical activity habits.

- You may consider gastric surgery to promote weight loss if you are more than 80 pounds overweight. The surgery, sometimes called bariatric surgery, causes weight loss in one of two ways:

  1. by limiting the amount of food your stomach can hold by closing off or removing parts of the stomach, or

  2. by causing food to be poorly digested by bypassing the stomach or part of the intestines.

After surgery, patients usually lose weight quickly. While some weight is often regained, many patients are successful in keeping off most of their weight. In some cases, the surgery can lead to problems that require follow-up operations. Surgery may also reduce the amount of vitamins and minerals in your body and cause gallstones. If you are considering a weight loss program and you have medical problems, or if you are severely overweight, programs run by trained health professionals may be best for you. These professionals are more likely to monitor you for possible side effects of weight loss and to talk to your doctor when necessary.

Whether you decide to use the do-it-yourself, non-clinical, or clinical approach, the program should help you lose weight and keep it off by teaching you healthy eating and physical activity habits that you will be able to follow for the rest of your life.

## Diet

The word "diet" probably brings to mind meals of lettuce and cottage cheese. By definition, "diet" refers to what a person eats or drinks during the course of a day. A diet that limits portions to a very small size or that excludes certain foods entirely to promote weight loss may not be effective over the long term. Rather, you are likely to miss certain foods and find it difficult to follow this type of diet for a long time. Instead, it is often helpful to gradually change the types and amounts of food you eat and maintain these changes for the rest of your life. The ideal diet is one that takes into account your likes and dislikes and includes a wide variety of foods with enough calories and nutrients for good health.

How much you eat and what you eat play a major role in how much you weigh. So, when planning your diet, you should consider:

- What calorie level is appropriate?
- Is the diet you are considering nutritionally balanced?
- Will the diet be practical and easy to follow?
- Will you be able to maintain this eating plan for the rest of your life?

The following information will help you answer these questions.

## Calorie Level

*Low-Calorie Diets.* Most weight loss diets provide 1,000 to 1,500 calories per day. However, the number of calories that is right for you depends on your weight and activity level. At these calorie levels, diets are referred to as low-calorie diets. Self-help diet books and clinical and non-clinical weight loss programs often include low-calorie diet plans.

The calorie level of your diet should allow for a weight loss of no more than 1 pound per week (after the first week or two when weight loss may be more rapid because of initial water loss). If you can estimate how many calories you eat in a day, you can design a diet plan that will help you lose no more than 1 pound per week. You may need to work with a trained health professional, such as a registered dietitian. Or, you can use a standardized low-calorie diet plan with a fixed calorie level. The selected calorie level, however, may not produce the recommended rate of weight loss, and you may need to eat more or less.

# Good Nutrition

Make sure that your diet contains all the essential nutrients for good health. Using the Food Guide Pyramid and the Nutrition Facts Label that is found on most processed food products can help you choose a healthful diet. The Pyramid shows you the kinds and amounts of food that you need each day for good health. The Nutrition Facts Label will help you select foods that meet your daily nutritional needs. A healthful diet should include:

- Adequate vitamins and minerals. Eating a wide variety of foods from all the food groups on the Food Guide Pyramid will help you get the vitamins and minerals you need. If you eat less than 1,200 calories per day, you may benefit from taking a daily vitamin and mineral supplement.

- Adequate protein. The average woman 25 years of age and older should get 50 grams of protein each day, and the average man 25 years of age and older should get 63 grams of protein each day. Adequate protein is important because it prevents muscle tissue from breaking down and repairs all body tissues such as skin and teeth. To get adequate protein in your diet, make sure you eat 2-3 servings from the Meat, Poultry, Fish, Dry Beans, Eggs, and Nuts Group on the Food Guide Pyramid every day. These foods are all good sources of protein.

## One Serving Equals

### Bread, Cereal, Rice, and Pasta Group

1 slice of bread
1 ounce of ready-to-eat cereal
1/2 cup of cooked cereal, rice, or pasta

### Vegetable Group

1 cup of raw leafy vegetables
1/2 cup of other vegetables-cooked or chopped raw
3/4 cup of vegetable juice

### Fruit Group

1 medium apple, banana, or orange
1/2 cup of chopped, cooked, or canned fruit
3/4 cup of fruit juice

217

## Milk, Yogurt, and Cheese Group

1 cup of milk or yogurt

1 1/2 ounces of natural cheese

2 ounces of processed cheese

## Meat, Poultry, Fish, Dry Beans, Eggs, and Nuts Group

2-3 ounces of cooked lean meat, poultry, or fish

1/2 cup of cooked dry beans or 1 egg counts as 1 ounce of lean meat. Two tablespoons of peanut butter or 1/3 cup of nuts count as 1 ounce of meat.

Adequate carbohydrates. At least 100 grams of carbohydrates per day are needed to prevent fatigue and dangerous fluid imbalances. To make sure you get enough carbohydrates, eat 6-11 servings from the Bread, Cereal, Rice, and Pasta Group on the Food Guide Pyramid every day.

A daily fiber intake of 20 to 30 grams. Adequate fiber helps with proper bowel function. If you were to eat 1 cup of bran cereal, 1/2 cup of carrots, 1/2 cup of kidney beans, a medium-sized pear, and a medium-sized apple together in 1 day, you would get about 30 grams of fiber.

No more than 30 percent of calories, on average, from fat per day, with less than 10 percent of calories from saturated fat (such as fat from meat, butter, and eggs). Limiting fat to these levels reduces your risk for heart disease and may help you lose weight. In addition, you should limit the amount of cholesterol in your diet. Cholesterol is a fat-like substance found in animal products such as meat and eggs. Your diet should include no more than 300 milligrams of cholesterol per day (one egg contains about 215 milligrams of cholesterol, and 3.5 ounces of cooked hamburger contain 100 milligrams of cholesterol).

At least 8 to 10 glasses, 8 ounces each, of water or water-based beverages, per day. You need more water if you exercise a lot.

These nutrients should come from a variety of low-calorie, nutrient-rich foods. One way to get variety—and with it, an enjoyable and nutritious diet—is to choose foods each day from the Food Guide Pyramid.

## Types of Diets

**Fixed-menu diet.** A fixed-menu diet provides a list of all the foods you will eat. This kind of diet can be easy to follow because the foods are selected for you. But, you get very few different food choices which may make the diet boring and hard to follow away from home. In addition, fixed-menu diets do not teach the food selection skills necessary for keeping weight off. If you start with a fixed-menu diet, you should switch eventually to a plan that helps you learn to make meal choices on your own, such as an exchange-type diet.

**Exchange-type diet.** An exchange-type diet is a meal plan with a set number of servings from each of several food groups. Within each group, foods are about equal in calories and can be interchanged as you wish. For example, the "starch" category could include one slice of bread or 1/2 cup of oatmeal; each is about equal in nutritional value and calories. If your meal plan calls for two starch choices at breakfast, you could choose to eat two slices of bread, or one slice of bread and 1/2 cup of oatmeal. With the exchange-type diet plans, you have more day-to-day variety and you can easily follow the diet away from home. The most important advantage is that exchange-type diet plans teach the food selection skills you need to keep your weight off.

**Prepackaged-meal diet.** These diets require you to buy prepackaged meals. Such meals may help you learn appropriate portion sizes. However, they can be costly. Before beginning this type of program, find out whether you will need to buy the meals and how much the meals cost. You should also find out whether the program will teach you how to select and prepare food, skills that are needed to sustain weight loss.

**Formula diet.** Formula diets are weight loss plans that replace one or more meals with a liquid formula. Most formula diets are balanced diets containing a mix of protein, carbohydrate, and usually a small amount of fat. Formula diets are usually sold as liquid or a powder to be mixed with liquid. Although formula diets are easy to use and do promote short-term weight loss, most people regain the weight as soon as they stop using the formula. In addition, formula diets do not teach you how to make healthy food choices, a necessary skill for keeping your weight off.

**Questionable diets.** You should avoid any diet that suggests you eat a certain nutrient, food, or combination of foods to promote easy weight loss. Some of these diets may work in the short term because they are low in calories. However, they are often not well balanced and may cause nutrient deficiencies. In addition, they do not teach eating habits that are important for long-term weight management.

219

**Flexible diets.** Some programs or books suggest monitoring fat only, calories only, or a combination of the two, with the individual making the choice of both the type and amount of food eaten. This flexible type of approach works well for many people, and teaches them how to control what they eat. One drawback of flexible diets is that some don't consider the total diet. For example, programs that monitor fat only often allow people to take in unlimited amounts of excess calories from sugars, and therefore don't lead to weight loss.

It is important to choose an eating plan that you can live with. The plan should also teach you how to select and prepare healthy foods, as well as how to maintain your new weight. Remember that many people tend to regain lost weight. Eating a healthful and nutritious diet to maintain your new weight, combined with regular physical activity, helps to prevent weight regain.

## Physical Activity

Regular physical activity is important to help you lose weight and build an overall healthy lifestyle. Physical activity increases the number of calories your body uses and promotes the loss of body fat instead of muscle and other nonfat tissue. Research shows that people who include physical activity in their weight loss programs are more likely to keep their weight off than people who only change their diet. In addition to promoting weight control, physical activity improves your strength and flexibility, lowers your risk of heart disease, helps control blood pressure and diabetes, can promote a sense of well-being, and can decrease stress.

Any type of physical activity you choose to do—vigorous activities such as running or aerobic dancing or moderate-intensity activities such as walking or household work—will increase the number of calories your body uses. The key to successful weight control and improved overall health is making physical activity a part of your daily life.

For the greatest overall health benefits, experts recommend that you do 20 to 30 minutes of vigorous physical activity three or more times a week and some type of muscle strengthening activity, such as weight resistance, and stretching at least twice a week. However, if you are unable to do this level of activity, you can improve your health by performing 30 minutes or more of moderate-intensity physical activity over the course of a day, at least five times a week. When including physical activity in your weight loss program, you should choose a variety of activities that can be done regularly and are enjoyable for you. Also, if you have not been physically active, you should see your doctor before you start, especially if you are older than 40 years of age, very overweight, or have medical problems.

### *Vigorous Activities*

aerobic dancing    running    brisk walking    cycling    swimming

### *Moderate-Intensity Activities*

walking up the stairs instead of taking the elevator
walking part or all of the way to work
using a push mower to cut the grass
playing actively with children

## Behavior Change

Behavior change focuses on learning eating and physical activity behaviors that will help you lose weight and keep it off. The first step is to look at your eating and physical activity habits, thus uncovering behaviors (such as television watching) that lead you to overeat or be inactive. Next you'll need to learn how to change those behaviors.

Getting support from others is a good way to help you maintain your new eating and physical activity habits. Changing your eating and physical activity behaviors increases your chances of losing weight and keeping it off. For additional information on behavior change, you may wish to ask a weight loss counselor or refer to books on this topic, which are available in local libraries.

## What Works for You?

A variety of options exist to help you lose weight and keep it off. The key to successful weight loss is making changes in your eating and physical activity habits that you will be able to maintain for the rest of your life.

## Additional Reading

### *Binge Eating Disorder*
NIH Publication No. 94-3589

This fact sheet describes the symptoms, causes, complications, and treatment of binge eating disorder, along with a profile of those at risk for the disorder. 1993. Available from WIN.

## Dieting, and Gallstones
NIH Publication No. 94-3677

This fact sheet describes what gallstones are, how weight loss may cause them, and how to lessen the risk of developing them. 1993. Available from WIN.

## Gastric Surgery for Severe Obesity
NIH Publication No. 96-4006

This fact sheet describes the different types of surgery available to treat severe obesity. It explains how gastric surgery promotes weight loss and the benefits and risks of each procedure. 1996. Available from WIN.

## Physical Activity and Weight Control
NIH Publication No. 96-4031

This fact sheet explains how physical activity helps promote weight control and other ways it benefits one's health. It also describes the different types of physical activity and provides tips on how to become more physically active. 1996. Available from WIN.

## Prescription Medications for the Treatment of Obesity
NIH Publication No. 97-4191

This fact sheet presents information on appetite suppressant medications. These medications may help some obese patients lose more weight than with non-drug treatments. The types of medications and the risks and benefits associated with the use of these medications are described. Revised 1997. Available from WIN.

## Very Low-Calorie Diets
NIH Publication No. 95-3894

Information on who should use a very low-calorie diet (VLCD) and the health benefits and possible adverse effects of VLCDs is provided in this fact sheet. 1995. Available from WIN.

## Weight Cycling
NIH Publication No. 95-3901

Based on research, this fact sheet describes the health effects of weight cycling, also known as "yo-yo" dieting, and how it affects obese individuals' future weight loss efforts. 1995. Available from WIN.

### *"Are You Eating Right?"*
Consumer Reports. October 1992, pp. 644-55

This article summarizes advice from 68 nutrition experts, including a discussion on weight control and health risks of obesity. Available from WIN.

### *"Losing Weight: What Works. What Doesn't" and "Rating the Diets."*
Consumer Reports. June 1993, pp. 347-57

These articles report on a survey of readers' experiences with weight loss diets, discuss research related to weight control, and outline pros and cons of different diet programs. Available in public libraries.

### *"The Facts About Weight loss Products and Programs"*
DHHS Publication No. (FDA) 92-1189

This pamphlet provides basic facts about the weight loss industry and what the consumer should expect from a diet program and/or product. Available from the Food and Drug Administration, Office of Consumer Affairs, HFE-88, Rockville, MD 20857.

### *"Nutrition and Your Health: Dietary Guidelines for Americans, Fourth Edition."*
Home and Garden Bulletin No. 232. 1995

This booklet answers some of the basic questions about healthy eating and the link between poor nutrition and disease. It stresses the importance of a balanced diet and a healthy lifestyle. Available from WIN.

### *A Report of the Surgeon General: Physical Activity and Health. 1996*
Produced by the Centers for Disease Control and Prevention

This report compiles decades of research concerning physical activity and health. It addresses the nationwide health problems associated with physical inactivity and outlines the benefits of becoming more physically active. Available for $19.00 from the U.S. Government Printing Office, Superintendent of Documents, Washington, DC 20402; (202) 512-1800. Stock Number 017-023-00196-5.

### *Weight-Control Information Network*
1 Win Way
Bethesda, MD 20892-3665 *(continued on next page)*

*Weight-Control Information Network* (*continued*)
Toll-free number: (800) 946-8098
Tel: (301) 984-7378
Fax: (301) 984-7196
E-mail: WIN@info.niddk.nih.gov
Internet: http://www.niddk.nih.gov/NutritionDocs.html

The Weight-control Information Network (WIN) is a service of the National Institute of Diabetes and Digestive and Kidney Diseases, part of the National Institutes of Health, under the U.S. Public Health Service. Authorized by Congress (Public Law 103-43), WIN assembles and disseminates to health professionals and the general public information on weight control, obesity, and nutritional disorders. WIN responds to requests for information; develops, reviews, and distributes publications; and develops communication strategies to encourage individuals to achieve and maintain a healthy weight.

Publications produced by WIN are reviewed for scientific accuracy, content, and readability. Materials produced by other sources are also reviewed for scientific accuracy and are distributed, along with WIN publications, to answer requests.

# Part Five

# Specific Concerns Related to Children and Adolescents

Chapter 30

# Eating Disorders among Children

An estimated 25% of children suffer from eating disorders that could impede their development. Post-traumatic feeding disorder often occurs in babies who have been kept alive through intensive medical intervention. Infantile anorexia often occurs in willful babies with anxious parents.

Martina Lisi is three years old-and weighs just 19 lb. To her parents, that is a victory. Born with Down's syndrome and four heart defects, Martina underwent open-heart surgery at five months and remained hospitalized on and off for almost half a year after that because of congestive heart failure. Lacking the energy to suck a bottle, she was fed through tubes pushed down her throat and later through her nose and into her stomach. When the worst of her medical problems appeared to be behind her, she was released from hospital. But then another problem emerged: Martina refused to eat, forcing doctors to fit her with a feeding tube that went directly to her stomach. It was not until the age of 2 1/2 that Martina, on her own, swallowed her first bite: pureed pears. "After two years of trying to get this child to eat I was starting to lose it," says her mother, Angela, 27, of Cambridge, Ont. "I would look at other kids and I would think it's so easy for them and so hard for her. I felt like I was going to die."

Martina is part of a small but growing group of very young children who suffer from serious eating disorders that threaten to stunt

"The First Bite: Kid's Eating Disorders are a Serious Concern," by Tracy Nesdoly, ©1996 Tracy Nesdoly, from *Maclean's*, June 17, 1996, Vol. 109, No. 25, Pg. 48(1); reprinted with permission.

their development. In Martina's case, the problem is known as post-traumatic feeding disorder, which usually afflicts children who have survived infancy because of intense medical intervention. The condition was first identified in the late 1970s and, according to Dr. Diane Benoit, a child psychiatrist at Toronto's Hospital for Sick Children, it "affects more and more babies who were born extremely ill but who survive by being hooked up to machines and tubes. They learn that anything that gets to the back of their throat is frightening—they see food and they literally panic."

Doctors are wary of estimating the extent of post-traumatic eating disorder. What is known, though, is that about 25 per cent of children suffer from feeding problems. That represents a broad spectrum, from children who are unusually picky or selective about what they eat—not touching anything but Chicken McNuggets, for example—to those who absolutely refuse to eat or drink. And in the latter category, post-traumatic feeding disorder is only one condition affecting children. Dr. Irene Chatoor of the Children's National Medical Center in Washington is now studying infantile anorexia. Like anorexia in older children, she says, this disorder is often a result of a power struggle or an issue of control between particularly sensitive children and their often high-strung parents.

In that battleground, food becomes a weapon. "Parents will tell me they have tried everything—coaxed, distracted, bribed, tried this food, that food, bottles, anything short of standing on their heads to get their children to eat," says Chatoor, who adds that the problem often shows up during a child's so-called terrible twos. Although little has so far been published about the condition, she says that those at risk are usually very intense, bright, perceptive and curious—but also extremely willful. Couple that with parents who are overly anxious, and one has a recipe for disaster. "The baby of a relaxed parent will not develop infantile anorexia," Chatoor says.

Treatment for serious children's eating disorders is a long and difficult process, and often begins with a doctor's observation of the "feeding relationship" between parent and child. And while not all kids respond, there are success stories. Martina Lisi is among them. She and her mother underwent a six-month program in Toronto, developed by Benoit. Benoit and her team first videotape feeding sessions to assess the situation, and then help parents learn new tricks—among them, changing the flavor or texture of food to make it more palatable. "In the program, we were constantly reassured, and they always had new ideas for things to try," says Angela Lisi. "Now Martina is as good an eater as any kid. I don't know how much longer

I could have handled the strain—now she sits and eats and we're over the moon."

## Food For Thought

Most children's feeding problems are not overly serious—but parents should still be on the lookout for signs of trouble. Some hints:

- Avoid overreacting—if an otherwise healthy child refuses to eat his peas, don't make a mountain out of a molehill.

- Remember that children have fluctuating appetites. "If you ride the fluctuation out," says Dr. Glenn Berall, chief of pediatrics at Toronto's Doctors Hospital, "most children will take what they need."

- Seek help early for persistent problems that could develop into larger troubles.

- Keep an eye out for the following warning signs:

  a child is either losing or not gaining weight consistently

  a child's refusal to eat compels parents to try force-feeding

  a child will only eat if coercion or elaborate games are used

  parents consistently find that they are, in Berall's words, "doing the restaurant" for their child. "That's when the child says he wants macaroni and when you serve that, he says no, he wants a tuna sandwich and then he says no, he wants scrambled eggs," Berall says.

All of the above are signs of problems that need to be addressed. "Parents need to go to the family doctor or pediatrician so the situation can be evaluated," he adds.

Chapter 31

# School-Based Programs for Preventing Eating Disorders

Numerous studies have addressed the importance of prevention,[1-10] while others have studied factors associated with eating disturbances.[11-15] Surprisingly, limited research has addressed implementation and evaluation of school-based programs aimed at the prevention of eating disturbances.[16-21] In this paper, school-based approaches for prevention of eating disturbances are addressed in the context of why, what, who, and how. A model of a comprehensive school-based program aimed at the primary and secondary prevention of eating disturbances is proposed and described.

## Factors to be Addressed

Factors to be addressed in school-based prevention programs include those which play an etiological role in the development of eating disturbances, are amenable to change, and are suitable for addressing in a school setting. There is general consensus that eating disturbances are multifactorial and that sociocultural, developmental, cognitive, behavioral, genetic, psychological, and familial factors contribute to their etiology.[35,44] However, different viewpoints exist as to why certain individuals progress from experimentation with weight loss diets to more severe eating disorders. Those who favor the sociocultural

Excerpted from "School-Based Programs for Preventing Eating Disturbances," by Dianne Neumark-Sztainer, © 1996 American School Health Association, Kent, Ohio, from *Journal of School Health*, Feb. 1996, Vol. 66, No. 2, Pg. 64(8); reprinted with permission.

point-of-view state that dieters who internalize sociocultural values emphasizing thinness are more likely to develop a severe eating disorder,[19] while others emphasize the finding that dieters only progress toward more severe eating disorders in the presence of psychiatric disturbances.[45] Likewise, it remains unclear whether obesity is due mainly to a genetic tendency, eating patterns, or sedentary lifestyle. Research should explore further etiological processes leading to various eating disturbances. However, enough is known to develop prevention programs and to begin research on comparing different approaches.

Body dissatisfaction, a strong predictor of both mild and severe eating disturbances,[11,12] needs to be addressed in prevention programs. The large gender differences in body dissatisfaction; increasing rates of body dissatisfaction in countries influenced by western values; and high prevalence of body dissatisfaction among young women in western societies, particularly those in professions such as dancing and modeling, strongly suggest sociocultural norms have a strong influence on body image.[46]

Prevention programs should aim toward increasing adolescents' understanding of the role of sociocultural factors on body image, and should include activities in which adolescents critically examine social norms. Normal physical development may be viewed by adolescent females as problematic, in light of social norms which emphasize small hips and breasts, and efforts should be made to view these bodily changes as normal and positive. However, significant improvements in body image are unlikely to occur without modification in social norms more accepting of a range of body shapes and sizes. Thus, prevention programs need to aim at changing both individual and environmental determinants of body image.

Cognitive factors such as knowledge and attitudes regarding nutrition and weight loss behavior influence eating patterns such as skipping meals and overall nutritional intake.[6] School settings are suitable frameworks for cognitive learning, and knowledge seems to be necessary but not sufficient for behavior change so prevention programs should promote increased understanding of healthy eating and exercise behavior, healthy methods of weight control; consequences of dieting, eating disorders, and obesity; and understanding the multicausality of eating disorders and obesity. Programs should aim to improve attitudes of both students and staff toward overweight individuals who are stigmatized in western societies,[47-49] and the genetic tendency toward obesity should be discussed. Skill acquisition in developing a healthy and enjoyable eating and exercise plan is important, and programs emphasizing gradual change are more likely to improve self-efficacy and successful behavior modification.[50]

Psychological and familial issues also play a role in eating disorders. While psychological issues such as self-esteem and body image, and familial issues such as communication patterns and autonomy may be suitable for discussion in classrooms or small groups, these settings are not suitable for severe psychological or familial disturbances, such as clinical depression or sexual and physical abuse. However, classroom discussion may lead to identification of high-risk adolescents and should lead to referral to appropriate treatment centers.

## Target Audiences

Before developing prevention programs, target audiences need to be identified. Issues include the target population's risk for developing an eating disturbance, their interest and motivation in the material, and available time and resources.

Prevention needs to address students of all ages (preschool through college), at least through opportunities for healthy eating and exercise; informal messages encouraging acceptance of different body shapes and sizes; and learning methods which encourage healthy relationships, gender equality, autonomy, critical thinking, social skills, and empowerment. However, it may be most efficacious to target school-based prevention programs per se on adolescents in middle school. In determining the appropriate grade level for school-based prevention programs, strike a balance between having enough students interested in the material, yet not too many who have engaged in the outcome behavior, because programs may be more effective in prevention of health-compromising behaviors than in their modification.[16]

### Should both males and females be targeted for intervention or should the focus be on females?

While prevalence rates for eating disturbances are higher among females, male adolescents are not immune to developing body and eating concerns. Furthermore, males are part of the greater culture emphasizing thinness, and by their inclusion in educational programs, they may have a positive influence on their female peers. In one experience working with mixed-gender classes, discussions on desired body shapes revealed that girls aspired to thinner body shapes than boys found to be attractive.[16] Yet, in certain classes, boys were not interested in the material and disturbed the intimacy of the discussion. The decision of whether to include both males and females should influence the approach employed, to make the program relevant for all participants.

A related question involves whether the target audience should include all students or be limited to those at highest risk for certain behaviors or outcomes.[3,6,16,17] With primary prevention, all students are reached and positive changes occur in social norms, at least within the peer group, regarding acceptable body weights, weight control methods, and eating and exercise behaviors. Primary prevention efforts also afford more opportunity for reaching the larger community and advocating changes in advertisements in the media. The larger social environment is a key contributor to adolescent behavior.[51]

One school-based primary prevention program was moderately successful in preventing onset of binge eating and unhealthy dieting but not in modifying already existing behaviors.[16]

An advantage of secondary prevention is that limited time and resources may be directed toward those at greatest risk for eating disturbances. Attitudes and behaviors are difficult to change and strategies such as individual counseling and small group work may be necessary. Some students at risk for these conditions may not be interested in their modification, but many may be motivated toward change and would be interested in receiving individual attention. In determining risk for eating disturbances, factors include age, gender, level of body dissatisfaction, body weight, weight loss behaviors, eating and exercise behaviors, other health concerns, and family history of weight-related problems. Unfortunately, clear guidelines do not exist for identifying at-risk adolescents. Methods for identifying those needing secondary (or tertiary) prevention include careful observation of weight changes, eating rituals, excessive exercise, academic performance, social involvement, style of dress, or overall appearance; discussions with the adolescent's peer group and family; and sensitive talks with adolescents in which assessment tools may be employed.

While it is important to consider advantages and disadvantages of primary and secondary prevention, both need to be integrated into school-based prevention programs.

## Approaches to Prevention

Options for prevention range from one-time classroom lectures on eating disorders to implementation of a comprehensive school-based program with linkages within the school and between the school and community. Intermediate options also exist, such as introducing an educational program (5-15 sessions) specifically aimed at preventing eating disturbances. The topic may be approached through a focus on nutrition and health; gender equality; and/or life skills training. Another option involves integrating relevant topics into existing classes or other activities such as discussing the prevalence, etiology, and prevention of eating disorders in health classes; reviewing development of the feminist movement and feminist theories on eating disorders in social science and history classes; and critiquing advertisements and responding to them through correspondence with local media stations in journalism or language arts classes. Physical education classes and extracurricular sport activities provide another unused, or often misused option as well.

Another option, which can stand alone or precede other interventions, involves focusing on staff including teachers, counselors, nurses, and food service providers. Through work with an interdisciplinary staff, a health-promoting school environment can be encouraged. The scope of the intervention chosen will depend on resources and perceived severity of the problem in a particular school. It may be necessary to begin with a small-scale program; however that should be viewed as a first step toward implementation of a comprehensive program. Even small-scale interventions should include primary prevention aimed at the entire student body and opportunities for secondary prevention.

Prevention in relation to eating disturbances is still in its infancy, and little is known about effectiveness of different approaches, so evaluation of prevention strategies is highly encouraged. Evaluation should address both the strengths and weaknesses of programs to help improve future interventions. Program objectives will vary by approach, but realistic objectives should be specified clearly preceding program development. A one-time session with students should not aim for changes in body image and eating behavior but could aim for an increased awareness of the dangers of eating disorders and toward seeking help for students with weight and eating concerns. Objectives for a comprehensive program may include improvement in body image and eating behavior; implementation of outreach activities with peers, families, and communities; and modification in the social and physical school environment.

Eating disturbances often develop over many years, so it is unrealistic to expect brief interventions to be effective in preventing these conditions. To affect prevalence and severity of these conditions, long-term programs which are comprehensive and employ an integrated approach are necessary. Linkages within the school such as between teachers from different disciplines or between health care and food service providers are important. Linkages with community health services are needed to ease the referral process of adolescents needing treatment and for smooth transition of adolescents who have received treatment back into the school environment. Programs to prevent eating disturbances which have been evaluated were relatively short-term.[16-21] These programs focused primarily on the individual level. Limited success of these programs and the strong influence of social and physical environments on health behavior suggest an ecological approach[52] aimed at changes at both the individual and environmental levels.

Allensworth and Kolbe[53] developed a conceptual model for a comprehensive school health program with eight components: school environment, school health education, school health services, physical education, school counseling, school worksite health promotion, integrated school and community programs, and school food service programs. Based on this model, approaches have been suggested for school-based programs to increase fruit and vegetable consumption[54] and for comprehensive school-based nutrition education and services.[55] This model also may guide development of comprehensive programs for preventing eating disturbances.

A comprehensive program for preventing eating disturbances includes:

1. staff training

2. a module for preventing eating disturbances and obesity for junior high students

3. formal and informal integration of material into existing curricula for all students

4. individual counseling and small group work for high-risk adolescents

5. a referral system within the school and between the school and community health services

6. opportunities for healthy eating at school

7. modifications in physical education and sport activities to encourage opportunities for physical activity for all students and policies preventing extreme weight fluctuations in the interest of improving team or individual competitiveness

8. outreach activities in the school and the community by students as part of the curriculum and by staff and interested parents.

Evaluation should be an integral part of comprehensive programs and focus on the entire program and on its separate components to identify needed modifications. Both process and impact evaluations are important in the early stages of program implementation. Process evaluation should focus on the program itself: whether or not it was implemented as planned, barriers to implementation, and provider and participant satisfaction. Impact evaluation should be in accordance with the specific objectives for each program component. Thus, in evaluating impact of staff training, examine changes in staff knowledge, attitudes, and behavior related to eating disturbances and assess intentions to implement, and actual implementation, of activities with students. Program components depend on the individual school. Time and resources usually are limited, so it is essential to use the existing infrastructure within the school and community. A plan should be formulated by a committee including teachers from different disciplines, school counselors, school health care providers, coaches, students, health care workers from the community, and parents. While the committee should be large enough to include all relevant parties, a coordinator or smaller group should be responsible for program implementation, integration of program components, and evaluation.

## Conclusion

Research on prevalence of eating disturbances, consequences of these conditions, and difficulties encountered in treatment strongly indicate why prevention is necessary. Research on etiology of the conditions, while far from conclusive, provides a basis for determining what factors should be addressed in intervention programs. However, although populations at greatest risk for developing eating disturbances have been identified, research has not adequately addressed the question of who should be targeted for prevention and how the topic of prevention should be approached. Results from preliminary programs already evaluated suggest that, for school-based programs to be effective, they need to be more intensive, in particular for those at higher risk, they need to be long-term, and they need to reach beyond the classroom to the larger school and community environments.

School-based programs should serve as catalysts for broader societal changes if eating disturbances are to be prevented. Such changes should include the way in which women are portrayed in the media; expectations regarding roles of both genders; acceptance of a wider range of body weights and shapes; and increased opportunities for healthy eating and exercise, in particular in low-income areas where exercise facilities are not available. A high priority in research and funding for research projects should be placed on developing, implementing, and evaluating programs to prevent eating disturbances and obesity to determine how best to prevent these conditions.

## References

1. Jackson MY, Proulx JM, Pelican S. Obesity prevention. *Am J Clin Nutr.* 1991;53:1625S-1630S.

2. Shisslak CM. Crago M. Neal ME, Swain B. Primary prevention of eating disorders. *J Consult Clin Psychol.* 1987;55:660-667.

3. Crisp AH. Some possible approaches to prevention of eating and body weight/shape disorders, with particular reference to anorexia nervosa. *Int J Eating Disord.* 1988;7:1-17.

4. Connolly C, Corbett-Dick PC. Eating disorders: A framework for school nursing initiatives. *J Sch Health,* 1990;60:401-405.

5. Chitty KK. The primary prevention role of the nurse in eating disorders. *Nurs Clin North Am.* 1991;26:789-800.

6. Neumark-Sztainer D. Excessive weight preoccupation. *Nutr Today.* 1995;30(2):68-74.

7. Fairburn CG. The prevention of eating disorders. In Brownell KD, Fairburn CG. *Eating Disorders and Obesity: A Comprehensive Handbook.* New York, NY: The Guilford Press; 1995:289-293.

8. Steiner-Adair C. The politics of prevention. In Fallon P, Katzman MA, Wooley SC. *Feminist Perspectives on Eating Disorders.* New York, NY: The Guilford Press; 1994:381-394.

9. Kilbourne J. Still killing us softly: Advertising and the obsession with thinness. In Fallon P, Katzman NM, Wooley SC. *Feminist Perspectives on Eating Disorders.* New York, NY: The Guilford Press; 1994:395-418.

10. Shisslak CM, Crago M. Toward a new model for the prevention of eating disorders. In Fallon P, Katzman MA, Wooley SC. *Feminist Perspectives on Eating Disorders.* New York, NY: The Guilford Press, 1994:419-437.

11. Emmons L. Predisposing factors differentiating adolescent dieters and nondieters. *J Am Diet Assoc.* 1994;94(7):725-731.

12. Leon GR, Fulkerson JA, Perry CL, Cudeck R. Personality and behavioral vulnerabilities associated with risk status for eating disorders in adolescent girls. *J Ab Psychol.* 1993;102(3): 438-444.

13. Attie I, Brooks-Gunn J. Development of eating problems in adolescent girls: A longitudinal study. *Dev Psychol.* 1989;25(1):70-79.

14. Crandall CS. Social contagion of binge eating. *J Person Soc Psychol.* 1988;55(4):588-598.

15. Rosen JC, Gross J, Vara L. Psychological adjustment of adolescents attempting to lose or gain weight. *J Consult Clin Psychol.* 1987;55(5):742-747.

16. Neumark-Sztainer D, Butler R, Palti H. Eating disturbances among adolescent girls: Evaluation of a school-based primary prevention program. *J Nutr Educ.* 1995;27(1):24-31.

17. Killen JD, Taylor CB, Hammer LD, et al. An attempt to modify unhealthful eating attitudes and weight regulation practices of young adolescent girls. *Int J Eat Disord.* 1993;13(4):369-384.

18. Moriarty D, Shore R, Maxim N. Evaluation of an eating disorder curriculum. *Eval Prog Plan.* 1990; 13:407-413.

19. Shisslak CM, Crago M, Neal ME. Prevention of eating disorders among adolescents. *Am J Health Prom.* 1990;5:100-106.

20. Paxton SJ. A prevention program for disturbed eating and body dissatisfaction in adolescent girls: A 1-year follow-up. *Health Educ Res.* 1993;8:43-51.

21. Moreno AB, Thelen MH. A preliminary prevention program for eating disorders in a junior high school population. *J Youth Adolesc.* 1993;22:109-124.

22. American Psychiatric Association. *Diagnostic and Statistical Manual of Mental Disorders,* 4th ed. Washington, DC: American Psychiatric Association; 1994.

23. Brownell KD, Fairburn CG. Preface. In Brownell KD, Fairburn CG. *Eating Disorders and Obesity: A Comprehensive Handbook.* New York, NY: The Guilford Press; 1995.

24. Kreipe RE, Golden NH, Katzman DK, et al. Eating disorders in adolescents: A position paper of the Society for Adolescent Medicine. *J Adolesc Health.* 1995;16(6):476-480.

25. Fisher M, Golden NH, Katzman DK, et al. Eating disorders in adolescents: A background paper. *J Adolesc Health.* 995;16(6): 420-437.

26. Lucas AR, Beard CM, O'Fallon WM, Kurland LT. 50-year trends in the incidence of anorexia nervosa in Rochester, Minnesota: A population-based study. *Am J Psychiatry.* 1991;148: 917-922.

27. Nylander I. The feeling of being fat and dieting in a school population: An epidemiological investigation. *Acta Soc Med Scand.* 1971;1:17-26.

28. Stein DM. The prevalence of bulimia: A review of the empirical research. *J Nutr Educ.* 1991;23:205-213.

29. Killen JD, Taylor CB, Telch MJ, Saylor KE, Maron DJ, Robinson TN. Self-induced vomiting and laxative and diuretic use among teenagers: Precursors of the binge-purge syndrome? *JAMA.* 1986;255(11):1447-1449.

30. Neumark-Sztainer D, Palti H, Butler R. Weight concerns and dieting behaviors among high school girls in Israel. *J Adolesc Health.* 1995;16(1):53-59.

31. Neumark-Sztainer D, Story M, Resnick MD, Garwick A, Blum RW. Body dissatisfaction and unhealthy weight control behaviors among adolescents with and without chronic illness: A population-based study. *Arch Pediatr Adolest Med.* 1995;149:1330-1335.

32. Gortmaker SL, Dietz WH, Sobol AM, Wehler CA. Increasing pediatric obesity in the United States. *Am J Dis Child.* 1987;141:531-540.

33. US Dept of Health and Human Services. *Healthy People 2000: National Health Promotion and Disease Prevention Objectives.* Washington, DC: US Dept of Health and Human Services; 1990.

34. Herzog DB, Copeland PM. Eating disorders. *N Engl J Med.* 1985;313(5):295-303.

35. Patton GC. Eating disorders: Antecedents, evolution and course. *Ann Med.* 1992;24:281-285.

36. Pugliese MT, Lifshitz F, Grad G, Fort P, Marks-Katz M. Fear of obesity: A cause of short stature and delayed puberty. *N Engl J Med.* 1983;309:513-518.

37. MacDonald LA, Wearring GA, Moase O. Factors affecting the dietary quality of adolescent girls. *J Am Diet Assoc.* 1983;82: 260-263.

38. Neumark-Sztainer D, Butler R, Palti H. Dieting and binge eating: Which dieters are at risk? *J Am Diet Assoc.* 1995;95(5): 586-589.

39. Bull NL. Studies of the dietary habits, food consumption and nutrient intakes of adolescents and young adults. *World Rev Nutr Diet.* 1988;57:24-74.

40. Dietz WH. Childhood obesity: Prevalence and effects. In Brownell KD, Fairburn CG. *Eating Disorders and Obesity: A Comprehensive Handbook.* New York, NY: The Guilford Press; 1995:438-440.

41. Gortmaker SL, Must A, Perrin JM, Sobol A, Dietz WH. Social and economic consequences of overweight in adolescence and young adulthood. *N Engl J Med.* 1993;329(14):1008-1012.

42. Steinhausen H. The course and outcome of anorexia nervosa. In Brownell KD, Fairburn CG. *Eating Disorders and Obesity: A Comprehensive Handbook.* New York, NY: The Guilford Press; 1995:234-237.

43. Burgard D, Lyons P. Alternatives in obesity treatment: Focusing on health for fat women. In Fallon P, Katzman MA, Wooley SC. *Feminist Perspectives on Eating Disorders.* New York, NY: The Guilford Press; 1994:212-230.

44. Johnson C, Maddi KL. Factors that affect the onset of bulimia. *Sem Adolesc Med.* 1986;2(1):11-19.

45. Patton GC, Johnson-Sabine E, Wood K, Mann AH, Wakeling A. Abnormal eating attitudes in London schoolgirls—a prospective epidemiological study: Outcome at twelve-month follow-up. *Psychol Med.* 1990;20:383-394.

46.  Rolls BJ, Fedoroff IC, Guthrie JF. Gender differences in eating behavior and body weight regulation. *Health Psychol.* 1991;10(2):133-142.

47.  Rothblum ED. I'll die for the revolution but don't ask me not to diet: Feminism and the continuing stigmatization of obesity. In Fallon P, Katzman MA, Wooley SC. *Feminist Perspectives on Eating Disorders.* New York, NY: The Guilford Press; 1994:53-76.

48.  Agell G, Rothblum ED. Effects of clients' obesity and gender on the therapy judgements of psychologists. *Professional Psychology: Theory, Research and Practice.* 1991;22:223-229.

49.  Middlebrook DL, Coleman LM. Assessing the stigmatizing effects of body image in overweight individuals. Presented at the annual convention of the American Psychological Association, Los Angeles, California. August 1994.

50.  Glanz K, Marcus Lewis F, Rimer BK. Theory, research, and practice in health education: Building bridges and forging links. *Health Behavior and Health Education: Theory, Research and Practice.* San Francisco, Calif: Jossey-Bass Publishers; 1990:17-32.

51.  Roski J. The influence of the social environments of school and communities on adolescent alcohol and drug use. Minneapolis, Minn: University of Minnesota; 1995. Thesis.

52.  McLeroy KR, Bibeau D, Steckler A, Glanz K. An ecological perspective on health promotion programs. *Health Educ Q.* 1988;15(4):351-377.

53.  Allensworth DD, Kolbe LJ. The comprehensive school health program: Exploring an expanded concept. *J Sch Health.* 1987;57(10):409-412.

54.  Neill K, Allensworth DD. A model to increase consumption of fruit and vegetables by implementing the "5-A-Day" initiative. *J Sch Health.* 1994;64(4):150-155.

55.  Story M, Neumark-Sztainer D. School-based nutrition education programs and services for adolescents. *Adolesc Med: State of the Art Rev.* In press.

Chapter 32

# The Dietitians Role: Childhood Eating Disorders

During her dietetic internship, Monika M. Woolsey, MS, RD, had to follow a series of therapeutic diets to learn "the other side" of a diet prescription. The experience convinced her that, whenever possible, she would help clients be healthy without imposing restrictions on them. Realizing she was most interested in preventive care, she earned a master's degree in kinesiology and began working as a sports nutritionist. Many of the athletes she counseled were being referred to her for eating disorder diagnoses, but Woolsey felt frustrated as she tried to intervene without access to a multidisciplinary team that could support her efforts. Drawn to the field of eating disorders, she became the director of dietary services at an inpatient treatment center where, for 3 1/2 years, she was part of a multidisciplinary group planning care for more than 1,000 patients. Invigorated by the work, she was also saddened to see women enter the program weighing only half or more than 3 times their goal weight and longed for opportunities to intervene sooner. Two years ago she decided to pursue her passion for preventive intervention and today is president and founder of A Better Way Health Consulting, Inc, in Glendale, Ariz, where she specializes in helping children and teens with eating disorders. Following are a series of questions and answers about her efforts to treat, and prevent, this complex disease.

---

Excerpted from "When food becomes a cry for help: how dietitians can combat childhood eating disorders," by Nancy I. Hahn, ©1998 American Dietetic Association. Reprinted by permission from *Journal of the American Dietetic Association,* April 1998, Vol. 98, No. 4, Pg. 395(3).

## What goals do you try to achieve when working with a child who has an eating disorder?

I focus mainly on the "3 Cs": communication (how to recognize and express feelings), conflict resolution (how to ask for your needs when they are not being met), and coping (what to do when a problem cannot be directly fixed but just needs some "riding through"). Children able to master the 3 Cs are less likely to turn to food as an outlet for emotional stress. For example, a teenage girl arrived at one of my group sessions upset because her sister had locked her out of the girl's bathroom at home. When she used the boy's bathroom, her brother charged her $5! By the time she arrived for our meeting, she was very angry and wanted to eat. As a group, we shared, and laughed about, how annoying brothers can be (I told stories too!); discussed alternative ways the girl could resolve her angry feelings; and prioritized which alternatives the girl would try. The next week, the girl returned in triumph, telling how she had asked her mother to intervene and not only got her $5 returned but also got the family's rules about bathroom use changed. How empowered she felt! We talked about how taking charge of the situation reduced her craving for food, a consequence the girl had not thought about but now was able to understand.

## Do your counseling strategies differ for children versus adults?

Children perceive the world in more concrete terms and do better with more expressive work. An 11-year-old girl I saw in a group program struggled with discussing her feelings in front of her peers. Privately, I agreed to exchange written stories with her. Her fictional story told me everything I needed to know about what was happening in her world. Many therapists like to use play therapy, which engages children in activities natural to them so they don't feel as if they are being analyzed or treated for some problem.

Disordered eating behaviors are similar for children and adults, but by adulthood the behaviors have typically been in use for many years and are more difficult to change. That's why it's so important to recognize when a child may be developing an eating disorder and to catch the problem as soon as possible.

Working with kids automatically means you will be working with the family system because a child doesn't develop such a dysfunctional behavior unless she has grown up in a dysfunctional system. Every member of the family must be involved in the behavior change, but often parents expect me to "fix" their child (usually with a diet!) without having to change themselves. This doesn't work. It's almost impossible for me to teach a child not to be afraid to eat if his mother is a chronic dieter who fills the house with diet foods.

*Describe some of your outreach efforts to families.*

I'm involved in a domestic violence intervention sponsored by the Girl Scout Council in Phoenix. While parents are offered classes in anger management, conflict resolution, job skills, and child development, their children are in Boy Scout or Girl Scout meetings. I was asked to teach a basic nutrition class to the Girl Scout troop but convinced the leaders that their population was at high risk for low self-esteem and, therefore, eating disorders. So now I'm helping the girls work on self-esteem badges using the "Teens & Diets—No Weigh" curriculum, an 8-week program developed by HUGS International that I frequently use when working with groups. (This program also includes an outcome study, which has proven valuable because we are seeking United Way grant money and now can validate effectiveness.) Currently, we have programs in 6 schools and are planning to expand into 2 of the city's worst housing projects.

I'm especially excited about this project because it blows away the assumption that eating disorders are only a problem for white, upper-socioeconomic groups. We've translated the program into Spanish and are providing what I think is the first Spanish-language eating disorders prevention program in the country. With the population data I collect for the outcome study, I hope to raise awareness that this problem crosses social, economic, and cultural boundaries.

*The partnership of dietitian and psychotherapist seems critical.*

Dietetics professionals are often the first place a parent will come seeking help, because the family sees a problem with food and assumes it can be fixed with a diet. Or the family may suspect there is a psychological issue but feels uncomfortable going to a mental health professional. Our culture still imposes a stigma on getting psychological help, so many people reach out to dietitians instead because our profession is less threatening and because they are hoping we can provide a simple solution, such as a diet, when their lives feel out of control.

245

When these clients show up in our offices, we need to recognize when dietary structure will help and when it will only exacerbate problems by increasing a sense of failure and helplessness. We must also recognize when a serious psychological disorder may exist and then build a relationship of trust until we can persuade the client to seek the psychological treatment he or she needs.

One of the dietitian's most important jobs is helping clients see the connection between mental health and physical well-being. During a patient assessment, I often ask questions that probe emotional issues, but not because I'm trying to practice psychotherapy. My job is to recognize underlying problems, (depression is the most common comorbidity in eating disorders) and refer clients to mental health experts for help. Dietitians are not used to marketing themselves to psychotherapists, but we must let mental health professionals know we are not competitors. Rather, our therapeutic efforts are interwoven, and we can refer new patients to each other.

### What skills do dietitians need to work in the eating disorders field?

First, one must have the heart to work with these clients. Many have been abused, abandoned, or neglected, and they are wounded and often very angry. All the knowledge in the world cannot replace compassion.

One must also be able to enforce limits in a compassionate way. These clients can be manipulative, but we can't allow ourselves to be drawn into their disease. If a patient refuses to maintain a minimum weight you have set, you must follow through with the consequence you promised (inpatient hospitalization). Your consistency will be valued even if a client is emotionally unable to demonstrate this at the time. One client became so angry, she threw a book at me. Another threw a can of Ensure! But years later, both women keep in touch and have told me that although they hated me then, they knew they were safe with me because I stood behind my words. One even counts the day she began to trust me as an important anniversary.

Basic competency in mental health is also required. I don't have a degree in counseling, but I read the literature, and I've practiced with trained counselors to develop listening skills. Dietitians are taught to talk, but in this specialty, we must learn to listen. Dietitians also need an understanding of neuroendocrinology. These diseases are not merely behavioral, they affect central nervous system function. Symptoms are not seen in blood values, but in behavior. We must learn to distinguish what is physiologic from what is psychological. Otherwise, we may expect a client to implement a behavior she is incapable of performing.

## Dietitian's Role In Treatment

Treating an eating disorder requires the expertise of a team of health professionals, including a psychiatrist, psychologist, therapist/ social worker, physician, dentist, and dietitian.

* Identify the disordered eating behaviors and interpret the underlying message these behaviors are communicating.

* Refer information about the underlying stress issues to the mental health therapist. Work with the therapist to help the child and family learn alternative ways to communicate and resolve conflicts.

* Evaluate the diet and share with the psychiatrist and physician important nutrition information that may affect medication needs (is the client caffeine-dependent or taking St John's Wort?).

* Offer active learning activities (such as cooking or going out to eat together) that help clients learn new behaviors and confront fears of environments such as grocery stores or restaurants.

* Model normal eating. Don't just talk about it—help clients get over their fear by letting them see you eat a burger and fries or pizza.

* Communicate frequently with other members of the team to determine whether a nutrition intervention is appropriate, given the client's emotional stability.

Chapter 33

# Adolescent Vegetarians: A Behavioral Profile

Adolescents who describe themselves as vegetarian may have higher rates of eating disorders. Researchers in Minnesota surveyed 107 school-aged vegetarian adolescents and 214 similar nonvegetarian youth. Vegetarianism was very uncommon, and 81% of vegetarians were female. Vegetarians were more likely to eat fruits and vegetables and less likely to eat sweet or salty snack foods. However, vegetarians had significantly higher rates of dieting, binge eating, intentional vomiting, and laxative use. Some adolescents may adopt vegetarian eating to lose weight or express independence.

A vegetarian eating style may be adopted for various reasons. Vegetarian adolescents may simply be following the eating patterns of their family or may choose to follow a vegetarian diet for the same reasons as adult populations (e.g., religious affiliation, health promotion, ecological concerns, animal welfare, or food preferences).[1] However, adolescence is a period of increased autonomy and self-identification; one expression of this process is via the selection of eating patterns that may differ from one's family or from that of society. Thus, some adolescents may choose to adopt a vegetarian diet as an expression of their independence, as they explore new ideals, or as they experiment with an unconventional lifestyle. Other adolescents with excessive

Excerpted from "Adolescent Vegetarians: A Behavioral Profile of a School-Based Population in Minnesota," by Dianne Neumark-Sztainer, Mary Story, Michael D. Resnick, and Robert W. Blum, ©1997 American Medical Association, from *Archives of Pediatrics & Adolescent Medicine*, August 1997, Vol. 151, No. 8, Pg. 833(6); reprinted with permission.

weight concerns may choose to adopt a vegetarian diet to reduce fat and overall energy intake in a socially acceptable manner. Given their interest in self-expression, members of the first group may differ from nonvegetarians in behaviors other than food consumption patterns, while the second group of youth may be at increased risk for the development of an eating disorder. While vegetarians may have healthier behaviors because of greater health awareness, they may also be engaging in a range of eating disorder-related behaviors or alternative behaviors, some of which may not be conducive to health.[2,3]

Although health professionals working with vegetarian adolescents frequently have questions about the health behaviors and health status of this group, relatively few studies have addressed these issues. Existing studies have tended to focus on the nutritional intake (e.g., food groups and nutrients) and on the health status parameters (e.g., the onset of menarche, height, weight, and hemoglobin levels) of vegetarian youth.[1,4-11] Although somewhat inconsistent, findings suggest that vegetarian diets may have benefits such as decreased fat intake.[1] However, they may also place the adolescent at greater risk for lower intake of nutrients such as calcium, iron, and zinc.[1,12] While providing important information, these studies have been somewhat limited in scope and have not provided answers to these questions: Who are adolescent vegetarians? Are they adolescents who are interested in controlling their weight and have adopted an eating style conducive to fat reduction? Are they adolescents who in general have adopted a health-promoting lifestyle? Or are they risk-seeking adolescents who tend to experiment with a range of unconventional behaviors? In part, these questions may be answered through the examination of a range of behaviors among adolescents following a vegetarian diet and a comparison with nonvegetarian youth with similar sociodemographic and personal characteristics.

A study was undertaken to learn more about adolescent vegetarians. Specifically, we wanted to increase our knowledge about behavioral patterns of vegetarian and nonvegetarian adolescents. Therefore, adolescent vegetarians and nonvegetarians were compared for a range of health behaviors: food intake patterns, disordered eating behaviors, and non-food-related health-compromising and health-promoting behaviors.

This study compared vegetarian with nonvegetarian adolescents for a range of health behaviors. Through a comparison of behavior profiles, we hoped to increase our understanding of adolescents who have adopted a vegetarian eating style and to identify concerns that need to be addressed in the health care setting.

Vegetarians had several positive food consumption behaviors compared with a randomly matched comparison group of nonvegetarian youth. Fruit and vegetable consumption was considerably higher among the vegetarians. Another positive behavior among the vegetarians was their relatively low consumption of sweet and salty snack foods compared with the nonvegetarian youth. However, of potential concern were the relatively low consumption patterns of foods high in protein, iron, and zinc (poultry, fish, beans, peas, peanut butter, and eggs) and of sources of protein and calcium (dairy foods). Our findings, and the findings from previous studies on the nutritional intake of adolescent and adult vegetarians,[1,11,13] suggest that the vegetarian diet may offer important advantages; however, health professionals should screen for the consumption of nonmeat alternatives and provide counseling about these alternatives to ensure the adequate intake of foods rich in calcium, zinc, iron, and other essential nutrients. Iron and zinc status may be affected by the low intake of foods rich in these nutrients and by the high intake of foods high in compounds such as fiber, phytate, and oxalate, which may bind to minerals and decrease bioavailability.[24-26] Therefore, counseling should stress the importance of eating foods rich in these nutrients together with foods high in ascorbic acid. If the adolescent follows a vegetarian diet, the type of vegetarian diet followed should be assessed, as previous studies have suggested that individuals following a vegan diet are at greater risk for nutritional inadequacy than those following a lacto-ovo diet.[11]

Vegetarians were more likely to engage in all of the disordered eating behaviors examined in this study, which included frequent dieting, binge eating, self-induced vomiting, and laxative use. To our knowledge, this is the first population-based study in which these associations have been examined among adolescents, although clinical studies of patients with an eating disorder have reported high rates of vegetarianism.[2-3]

O'Connor et al[2] examined the medical records of 116 patients with anorexia nervosa and found that 54% were avoiding red meat. However, only 4 of the patients had followed a vegetarian diet before the onset of anorexia nervosa. Because of the cross-sectional nature of this study, causal relationships between vegetarianism and disordered eating behaviors could not be assessed. Nevertheless, the strong associations between vegetarianism and disordered eating behaviors should be considered in the counseling situation, as vegetarianism may be serving as a marker for potentially harmful weight control behaviors. Motives for embarking on a vegetarian eating style should be evaluated carefully. It is possible that the adolescent is using vegetarianism as a socially acceptable way to avoid fat intake and to reduce energy intake. Thus, weight concerns and eating patterns should be examined carefully among adolescents following a vegetarian diet.

To the best of our knowledge, the only other study that examined associations between vegetarianism and disordered eating behaviors among nonclinical populations was done with adult women by Janelle and Barr.[27] To be included in their study, women had to be aged 20 to 40 years, be weight stable, be nonsmokers, consume 1 alcoholic drink or less a day, and not be using oral contraceptives. They found that the nonvegetarians had higher dietary restraint scores (dietary restraint is a cognitive-based perception that may be accompanied by actual differences in behaviors) than the vegans and did not differ notably from the lactovegetarians. The nature of their study population, and its relatively small size, makes the drawing of conclusions somewhat difficult. Furthermore, dietary restraint per se was not assessed in the present study. Nevertheless, the contrast with our findings suggests that the association between vegetarianism and disordered eating behaviors may be unique to adolescent populations.

For the most part, associations were not found between vegetarianism and non-food-related health-promoting or health-compromising behaviors. The lack of notable findings is of interest as studies among adult populations, which have taken a broader approach toward studying behavioral profiles of vegetarians, have suggested that vegetarians are at lower risk for health-compromising behaviors.[28] Freeland-Graves et al[28,29] found that adult vegetarians were less likely to use tobacco and alcohol compared with a matched group of nonvegetarians; however, no differences in marijuana use were noted. They did not find differences in frequency of physical activity; however, differences in the types of physical activity were noted, with more vegetarians reporting bicycle riding and yoga.[29]

Slattery et al[30] found that young adults who reported eating red meat or poultry less than once a week were less likely to drink alcohol and reported more physical activity. Dwyer et al[31] studied behaviors among 100 vegetarians aged 15 to 35 years and found that vegetarians following more restrictive diets were less likely to use substances such as tobacco, alcohol, prescription and nonprescription drugs, and coffee than were those who had less restrictive diets. We are unaware of any studies of adolescents in which behavioral profiles of vegetarians and nonvegetarians, matched for sociodemographic variables, have been compared. Our findings suggest that vegetarian adolescents may differ from adult vegetarians; however, future research in which more comprehensive measures of assessing the vegetarian lifestyle is necessary to draw conclusions. An important strength of this study is that it focused on a nonclinical, population-based sample. Previous studies in which associations between vegetarianism and eating disordered behaviors have been examined have focused on clinical populations and thus have examined the association from a different perspective.[2,26] Other studies of adolescent populations have employed convenience samples, in which participants were recruited via publicity in the media, at health food stores, and in schools.[11] Clinical and convenience samples have the disadvantage of having biased and nonrepresentative study populations. Another strength of the study is that the study sample was drawn from a larger population, which allowed for a comparison group that was matched for key sociodemographic variables. This was of particular importance to this study, as the health-compromising and health-promoting behaviors that were included in the analysis vary by sex, age, and ethnicity.[12] Finally, the comprehensive nature of the survey allowed us to compare vegetarian with nonvegetarian youth for a range of behaviors.

During the past decade, it is highly possible that the reasons for following a vegetarian diet and the types of persons who choose to follow a vegetarian diet have changed; however, we are unaware of any more recent surveys on large populations of youth that would have allowed for the examination of associations between vegetarianism and other behaviors. Finally, the measures used to assess vegetarianism and nutritional intake were somewhat incomplete. The food frequency questionnaire was brief and did not allow for an assessment of nutrient intake or a comprehensive assessment of food item consumption. It would have been preferable to have adolescents self-identify as lacto-ovo vegetarians, semivegetarians, and vegans. The item assessing vegetarianism was phrased in a manner that may not have identified all vegetarians in the population. Indeed, the relatively low percentage of self-identified vegetarians (0.6% of the total population surveyed) suggests that not all youth following a vegetarian diet responded in the affirmative to this item. Although anecdotal reports suggest higher prevalence rates of vegetarianism, we were unable to locate prevalence rates of vegetarian youth. Slattery et al[30] studied 5111 young adults and found that less than 1% (n=32) ate no red meat or poultry and another 1% (n=47) ate red meat or poultry less than once a week. They did not ask the respondents to identify themselves as vegetarians.[30]

The increasing interest in vegetarianism and the striking findings of our study regarding factors associated with vegetarianism among adolescents point to the need for further research on this topic and for attention to this matter in clinical settings. Future research should consider the limitations of this study and employ better and more comprehensive measures of vegetarianism and other eating behaviors. Health care providers counseling vegetarian adolescents need to be alert to their higher risk for disordered eating behaviors.

## References

1.  Johnston PK, Haddad E, Sabate J. The vegetarian adolescent. *Adolesc Med State Art Rev.* 1992;3:417-437.

2.  O'Connor MA, Touyz SW, Dunn SM, Beumont PJV. Vegetarianism in anorexia nervosa? A review of 116 consecutive cases. *Med J Aust* 1987;147:540-542.

3.  Huse DM, Lucas AR. Dietary patterns in anorexia nervosa. *Am Clin Nutr.* 1984;40:251-254.

4.  Tayter M, Stanek KL. Anthropometric and dietary assessment of omnivore and lacto-ovo-vegetarian children. *J Am Diet Assoc.* 1989;89:1661-1663.

5.  Kissinger DG, Sanchez A. The association of dietary factors with the age of menarche. *Nutr Res.* 1987;7:471-479.

6.  Hanne N, Olin R, Rotstein A. Physical fitness, anthropometric and metabolic parameters in vegetarian athletes. *J Sports Med.* 1986;26:180-185.

7.  Dagnelie PC, van Staveren WA. Macrobiotic nutrition and child health. *Am J Clin Nutr.* 1994;59(suppl):1187S-1196S.

8.  Sabate J, Llorca MC, Sanchez A. Lower height of lacto-ovo-vegetarian girls at preadolescence. *J Am Diet Assoc.* 1992;92:1263-1264.

9.  Sabate J, Lindsted KID, Harris RD, Johnston PK. Anthropometric parameters of schoolchildren with different life-styles. *AJDC.* 1990;144:1159-1163.

10. Treuherz J. Possible inter-relationship between zinc and dietary fibre in a group of lacto-ovo-vegetarian adolescents. *D Plant Foods.* 1982;4:89-93.

11. Donovan UM, Gibson RS, Dietary intakes of adolescent females consuming vegetarian, semi-vegetarian, and omnivorous diets. *J Adolesc Health.* 1996;18:292-300.

12.  Dwyer J. Nutritional consequences of vegetarianism. *Ann Rev Nutr.* 1991;11:61-91.

13.  Blum R, Haris LJ, Resnick MID, Rosenwinkel K. Technical Report on the Adolescent Health Survey. Minneapolis: University of Minnesota; 1989.

14.  Blum R, Resnick M, Geer L, et al. The State of Adolescent Health in Minnesota. Minneapolis: University of Minnesota Adolescent Health Program; 1989.

15.  Story M, Rosenwinkel K, Himes JH, Resnick M, Harris LJ, Blum RW. Demographic and risk factors associated with chronic dieting in adolescents. *AJDC.* 1991;145:994-998.

16.  Resnick MD, Harris LJ, Blum FIN. The impact of caring and connectedness on adolescent health and well-being. *J Pediatr Child Health.* 1993;29(suppl 1):S3-S9.

17.  Blum R, Geer L, Hutton L, et al. Summary: The Minnesota Adolescent Health Survey: implications for physicians. *Minn Med.* 1988;71:143-146.

18.  Neumark-Sztainer D, Story M, Resnick M, Garwick A, Blum RW. Body dissatisfaction and unhealthy weight-control practices among adolescents with and without chronic illness: a population-based study. *Arch Pediatr Adolesc Med.* 1995;149: 1330-1335.

19.  Must A, Dallal GE, Dietz WH. Reference data for obesity: 85th and 95th percentiles of body mass index (wt/ht.sup.2) and triceps skinfold thickness. *Am J Clin Nutr.* 1991;53:839-846.

20.  Must A, Dallal GE, Dietz WH. Reference data for obesity: 85th and 95th percentiles of body mass index (wt/ht.sup.2): a correction. *Am J Clin Nutr.* 1991;54:773.

21.  Himes JH, Dietz WH. Guidelines for overweight in adolescent preventive services: recommendations from an expert committee. *Am J Clin Nutr.* 1994;59:307-316.

22.  SPSS Inc. SPSS 6.1 *Base System User's Guide, Part 1 & 2,* Macintosh Version. Chicago, III: SPSS Inc; 1994.

23.  Shultz TD, Leklem JE. Dietary status of Seventh-day Adventists and nonvegetarians. *J Am Diet Assoc.* 1983;83:27-33.

24.  Freeland-Graves J. Mineral adequacy of vegetarian diets. *Am J Clin Nutr* 1988;48:859862.

25. Freeland-Graves JH, Bodzy PW, Eppright MA. Zinc status of vegetarians. *J Am Diet Assoc.* 1980;77:655-661.

26. Weaver CM, Plawecki KL. Dietary calcium: adequacy of a vegetarian diet. *Am J Clin Nutr.* 1994;59(suppl):1238S-1241S.

27. Janelle KC, Barr S. Nutrient intakes and eating behavior scores of vegetarian and nonvegetarian women. *J Am Diet Assoc.* 1995;95:180-186.

28. Freeland-Graves JH, Greninger SA, Young RK. A demographic and social profile of age- and sex-matched vegetarians and nonvegetarians. *J Am Diet Assoc.* 1986;86:907913.

29. Freeland-Graves JH, Greninger SA, Young RK. Health practices, attitudes, and beliefs of vegetarians and nonvegetarians. *J Am Diet Assoc.* 1986;86:913-918.

30. Slattery ML, Jacobs DR Jr, Hilner JE, et al. Meat consumption and its associations with other diet and health factors in young adults: the CARDIA study. *Am J Clin Nutr.* 1991;54: 930-935.

31. Dwyer JT, Mayer LDVH, Kandel RF, Mayer J. Who are they? the new vegetarians. *J Am Diet Assoc.* 1973;62:503-509.

32. Neumark-Sztainer D, Story M, French S, Cassuto N, Jacobs DR Jr, Resnick MD. Patterns of health-compromising behaviors among Minnesota adolescents: sociodemographic variations. *Am J Public Health.* 1996;86:1599-1606.

33. Walker J, Harris L, Blum R, Schneider B, Resnick M. Outlooks and Insights: Understanding Rural Adolescents, Minneapolis: University of Minnesota; 1990.

Chapter 34

# Abnormal Psychosocial Situations and Eating Disorders in Adolescence

It has long been known that many psychiatric illnesses do not strike at random but are related to biological changes in the individual or to alteration in the environment, or both. Many attempts have been made to measure the influence of these two main factors with respect to the major psychiatric syndromes such as schizophrenia, mood disorders, and anxiety states. This chapter addresses stressful life events (SLE), one of the major psychological aspects of the psychobiological model.

The last two decades have seen a growing interest in the association between life events, stress, and psychopathology in both adults and children and adolescents. Adult studies in this area have shown that life events constitute stress and require adjustment on the part of the individual to disturbing physiological and psychological events. Thus SLE may lead to the development of both psychological and physical symptoms in vulnerable individuals. For instance, accumulation of life events may lead to psychiatric illness. The greater the number and severity of the life events, the more severe the psychopathology. This association has been shown for the neuroses, for anxiety, for obsessive-compulsive disorder, for acute schizophrenic episodes, and for depression.

Excerpted from "Abnormal Psychosocial Situations and Eating Disorders in Adolescence," by Netta Horesh, Alan Apter, Jo Ishai, Yardena Danziger, Mario Miculincer, Daniel Stein, Eli Lepkifker, and Marc Minouni, © 1996 American Academy of Child and Adolescent Psychiatry, from *Journal of the American Academy of Child and Adolescent Psychiatry*, July, 1996, Vol. 35, No. 7, Pg. 921(7); reprinted with permission.

There has been much less research on the effects of SLE in childhood psychopathology than there has been for adult psychopathology. Nevertheless there appears to be general agreement that many different kinds of life events may increase the risk of psychopathology in children and make them more vulnerable to pressures from the environment. One such example is the demand for achievement at school. SLE may occur because of lack of protection from families or they may be brought about by the child's own behavior. Some children seem to be protected from the harmful effects of life events by their own inner strengths. The relative importance of the chronic accumulation of life events as opposed to the potentiation of several life events occurring over a short period of time remains to be determined.

Cultural and sociological factors are of paramount importance in the understanding of the development of eating disorders. It is thus surprising that there has been little systematic research into the association between life events and these disorders. A series of experiments have shown that life stress influences motivation to eat, idealization of thinness, as well as self-image, and that patients with personality features seen in anorexics report high levels of life stress. Sohlberg and Norring (1992) maintain that life events explain a substantial 30% of the variability on follow-up status in adults with eating disorders. Thus SLE influence the outcome of adult eating disorders.

Subjects with eating disorders in Armstrong and Roth's (1991) study report high levels of separation and attachment difficulties, which may be related to their past history. The importance of separation from primary attachment figures is of course a cornerstone in the psychoanalytic theory of anorexia nervosa. Nonetheless only two studies have examined the relationship between various kinds of life events unrelated to sex abuse and anorexia nervosa in a systematic manner. Mynors-Wallace et al. (1992) found that late-onset cases were more likely to be preceded by SLE and to occur against a background of chronic stress than other anorexia nervosa patients. Patients with anorexia nervosa showed significantly higher negative life event scores than healthy controls in all the areas of life events examined. In addition, they showed significantly more negative life events concerning parents than did patients in the other psychiatric diagnostic categories.

Finally, it seems that our results support empirical findings that certain negative emotions characterize the parent-child relationships of patients with eating disorders. These may be directly related to criticisms related to weight and body shape, to a lack of emotional support in the family, or to disturbed family cohesion in general.

Humphrey (1986, 1987) reported that parents of girls with eating disorders were insufficiently nurturing and empathic. This in turn causes a negative response from the daughters so that cause-and-effect relationships are difficult to unravel. In the laboratory these families show enmeshed intrusive and hostile patterns of interaction with lack of attention paid to the child's emotional needs.

This study also showed that sexual abuse was more common in the eating disorder and in the psychiatric patient controls than it was in the histories of the healthy controls. Sexual abuse was not more common in the eating disorder patients than in the other psychiatric patients. These findings are in accord with the most recent literature.

## References

Armstrong, M.G., Roth, D.M. (1991), Attachment and separation difficulties in eating disorders: a preliminary investigation. *Int J Eat Disord* 8:141-155.

Humphrey, L.L. (1986), Structural analysis of parent-child relationships in eating disorders. *J Abnorm Psychol* 95:395-402.

Humphrey, L.L. (1987), Comparison of bulimic-anorexic and non-distressed families using structural analysis of social behavior. *J Am Acad Child Adolest Psychiatry* 26:248-255.

Mynors-Wallace, L., Treasure, J., Chee, D. (1992), Life events and eating disorders: differences between early and late onset cases. *Int J Eat Disord* 11:369-375.

Sohlberg, S., Norring, C. (1992), A three year prospective study of life events and course with adults with anorexia nervosa/bulimia nervosa. *Psychosom Med* 54:59-70.

Chapter 35

# Strategies to Enhance Self-Esteem

Students can be taught positive health behaviors through methods that increase their self-esteem. Activities that utilize media portrayals of body parts, recollections of feelings when self-esteem was lowered, and discussion of positive events in life can be adapted to various middle grade and high school levels. These activities can be used with health units on violence, eating disorders, sexuality, and other relevant topics.

Health educators are in a unique position to positively influence the self-esteem of students. Alienation, insecurity, and feelings of inadequacy can be lessened when educators develop self-esteem enhancement strategies for students. High self-esteem in youth typically occurs when they feel comfortable, confident, and supported in their learning environment.[1] In a study by Miller et al,[1] negative health behaviors such as risky sexual behavior, drug use, and suicide were perceived by teachers to be related to low self-esteem, depression, and peer pressure. Other research[2,3] indicates that high self-esteem is directly related to positive health choices and behaviors. Though time and effort are required for educators to design and structure activities to improve students' self-esteem, the positive gains made by students more than offsets the energy expended to incorporate this element into the learning situation.[1]

"Distract Me from My Dreaded Self: Strategies to Enhance Self-Esteem," by Diane Hamilton and Sara Oswalt, © 1998 American School Health Association, Kent, Ohio, from *Journal of School Health*, Sept., 1998, Vol. 68, No. 7, Pg. 301(3); reprinted with permission.

It is not enough to "talk" an adolescent into better self-esteem. Rather, this growth process requires dialogue, sharing among peers, and experiential learning activities. Communication allows students to clarify their opinions, articulate their ideas, and receive feedback.

## Self-Esteem Enhancement to Reinforce Positive Health Behaviors

### Lesson Objectives

1. Identify positive and negative life experiences and indicate how those experiences influence self-esteem.

2. Describe the internal and external factors influencing self-esteem.

3. Utilize self-affirmation strategies to enhance self-esteem.

4. Explain the role of body image in self-esteem development.

5. Discuss how individuals can support the self-esteem of others.

This three-activity lesson begins with "Pieces and Parts" which examines cultural standards of beauty, questions students' attitudes about their body image, and addresses the effect of nonappearance affirmations in enhancing self-esteem. Activity two, "Self-Esteem Rip Off," helps students recall occasions when others' comments influenced their self-esteem and explores the use of positive self-talk. "Affirmation Breeds Success," the third and concluding activity, allows students to receive support from others while reflecting on their personal strengths.

### Assessment Criteria

Following the lesson, each student writes a letter to themselves that focuses on the following questions:

1. What are three things you like about yourself that do not relate to your appearance?

2. How do your feelings about your body influence your self-esteem?

3. What positive and negative life experiences have influenced your self-esteem?

4. What factors in your environment and within you have affected your self-esteem?

5. How could you use self-affirmation strategies in your everyday life?

6. What activities can you do to enhance the self-esteem of others?

## Activities and Strategies

### Activity One: "Pieces and Parts"

Images of bodies and body parts pervade our culture. Magazines such as *Glamour, Seventeen, Essence,* and *Muscle Fitness* often portray standards of attractiveness and body types unattainable by most people. Self-comparisons with these unrealistic ideals often reveal a gap between the actual and ideal which can diminish one's self-esteem.

This activity allows students to question their attitudes about their body image as well as the cultural "ideal," and addresses the effect of nonappearance affirmations in enhancing self-esteem.

1. Cut out body parts from magazines. Create an envelope for male body parts and one for female body parts. Each envelope should contain five to six heads, torsos, legs, and feet. Include cut-outs that represent a variety of ages, ethnicities, and appearances. Label each envelope as male or female. Distribute an envelope to groups of five to six students.

2. Ask the groups to construct the ideal man or woman from the body parts provided.

3. After the groups have finished, ask each group how they arrived at this ideal and how they selected the particular body parts.

### Discussion Questions:

1. Describe the people you know. How many of them look like this "ideal?" How realistic do you think this ideal is?

2. What, if anything, about creating this "ideal" bothers you? How does it affect your self-esteem? Explain.

3. Explain how you see your body—as a whole or in parts as this activity depicts.

263

4. Pretend you are going on your dream date. How much time and energy would you expend trying to look like this ideal? How many products would you use before you left the house? Why do you think people attempt to achieve this ideal?

5. What can we do to get beyond this ideal?

### Activity Two: "Self-Esteem Rip Off"

Others' remarks may influence a student's self-esteem positively or negatively. This activity allows students to recall occasions when comments influenced their self-esteem and explores use of affirmations and positive self-talk to lessen the effect of negative feedback.

1. Distribute a sheet of paper with "Your Self-Esteem" printed in large print.

2. Read these directions: Statements that relate to your self-esteem will be read. As sentences are read, if the statement applies to you, tear off a piece of paper. The greater the effect of the statement on your self-esteem, the larger the tear should be. As you think about incidents from the past, focus on spoken messages as well as the unspoken ones implied by the situation.

3. Read these statements:

   A. Someone blamed you for something you did not do.

   B. Someone told you that you are not smart enough.

   C. Someone said you were ugly.

   D. Someone told you that you were incompetent.

   E. Someone stated they didn't trust you.

   F. You were left out of doing things with your friends.

   G. Someone told you they did not like you.

4. Discuss with the students how they felt while tearing off the strips of paper and if they relived the feelings associated with the incident. Explore with students what thoughts emerged and what situations were recalled. Ask students how they were influenced by others tearing their self-esteem sheets.

5. Read these directions: Again, statements that relate to your self-esteem will be read, however, this time, as the sentences are read, if the statement applies to you, replace a piece of paper

and rebuild your self-esteem. The greater the effect of the statement on your self-esteem, the larger the replacement piece should be.

6.  Read these statements:

    A. You felt confident about a decision you made.

    B. Someone told you they loved you.

    C. You felt proud to accomplish a goal.

    D. Someone told you that you are fun to be with.

    E. Someone complimented your sense of humor.

    F. Someone said they trusted you.

    G. You were appreciated for a job well done.

7.  Discuss with the class how they felt while replacing the strips of paper and repeat discussion points for part one. Ask students whether the positive or negative statements had a more powerful effect on their self-esteem.

### *Activity Three: "Affirmation Breeds Success"*

In daily living, small accomplishments often go unnoticed and unappreciated by ourselves as well as others. In this closing activity, students reflect on their strengths and make a positive self-statement to the class. As a result, they leave the class appreciating themselves and feeling affirmed by their peers.

1.  Students are asked to volunteer to be the focus person. As the focus person, the individual stands and makes a positive statement about something in his or her life. Examples include something they are proud of or have recently accomplished, a goal they have set for the future, a decision they have made, or an obstacle they have overcome.

2.  After each focus person makes a statement the class cheers, celebrates, and offers affirmation. Allot adequate time to ensure that all students who would like to participate have an opportunity to be the focus person.

## *Summary*

As one major effect of this lesson, students begin to view their self-esteem as personally meaningful rather than as an abstract concept.

Students are encouraged to continue working with these ideas and to deepen their awareness. The underlying theme of these activities encourages students to decrease their focus from external standards while increasing their personal levels of self-respect and self-worth. Changing self-esteem involves a gradual and challenging process; students and teachers should be patient and accept occasional setbacks as part of the process.

## Grade Level and Subject Area

This lesson can be adapted to a variety of middle grade and high school levels; however, the depth and scope of the discussion and impact will reflect the students' ability and maturity levels. Lessons on self-esteem can stand alone or be used in conjunction with units on sexuality, substance use/abuse, eating disorders, violence, and emotional health.

## Resources and Materials

Materials needed include cut out body parts from magazines for the "Pieces and Parts" activity and handouts for "Self-Esteem Rip Off." Other resources for self-esteem include:

*Building Self-esteem: A Comprehensive Program for Schools* by Robert Reasoner

*Stress Management and Self-Esteem Activities* by Patricia Rizzo Toner, and the Branden Institute for Self-Esteem in Beverly Hills, Calif.

## References

1. Miller DF, Telljohann SK, Symons CW. *Health Education*. Dubuque, Iowa: Times Mirror Higher Education Group; 1996:134, 119-120.

2. Lewis Harris and Associates. *An Evaluation of Comprehensive Health Education in American Public Schools*. New York, NY: Metropolitan Life Foundation; 1988.

3. Macgregor ID, Regis D, Balding J. Self-concept and dental health behaviors in adolescents. *J Clin Peridontol*. 1997;24(5):335-339.

266

Chapter 36

# The Educator's Role at the Onset of Anorexia Nervosa in Young Girls

Anorexia nervosa is a serious mental disorder that effects primarily women. The reported mortality rate for this disorder is over 10%. The onset of the disorder is during adolescence. Educators who are informed of the characteristic behaviors of these young girls, could help to identify them in the early stages of the disorder. This chapter describes some of the major characteristics of the disorder, in order to help the educator identify the anorectic among the population of teenage dieters. Early identification and referral to psychological services will increase the young girl's likelihood of a more favorable prognosis.

## Introduction

Anorexia nervosa is a serious mental disorder, with onset occurring during adolescent years, which predominantly affects women in approximately 90% of the cases. The young girl who is psychologically vulnerable, may be victim to this life-threatening disorder. The long-term mortality from anorexia nervosa is over 10%. These girls are among the student population in our nations' elementary and secondary schools. It is important that educators be familiar with the early stages of this disorder. However, more importantly, the educator must look for signs that indicate whether this student is just a typical dieter or

"Educators and the Onset of Anorexia Nervosa in Young Girls," by Felicia Romeo, ©1996 Project Innovation, from *Education*, Fall 1996, Vol. 117, No.1, Pg. 55(4); reprinted with permission.

a potential anorexic. Early identification increases the chances of a more favorable prognosis.

The purpose of this chapter is to present a case description of a young girl who is in the early stages of anorexia nervosa. The inception of this disorder is very subtle, as it resembles the dieting behaviors of the typical adolescent who engages in the pursuit of a reasonable expectation of weight loss. This case description intends to inform the educator about the symptoms of anorexia nervosa, as it blends into what appears to be a normal diet. The major symptoms of anorexia nervosa include the following:

- Refusal to maintain body weight at or above a minimally normal weight for age and height (body weight less than 85% of that expected).

- Intense fear of gaining weight or becoming fat, even though underweight.

- Exhibits a significant disturbance in the perception of the shape or size of his or her body, or denial of seriousness of the current bow body weight.

- Postmenarcheal female with this disorder are amenorrhia (absence of at least three consecutive menstrual cycles).

- Usually weight loss is accomplished primarily through reduction in total food intake.

- Increased or excessive exercises.

## The Young Girl

### The Initial Stages of Anorexia Nervosa

A young girl wakes up one morning eager to begin her day. What will she wear? She looks among the varied colors of clothes in her closet and chooses a blue skirt, a skirt which she has not worn for some time. Her choice gives her a feeling of success as she continues her morning preparations for school. When she puts on the blue skirt, she notices it fits a little snugly and that she is having difficulty buttoning it at the waist. Has she gained weight? Didn't one of her friends recently comment that she looked "chubby?" She moves quickly toward the bathroom and steps on the scale. Sure enough. That is it. Yes, she weighs four pounds more than she did a few days ago when she weighed herself. There is only one solution: she will have to go on a diet. Certainly she is not going to let herself weigh as much as another girl in school who everyone knows is as fat as a balloon!

## Breakfast

Our young dieter joins the family for breakfast and announces that she is going on a diet. This announcement is greeted by her family with benevolent amusement. A diet! She has decided that she will not eat any more junk food like potato chips and candy. Everyone in the family agrees that junk foods are not beneficial for you. Although she is not really overweight, they applaud her idea and agree with her initial plan.

She intends to lose just a few pounds. She will eat a little less than her usual amount. As she drinks her breakfast juice, she begins to silently ask herself a few questions: How many calories are there in orange juice, toast and eggs? What foods should she eat? How much should she eat? She makes a mental note to herself that later in the day she will go to the school library and look up information concerning nutrition and dieting. She exits from the breakfast table with fantastic speed and without eating her toast.

## School

During school she tells her friends that she has started a diet because she wants to lose six pounds. At lunch, the girls talk about the successes and failures of their own dieting attempts. They gleefully gossip about the shapes of other classmates who, of course, are not seated at the table. "Have you seen Jeanie's thighs? Wow, they are huge. She definitely wins the Ms. Thunderthighs of the Year award." The conversation continues along this topic for some time. A roster of girl's names is brought up and each girl's figure is critically evaluated for its weaknesses.

The conversation suddenly switches to just as careful an inspiration of the food which they are eating for lunch. "Do you know how many calories there are in that little cookie? Probably a million. Well, not really, but hundreds for sure. I would not touch that cookie. You might gain weight by just touching it with your fingers."

Our teenager dieter leaves that lunch table and goes directly to the school library. She checks out a few nutrition books. During her history class, she has difficulty resisting the temptation to read the books. After this class, she will have science. She considers showing her science teacher the library books and asking the teacher's opinion.

Our teenage dieter asks the science teacher for some advice about dieting. Also, she stops by a bookstore on the way home to buy the current best-selling diet book.

## A Diet Plan

As a result of reading the diet and nutrition books, our teenage dieter decides to make a diet plan. In general, she is going to decrease the number of calories she consumes, by one-half, and decrease the portion size of each meal, by half. Certain foods will be on her forbidden list, such as fatty foods and carbohydrates. They contain too many calories. Foods which will be considered "safe" must be labeled "dietetic."

This morning when our teenage dieter steps on the scale, she notices she has lost two pounds. She greets this news with mixed emotions. On the one hand, she is glad that she lost some weight, but on the other hand, she wishes that it was more at this point in her diet. Our young dieter jogged about a mile every day, now she decides that she will increase her mile to three miles a day. This way she would "burn off" more calories.

Exercise was definitely recommended and encouraged in every book that she had read concerning dieting. She will try to add another mile at the end of the week. She will never let anything interfere with her exercise schedule.

As she looks at the clock, she notices that it is still early and that most of her family is still in bed. Last night she woke up around one o' clock but managed to go back to sleep. Now it is only six o'clock. Our teenage dieter decides to do some sit-ups, jumping jacks and toe touches before she goes to breakfast, after all, she should take advantage of the available time. She knows that there is nothing to lose by exercising, but there is everything to gain. She quickly corrects herself and concludes there is more to gain if she does not exercise! With this thought, she softly accompanies each motion of her exercise with the rhythmical count: one, two, four, one, two ... and so on.

The young dieter almost finishes sixty sit-ups when she hears her mother call her for breakfast. She would love to skip breakfast. Plus, she is full of so much energy she believers that she could probably do at least a hundred more of these exercises.

Reluctantly, she goes down the stairs and gloomily looks at the breakfast meal. She eats half of everything on her plate and runs off to school. She has now lost more than 12 pounds and still fears that she is too fat. Her parents urge her finish her breakfast and tell her that she is too thin. Our young dieter staunchly declares that she is still too fat and that she must lose more weight.

## School

The young dieter has been on her diet for a few months and she has been successfully losing weight. Her school friends comment that she does everything else so successfully, i.e., school work, plays in the band, etc., that they are not surprised at her achievement. While the lunch conversation is still very much occupied with dieting and body shapers, one girl comments that throughout the morning she has been having terrible menstrual cramps, the other girls join in a chorus about the horrors the associated with their menstruation. This conversation brings to the attention of our teenage dieter for the first time that she has not menstruated in a few months. The young dieter reluctantly states to her friends that she has missed some menstrual periods, however she is not concerned.

## Parents and Adolescent Peers

Initially, the young dieter receives considerable praise from her friends and parents regarding her weight loss. They notice it. They notice her. Many people comment about the "slenderness" of her appearance and how "fashionable" she looks. Our teenage dieter begins to feel that others admire her resolve, and envy her. After all, glamorous models in fashion magazines, TV actresses and movie stars are all attractive and thin. She asks herself quietly, should she stop her dieting now, or should she continue until she loses just a few more pounds? She actively resists any suggestion from her peers or parents that she is too thin and must gain weight. Our young dieter believes that others are just jealous, and is firmly convinced that she still looks too fat! Although she has lost more than 20% of her original weight (which was normal by the Metropolitan Life Insurance Charts), she is still afraid to eat more for fear that she will be fat!

## Summary

This case description of a young girl in the early stages of anorexia nervosa and progressing further into the disorder. The educator can inquire, gently, with the young girl about her dieting behavior and listen for clues associated with the disorder. More importantly, the educator can also inquire of the young girls friends to learn about the young dieter's behavior outside the classroom. In a parent conference the educator is able to learn about the young dieter's behavior at home.

Educators, who are informed of the symptoms of anorexia nervosa, are able to identify potential anorectics and refer them to psychological services early in the onset of the disorder and increase the likelihood of a more favorable prognosis.

## References

*Diagnostics and Statistics Manual of Mental Disorders* (Fourth Edition), American Psychological Association; 1994, pp. 539-545.

Sours, John A.M.O. *Starving to Death in a Sea of Objects.* New York, Jasm Aronson, 1980.

Wesley, Myrna M., and Ruddy, Sue, Gibson. Anorexia Nervosa; an Obsession with Thinness, *Forecast for Home Economics,* September 1981.

# Part Six

# Additional Help and Information

Chapter 37

# *Glossary*

**Abdominal fat:** Fat (Adipose tissue) that is centrally distributed between the thorax and pelvis.

**Aerobic exercise:** A type of physical activity that includes walking, jogging, running, and dancing. Aerobic training improves the efficiency of the aerobic energy-producing systems that can improve cardio-respiratory endurance.

**Allotriophagy:** Eating strange things; an older term for pica (*see* pica).

**Anemia:** Not enough red blood, red blood cells, or hemoglobin in the body. Hemoglobin is a protein in the blood that contains iron.

**Amenorrhea:** The absence of menstruation when it would normally be expected.

**Anorexia:** Loss of appetite for food.

---

Definitions in this glossary were excerpted and adapted from "The Diabetes Dictionary," NIH Publication No. 94-3016; "The Digestive Diseases Dictionary," NIH Publication No. 97-2750; "Clinical Guidelines on the Identification, Evaluation, and Treatment of Overweight and Obesity in Adults," National Heart, Lung, and Blood Institute (NHLBI), 1998; "Eating Disorders," Office on Women's Health, U.S. Department of Health and Human Services, February 2000, and *Diet Information for Teens*, Omnigraphics, Inc. 2001.

**Anorexia nervosa:** An eating disorder in which people can literally starve themselves to death. People with this disorder have an intense and overpowering fear of body fat and weight gain. Anorexia is identified in part by refusal to eat, an intense desire to be thin, repeated dieting attempts, and excessive weight loss. To maintain an abnormally low weight, people with anorexia may diet, fast, or over exercise. They often engage in behaviors such as self-induced vomiting or the misuse of laxatives, diuretics, or enemas. People with anorexia believe that they are overweight even when they are extremely thin.

**Appetite:** Desire for something, especially food.

**Binge eating disorder (BED):** A disorder primarily identified by repeated episodes of uncontrolled eating. The overeating or bingeing does not typically stop until the person is uncomfortably full. Unlike anorexia nervosa and bulimia nervosa, however, BED is not associated with behaviors such as vomiting or excessive exercise to rid the body of extra food.

**Body dysmorphic disorder:** A disorder in which people suffer from preoccupations concerning imagined or slight defects in their physical appearance.

**Bulimia:** Refers to extreme hunger.

**Bulimia nervosa:** An eating disorder in which people follow a routine of secretive, uncontrolled or binge eating (ingesting an abnormally large amount of food within a set period of time) followed by behaviors to rid the body of food consumed. This includes self-induced vomiting and/or the misuse of laxatives, diet pills, diuretics (water pills), excessive exercise or fasting. As with anorexia nervosa, those with bulimia are overly concerned with food, body weight, and shape.

**Calorie:** Energy that comes from food. Some foods have more calories than others. Fats have many calories. Most vegetables have few.

**Carbohydrate:** One of the three main classes of foods and a source of energy. Carbohydrates are mainly sugars and starches that the body breaks down into glucose (a simple sugar that the body can use to feed its cells). The body also uses carbohydrates to make a substance called glycogen that is stored in the liver and muscles for future use.

# Glossary

**Cholesterol:** A fat-like substance found in blood, muscle, liver, brain, and other tissues in people and animals. The body makes and needs some cholesterol. Too much cholesterol, however, may cause fat to build up in the artery walls and cause a disease that slows or stops the flow of blood. Butter and egg yolks are foods that have a lot of cholesterol.

**Constipation:** A condition in which the stool becomes hard and dry. A person who is constipated usually has fewer than three bowel movements in a week. Bowel movements may be painful.

**Diabetes mellitus:** A disease that occurs when the body is not able to use sugar as it should. The body needs sugar for growth and energy for daily activities. It gets sugar when it changes food into glucose (a form of sugar). A hormone called insulin is needed for the glucose to be taken up and used by the body. Diabetes occurs when the body cannot make use of the glucose in the blood for energy because either the pancreas is not able to make enough insulin or the insulin that is available is not effective. The beta cells in areas of the pancreas called the islets of Langerhans usually make insulin.

There are two main types of diabetes mellitus: insulin-dependent (Type I) and noninsulin-dependent (Type II). In insulin-dependent diabetes (IDDM), the pancreas makes little or no insulin because the insulin-producing beta cells have been destroyed. This type usually appears suddenly and most commonly in younger people under age 30. Treatment consists of daily insulin injections or use of an insulin pump, a planned diet and regular exercise, and daily self-monitoring of blood glucose.

In noninsulin-dependent diabetes (NIDDM), the pancreas makes some insulin, sometimes too much. The insulin, however, is not effective. NIDDM is controlled by diet and exercise and daily monitoring of glucose levels. Sometimes oral drugs that lower blood glucose levels or insulin injections are needed. This type of diabetes usually develops gradually, most often in people over 40 years of age. NIDDM accounts for 90 to 95 percent of diabetes.

**Digestion:** The process the body uses to break down food into simple substances for energy, growth, and cell repair.

**Dietitian:** An expert in nutrition who helps people with special health needs plan the kinds and amounts of foods to eat. A registered dietitian (R.D.) has special qualifications.

**Disordered eating:** Refers to troublesome eating behaviors, such as restrictive dieting, bingeing, or purging, which occur less frequently or are less severe than those required to meet the full criteria for the diagnosis of an eating disorder.

**Dysphagia:** Problems in swallowing food or liquid, usually caused by blockage or injury to the esophagus.

**Eating disorders**: Complex, chronic illnesses with numerous physical, psychological, and social ramifications, including significant weight preoccupation, inappropriate eating behavior, and body image distortion. Many people with eating disorders experience depression, anxiety, substance abuse, and childhood sexual abuse. Eating disorders are often misunderstood and misdiagnosed. The most common eating disorders—anorexia nervosa, bulimia nervosa, and binge eating disorder—are on the rise in the United States and worldwide.

**Edema:** A swelling or puffiness of some part of the body such as the ankles. Water or other body fluids collect in the cells and cause the swelling.

**Enzymes:** A special type of protein. Enzymes help the body's chemistry work better and more quickly. Each enzyme usually has its own chemical job to do such as helping to change starch into glucose (sugar).

**Exercise:** Intentional physical activity performed for the purpose of achieving or maintaining fitness.

**Fats:** One of the three main classes of foods and a source of energy in the body. Fats help the body use some vitamins and keep the skin healthy. They also serve as energy stores for the body. In food, there are two types of fats: saturated and unsaturated.

Saturated fats are solid at room temperature and come chiefly from animal food products. Some examples are butter, lard, meat fat, solid shortening, palm oil, and coconut oil. These fats tend to raise the level of cholesterol, a fat-like substance in the blood.

Unsaturated fats, which include monounsaturated fats and polyunsaturated fats, are liquid at room temperature and come from plant oils such as olive, peanut, corn, cottonseed, sunflower, safflower, and soybean.

**Fiber:** A substance found in foods that come from plants. The two types of fiber in food are soluble and insoluble. Soluble fiber, found in beans, fruits, and oat products, dissolves in water. Insoluble fiber, found in whole-grain products and vegetables, passes directly through the digestive system, helping to rid the body of waste products.

**Geophagia:** A form of pica (*see* pica) characterized by eating substances from the earth, such as clay and dirt. Some cultures practice geophagia for traditional reasons. It can lead to iron deficiency.

**Heredity:** The passing of a trait such as color of the eyes from parent to child. A person "inherits" these traits through the genes.

**Hyperorexia:** Extreme appetite.

**Laxatives:** Medicines to relieve long-term constipation. Used only if other methods fail. Also called cathartics.

**Malnutrition:** A condition caused by not eating enough food or not eating a balanced diet.

**Metabolism:** The term for the way cells chemically change food so that it can be used to keep the body alive. It is a two-part process. One part is called catabolism—when the body uses food for energy. The other is called anabolism—when the body uses food to build or mend cells. Insulin is necessary for the metabolism of food.

**Nausea:** The feeling of wanting to throw up (vomit).

**Obesity:** When people have 20 percent (or more) extra body fat for their age, height, sex, and bone structure.

**Pica:** An eating disorder characterized by craving inedible substances not normally eaten. Examples include clay, dirt, chalk, dried paint, sand, toothpaste, and broken crockery.

**Polyphagia:** Great hunger; a sign of diabetes. People with this great hunger often lose weight.

**Protein:** One of the three main classes of food. Proteins are made of amino acids, which are called the building blocks of the cells. The cells need proteins to grow and to mend themselves. Protein is found in many foods such as meat, fish, poultry, and eggs.

Chapter 38

# Resources for Further Help and Information

## Federal Government

### Office on Women's Health
200 Independence Ave. SW, Room 730B
Washington, DC 20201
Tel: (202) 690-7650
Fax: (202) 690-7172
Internet: http://www.4woman.gov

### Food and Drug Administration
5600 Fishers Lane
Rockville, MD 20857-0001
Tel: (888) INFO-FDA (463-6332)
Internet: http://www.fda.gov

### National Institute of Mental Health
Public Inquiries Section
6001 Executive Boulevard, Rm. 8184, MSC 9663
Bethesda, MD 20892-9663
Tel: (301) 443-4513
Fax: (301) 443-4279
Internet: http://www.nimh.nih.gov

---

U.S. Department of Health and Human Services (DHHS), 2000. Contact information verified in March 2001.

281

## Weight-control Information Network (WIN)

A service of the National Institute of Diabetes and Diseases of the Kidney (NIDDK)
Weight-Control Information Network
1 Win Way
Bethesda, MD 20892-3665
Phone: (202) 828-1025 or (877) 946-4627
Fax: (202) 828-1028
Internet: http://www.niddk.nih.gov

## Other Resources

### National Eating Disorders Association, Inc.

603 Stewart Street
Suite 803
Seattle, WA 98101
Tel: (206) 382-3587
Internet: http://www.edap.org

### Harvard Eating Disorders Center

356 Boylston Street
Boston, MA 02116
Tel: (617) 236-7766
Internet: http://www.hedc.org
E-Mail: info@hedc.org

### National Association of Anorexia Nervosa and Associated Disorders

P.O. Box 7
Highland Park, IL 60035
Tel: (847) 831-3438
Fax: (847) 433-4632
Internet: http://www.anad.org
E-Mail: info@anad.org

### Pennsylvania Educational Network on Eating Disorders

3277 Cedar Run Road
Allison Park, PA 15101
Tel: (412) 366-9966

Chapter 39

# "Links" to More Information

## Links to Websites Providing Free Information

### Barton J. Blinder, MD
http://www.ltspeed.com/bjblinder/atpinx.htm

Dr. Blinder is a psychiatrist who has worked in the field of eating disorders for many years. His site includes scholarly, but very readable, articles on many different aspects of these perplexing disorders.

### The National Women's Health Information Center
http://www.4woman.gov

NWHIC is a health information and Federal publication referral service that provides a gateway to women's health information from other government agencies, public and private organizations, and consumer and health care professional groups. Of special interest is "Anorexics Sentenced to Death." Also available is an eating disorders information packet which was originally designed for middle-school educators. It can be downloaded.

### OBGYNnet: Women's Health
http://www.obgyn.net

A site that allows medical professionals, the medical industry, and women to publish information, access information, and interact on a global scale. One subsection is a terrific resource for general health information and a personal favorite of the ANRED staff.

### Eat Well, Live Well
http://www.healthyeating.org

Want to know what a healthy diet looks like? Want to see how nutritious your own meals are? Want to learn how to make nutrition acceptable for kids? Check these folks out. They have lots of good information in easily accessible form.

### The Academy for Eating Disorders
http://www.acadeatdis.org

The Academy for Eating Disorders is a multidisciplinary association of academic and clinical professionals with demonstrated interest and expertise in the field of eating disorders. A good resource for professionals.

### Something Fishy
http://www.something-fishy.org

Lots of well-organized information and lots of personal outreach.

### Mirror, Mirror, On the Wall . . .
http://www.mirror-mirror.org/eatdis.htm

Another well-organized and comprehensive site.

### Body Image Betrayal and Related Issues
http://www.bibri.com

Of special interest to people with eating disorders who have also survived domestic violence and sexual abuse. Lots of encouragement and support.

### Grant Me the Serenity . . .
http://open-mind.org

A directory for people wanting information about recovery from the compulsive use of drugs, alcohol, sex, and food. The site has a 12-step flavor but includes other resources as well.

### Addiction Resource Guide
http://www.addictionresourceguide.com

Many people are fighting an eating disorder plus chemical dependency. In treatment it seems to be more effective to begin with the substance abuse. This resource contains a directory of addiction treatment facilities, some of which also have special tracks for people with eating disorders.

### NEDIC: National Information Centre of Canada
http://www.nedic.on.ca

Established in 1985 to provide information and resources on eating disorders and weight preoccupation.

### Eating Disorders Referral and Information Center
http://www.edreferral.com

Good information plus a referral service for ED treatment providers in the USA and abroad. Be sure to read their disclaimers, and be a wise consumer of services.

### Cyclic Vomiting Syndrome Association
http://www.beaker.iupui.edu/cvsa/index.html

There is little information about this little known and under researched condition. The people who manage this site make an effort to collect available facts, hypotheses, and tips for sufferers.

### Harvard Eating Disorders Center
http://www.hedc.org

A large mental health website with information on psychological disorders and psychiatric medications. Also available are mental health chats, support groups, journals, diaries, online psychological tests, breaking mental health and medical news, and more.

### EDAP: Eating Disorders Awareness and Prevention
http://www.edap.org

ANRED's sister organization. Visit their Web site to learn about their extensive services and programs. EDAP offers a toll-free telephone number (1-800-931-2237) for people who want to speak to a real live person. The number provides a safe and confidential way to ask questions, receive free information, and receive referrals to an eating disorder professional in your area.

### National Centre for Eating Disorders
http://www.eating-disorders.org.uk

A resource for our friends in the U.K. The centre offers counseling, training, and information.

### Recovery Resources Online
http://www.soberrecovery.com

This organization provides thousands of links to mental health, eating disorders, and recovery resources: alcoholism, dual diagnosis, sober living, grief and loss, food addiction, sexual addiction, gambling addiction, twelve step meetings, sober chat, counseling and therapy, and treatment facilities. They also have information on treatment facilities.

### ZapHealth
http://www.zaphealth.com

A site that provides information to teens about a wide variety of health topics. They provide a wealth of articles and resources in easy-to-read format, and the site is intuitively navigable.

## Links to Websites Providing
## Fee-Based Services and Treatment Programs

### Gürze Books
http://www.gurze.com

This specialty bookseller provides books and videos about anorexia nervosa, bulimia nervosa, other eating disorders, obesity, self-image, and size acceptance. Gürze also publishes *Eating Disorders Digest,* a newsletter for professionals.

### Jean Kilbourne
http://www.jeankilbourne.com

Jean Kilbourne has been doing research on advertising, the media, and women's issues for many years. Her film "Killing Us Softly: Advertising's Image of Women" is a classic. She has just published her first book, *"Deadly Persuasion: Why Women and Girls Must Fight the Addictive Power of Advertising."* For information about the book, visit its Web site. To learn more about Jean Kilbourne, see her background page.

## CRIAW
http://www.criaw-icref.ca

The Canadian Research Institute for the Advancement of Women has issued two publications on young women and body image. *That Body Image Thing: Young Women Speak Out* is a collection of essays, written by young women in Canada. A parallel volume of essays, *Le corps en tête: Les jeunes femmes s'expriment,* was written by young francophone women.

## St. Joseph Medical Center
http://www.eating-disorders.com

A well-constructed site that offers information about eating disorders and also about the hospital's comprehensive, multidisciplinary treatment program.

## Rader Programs
http://www.raderprograms.com

Information about eating disorders and a Twelve Step treatment program.

## Rogers Memorial Hospital
http://www.rogershospital.org

This facility has the only program in the U.S. that we know of that treats male patients on an exclusively male unit in a residential setting.

## Monte Nido Residential Treatment Center
http://www.montenido.com

Located in Southern California. A facility designed and created by recovered professionals to help women suffering from anorexia nervosa, bulimia, and exercise addiction.

## Menninger Hospital and Clinic
http://www.menninger.edu

Located in Topeka, Kansas. This long-time provider of mental health care has expanded both its adult and child and adolescent eating disorders programs.

## Canopy Cove
http://canopycove.com

A residential day treatment program in Florida. Multi-disciplinary and comprehensive. The site includes a complete description of program components.

## Yale University Center for Eating and Weight Disorders
http://www.yale.edu/ycewd

The center serves both men and women. Located in New Haven, Connecticut, it provides services to the public, trains doctoral students, and conducts research.

## Radiance Magazine
http://www.radiancemagazine.com

A magazine full of information and support for people who do not have the unrealistically thin bodies featured in mainstream media.

## Geri's Recovery Music
http://www.geri.net

Geri is a recovering compulsive overeater and singer/songwriter. This attractive site tells her story and showcases the music that has been a part of her healing. Online ordering is available.

## Milestones in Recovery
http://business.msn.com/milestones

Provides residential and intensive outpatient programs for people suffering from compulsive eating, food addiction, bulimia, and related disorders. Milestones is a therapuetic community that offers a supportive environment where people can begin a new way of life called "recovery."

## Healthy Within
http://www.healthywithin.com

A day treatment and outpatient program for eating disorders that serves adolescent males and females plus adult males and females. A multidisciplinary team provides comprehensive treatment. Treatment plans are individualized, and therapy groups are small so people can practice new behaviors and learn new ways of relating to themselves and others.

## DietFreeSolution
http://www.dietfreesolution.com

Research shows that dieting does not work. Visit this organization which is dedicated to healthy, lifelong weight management WITHOUT dieting.

## Center for Discovery and Adolescent Change
http://www.centerfordiscovery.com

The center is a California state-licensed and JCAHO-accredited facility that specializes in the treatment of adolescents between the ages of eleven and seventeen who suffer from emotional and behavioral disorders, substance abuse, and eating disorders, and who can benefit from a psychological and residential treatment program.

## Eating Disorders Resource and Referral Service of San Diego
http://www.eatingdisorders-sd.com

This Southern California association of licensed psychotherapists specializes in the assessment and treatment of eating disorders. They also offer workshops, training, supervision, and consultation to therapists and other health professionals.

## Eating Disorders Recovery: Information and Links
http://www.joannapoppink.com

This site offers educational articles, access to a list of residential treatment programs, links to outpatient treatment sources, links to therapeutic information related to eating disorders (e.g., trauma and dissociative states), and other eating disorders resources on the Web.

## Laurel Hill Inn
http://www.laurelhillinn.com

Laurel Hill Inn is a private residential program for the treatment of eating disorders. Located in the greater Boston area, the program delivers personalized multidisciplinary treatment to a small group of residents. For more information, call 781-396-1116 or visit their website.

## COPE
http://www.wpic.pitt.edu/clinical/CLINSERV/eating.htm

The University of Pittsburgh Medical Clinic's Center for Overcoming Problem Eating conducts research and offers recovery programs for individuals with eating disorders. They are one of the oldest programs in the U.S. and one of the most respected. They offer treatment as well as opportunities for qualified volunteers to participate in up-to-date research studies.

### *Capital Health Authority Eating Disorders Program*
http://www.cha.ab.ca/healthsite/pk3149sh.asp

Alberta, Canada's only inpatient/outpatient program for people with severe eating disorders such as anorexia nervosa and bulimia. The program is located in the University of Alberta Hospital in Edmonton.

# Index

# *Index*

Page numbers followed by 'n' indicate a footnote. Page numbers in *italics* indicate a table or illustration.

## A

293

phenelzine 70
phenolphthalein 94
Phillips, Katharine A. 85–87
*Physical Activity and Weight Control* (NIH) 222
physical examination
  anorexia nervosa 54
  bulimia nervosa 60, 68–69
  night-eating syndrome 101
pica 106–8
  defined 279
Pizzulli, Cynthia 132, 138, 139, 140
podophyllin 91
polyphagia, defined 279
polysubstance abuse 65
polyunsaturated fats 278
Pomice, Eva 189
post-traumatic feeding disorder 227–28
post-traumatic stress disorder 65
potassium 29, 94
  bulimia nervosa 5
potassium loss *see* hypokalemia
power issues, eating disorders 23, 120, 159
Prader-Willi syndrome 109–10
pregnancy
  eating disorders 157–60
  pica 106, 107
*Prescription Medications for the Treatment of Obesity* (NIH) 222
Project Innovation 267n
proteins, defined 279
Prozac (fluoxetine) 30, 87
psychiatric illnesses, bulimia nervosa 65, 65–66
"Psychological Consequences of Food Restriction" 165n
psychological factors
  eating disorders 28, 41–42, 120, 233
  starvation 165–73
psychosexual development 49
psychotherapy
  anorexia nervosa 53, 55
  binge eating disorder 80
  bulimia nervosa 61, 71–72
  childhood eating disorders 245–46
  laxative abuse 98
psyllium 90–91, 96

purgatives 90, *92*
  listed 92
purging
  behavior complications 52
  defined 78
  methods 144
Putakian, Margot 137

**Q**

"Questionable dieting behaviors are used by young adults regardless of sex or student status" (Peters, et al.) 205n

**R**

Rader Programs, website 287
Radiance Magazine, website 288
"Rating the Diets" (*Consumer Reports*) 223
Reasoner, Robert 266
Recovery Resources Online, website 286
Reese, Jeff 136
renal failure *51*
*A Report of the Surgeon General: Physical Activity and Health. 1996* (CDC) 223
Resnick, Michael D. 249n
ritualistic behavior, anorexia nervosa 49
*RN* 25n
Rogers Memorial Hospital, website 287
Romeo, Felicia 267n
Rutgers Eating Disorders Clinic, contact information 82

**S**

saturated fats 278
Saylor, Billy Jack 137
"School-Based Programs for Preventing Eating Disturbances" (Neumark-Sztainer) 231n
secrecy, bulimia nervosa 5, 27, 60

# Health Reference Series
## COMPLETE CATALOG

## AIDS Sourcebook, 1st Edition

*Basic Information about AIDS and HIV Infection, Featuring Historical and Statistical Data, Current Research, Prevention, and Other Special Topics of Interest for Persons Living with AIDS*

*Along with Source Listings for Further Assistance*

Edited by Karen Bellenir and Peter D. Dresser. 831 pages. 1995. 0-7808-0031-1. $78.

"One strength of this book is its practical emphasis. The intended audience is the lay reader . . . useful as an educational tool for health care providers who work with AIDS patients. Recommended for public libraries as well as hospital or academic libraries that collect consumer materials."
—*Bulletin of the Medical Library Association, Jan '96*

"This is the most comprehensive volume of its kind on an important medical topic. Highly recommended for all libraries." —*Reference Book Review, '96*

"Very useful reference for all libraries."
—*Choice, Association of College and Research Libraries, Oct '95*

"There is a wealth of information here that can provide much educational assistance. It is a must book for all libraries and should be on the desk of each and every congressional leader. Highly recommended."
—*AIDS Book Review Journal, Aug '95*

"Recommended for most collections."
—*Library Journal, Jul '95*

## AIDS Sourcebook, 2nd Edition

*Basic Consumer Health Information about Acquired Immune Deficiency Syndrome (AIDS) and Human Immunodeficiency Virus (HIV) Infection, Featuring Updated Statistical Data, Reports on Recent Research and Prevention Initiatives, and Other Special Topics of Interest for Persons Living with AIDS, Including New Antiretroviral Treatment Options, Strategies for Combating Opportunistic Infections, Information about Clinical Trials, and More*

*Along with a Glossary of Important Terms and Resource Listings for Further Help and Information*

Edited by Karen Bellenir. 751 pages. 1999. 0-7808-0225-X. $78.

"Highly recommended."
—*American Reference Books Annual, 2000*

"Excellent sourcebook. This continues to be a highly recommended book. There is no other book that provides as much information as this book provides."
—*AIDS Book Review Journal, Dec-Jan 2000*

"Recommended reference source."
—*Booklist, American Library Association, Dec '99*

"A solid text for college-level health libraries."
—*The Bookwatch, Aug '99*

Cited in *Reference Sources for Small and Medium-Sized Libraries, American Library Association, 1999*

## Alcoholism Sourcebook

*Basic Consumer Health Information about the Physical and Mental Consequences of Alcohol Abuse, Including Liver Disease, Pancreatitis, Wernicke-Korsakoff Syndrome (Alcoholic Dementia), Fetal Alcohol Syndrome, Heart Disease, Kidney Disorders, Gastrointestinal Problems, and Immune System Compromise and Featuring Facts about Addiction, Detoxification, Alcohol Withdrawal, Recovery, and the Maintenance of Sobriety*

*Along with a Glossary and Directories of Resources for Further Help and Information*

Edited by Karen Bellenir. 613 pages. 2000. 0-7808-0325-6. $78.

"This title is one of the few reference works on alcoholism for general readers. For some readers this will be a welcome complement to the many self-help books on the market. Recommended for collections serving general readers and consumer health collections."
—*E-Streams, Mar '01*

"This book is an excellent choice for public and academic libraries."
—*American Reference Books Annual, 2001*

"Recommended reference source."
—*Booklist, American Library Association, Dec '00*

"Presents a wealth of information on alcohol use and abuse and its effects on the body and mind, treatment, and prevention." —*SciTech Book News, Dec '00*

"Important new health guide which packs in the latest consumer information about the problems of alcoholism." —*Reviewer's Bookwatch, Nov '00*

*SEE ALSO Drug Abuse Sourcebook, Substance Abuse Sourcebook*

## Allergies Sourcebook, 1st Edition

*Basic Information about Major Forms and Mechanisms of Common Allergic Reactions, Sensitivities, and Intolerances, Including Anaphylaxis, Asthma, Hives and Other Dermatologic Symptoms, Rhinitis, and Sinusitis*

*Along with Their Usual Triggers Like Animal Fur, Chemicals, Drugs, Dust, Foods, Insects, Latex, Pollen, and Poison Ivy, Oak, and Sumac; Plus Information on Prevention, Identification, and Treatment*

Edited by Allan R. Cook. 611 pages. 1997. 0-7808-0036-2. $78.

# Allergies Sourcebook, 2nd Edition

Basic Consumer Health Information about Allergic Disorders, Triggers, Reactions, and Related Symptoms, Including Anaphylaxis, Rhinitis, Sinusitis, Asthma, Dermatitis, Conjunctivitis, and Multiple Chemical Sensitivity

Along with Tips on Diagnosis, Prevention, and Treatment, Statistical Data, a Glossary, and a Directory of Sources for Further Help and Information

Edited by Annemarie S. Muth. 600 pages. 2001. 0-7808-0376-0. $78.

# Alternative Medicine Sourcebook

Basic Consumer Health Information about Alternatives to Conventional Medicine, Including Acupressure, Acupuncture, Aromatherapy, Ayurveda, Bioelectromagnetics, Environmental Medicine, Essence Therapy, Food and Nutrition Therapy, Herbal Therapy, Homeopathy, Imaging, Massage, Naturopathy, Reflexology, Relaxation and Meditation, Sound Therapy, Vitamin and Mineral Therapy, and Yoga, and More

Edited by Allan R. Cook. 737 pages. 1999. 0-7808-0200-4. $78.

"Recommended reference source."
—Booklist, American Library Association, Feb '00

"A great addition to the reference collection of every type of library." —American Reference Books Annual, 2000

# Alzheimer's, Stroke & 29 Other Neurological Disorders Sourcebook, 1st Edition

Basic Information for the Layperson on 31 Diseases or Disorders Affecting the Brain and Nervous System, First Describing the Illness, Then Listing Symptoms, Diagnostic Methods, and Treatment Options, and Including Statistics on Incidences and Causes

Edited by Frank E. Bair. 579 pages. 1993. 1-55888-748-2. $78.

"Nontechnical reference book that provides reader-friendly information."
—Family Caregiver Alliance Update, Winter '96

"Should be included in any library's patient education section." —American Reference Books Annual, 1994

"Written in an approachable and accessible style. Recommended for patient education and consumer health collections in health science center and public libraries." —Academic Library Book Review, Dec '93

"It is very handy to have information on more than thirty neurological disorders under one cover, and there is no recent source like it." —Reference Quarterly, American Library Association, Fall '93

SEE ALSO Brain Disorders Sourcebook

# Alzheimer's Disease Sourcebook, 2nd Edition

Basic Consumer Health Information about Alzheimer's Disease, Related Disorders, and Other Dementias, Including Multi-Infarct Dementia, AIDS-Related Dementia, Alcoholic Dementia, Huntington's Disease, Delirium, and Confusional States

Along with Reports Detailing Current Research Efforts in Prevention and Treatment, Long-Term Care Issues, and Listings of Sources for Additional Help and Information

Edited by Karen Bellenir. 524 pages. 1999. 0-7808-0223-3. $78.

"Provides a wealth of useful information not otherwise available in one place. This resource is recommended for all types of libraries."
—American Reference Books Annual, 2000

"Recommended reference source."
—Booklist, American Library Association, Oct '99

# Arthritis Sourcebook

Basic Consumer Health Information about Specific Forms of Arthritis and Related Disorders, Including Rheumatoid Arthritis, Osteoarthritis, Gout, Polymyalgia Rheumatica, Psoriatic Arthritis, Spondyloarthropathies, Juvenile Rheumatoid Arthritis, and Juvenile Ankylosing Spondylitis

Along with Information about Medical, Surgical, and Alternative Treatment Options, and Including Strategies for Coping with Pain, Fatigue, and Stress

Edited by Allan R. Cook. 550 pages. 1998. 0-7808-0201-2. $78.

"... accessible to the layperson."
—Reference and Research Book News, Feb '99

# Asthma Sourcebook

Basic Consumer Health Information about Asthma, Including Symptoms, Traditional and Nontraditional Remedies, Treatment Advances, Quality-of-Life Aids, Medical Research Updates, and the Role of Allergies, Exercise, Age, the Environment, and Genetics in the Development of Asthma

Along with Statistical Data, a Glossary, and Directories of Support Groups, and Other Resources for Further Information

Edited by Annemarie S. Muth. 628 pages. 2000. 0-7808-0381-7. $78.

"A worthwhile reference acquisition for public libraries and academic medical libraries whose readers desire a quick introduction to the wide range of asthma information." —Choice, Association of College and Research Libraries, Jun '01

"Recommended reference source."
—Booklist, American Library Association, Feb '01

## Back & Neck Disorders Sourcebook

Basic Information about Disorders and Injuries of the Spinal Cord and Vertebrae, Including Facts on Chiropractic Treatment, Surgical Interventions, Paralysis, and Rehabilitation

Along with Advice for Preventing Back Trouble

Edited by Karen Bellenir. 548 pages. 1997. 0-7808-0202-0. $78.

## Blood & Circulatory Disorders Sourcebook

Basic Information about Blood and Its Components, Anemias, Leukemias, Bleeding Disorders, and Circulatory Disorders, Including Aplastic Anemia, Thalassemia, Sickle-Cell Disease, Hemochromatosis, Hemophilia, Von Willebrand Disease, and Vascular Diseases

Along with a Special Section on Blood Transfusions and Blood Supply Safety, a Glossary, and Source Listings for Further Help and Information

Edited by Karen Bellenir and Linda M. Shin. 554 pages. 1998. 0-7808-0203-9. $78.

## Brain Disorders Sourcebook

Basic Consumer Health Information about Strokes, Epilepsy, Amyotrophic Lateral Sclerosis (ALS/Lou Gehrig's Disease), Parkinson's Disease, Brain Tumors, Cerebral Palsy, Headache, Tourette Syndrome, and More

Along with Statistical Data, Treatment and Rehabilitation Options, Coping Strategies, Reports on Current

Research Initiatives, a Glossary, and Resource Listings for Additional Help and Information

Edited by Karen Bellenir. 481 pages. 1999. 0-7808-0229-2. $78.

SEE ALSO Alzheimer's, Stroke & 29 Other Neurological Disorders Sourcebook, 1st Edition

## Breast Cancer Sourcebook

Basic Consumer Health Information about Breast Cancer, Including Diagnostic Methods, Treatment Options, Alternative Therapies, Self-Help Information, Related Health Concerns, Statistical and Demographic Data, and Facts for Men with Breast Cancer

Along with Reports on Current Research Initiatives, a Glossary of Related Medical Terms, and a Directory of Sources for Further Help and Information

Edited by Edward J. Prucha and Karen Bellenir. 600 pages. 2001. 0-7808-0244-6. $78.

SEE ALSO Cancer Sourcebook for Women, 1st and 2nd Editions, Women's Health Concerns Sourcebook

## Breastfeeding Sourcebook

Basic Consumer Health Information about the Benefits of Breastmilk, Preparing to Breastfeed, Breastfeeding as a Baby Grows, Nutrition, and More, Including Information on Special Situations and Concerns, Such as Mastitis, Illness, Medications, Allergies, Multiple Births, Prematurity, Special Needs, and Adoption

Along with a Glossary and Resources for Additional Help and Information

Edited by Jenni Lynn Colson. 350 pages. 2001. 0-7808-0332-9. $48.

SEE ALSO Pregnancy & Birth Sourcebook

## Burns Sourcebook

Basic Consumer Health Information about Various Types of Burns and Scalds, Including Flame, Heat, Cold, Electrical, Chemical, and Sun Burns

Along with Information on Short-Term and Long-Term Treatments, Tissue Reconstruction, Plastic Surgery, Prevention Suggestions, and First Aid

Edited by Allan R. Cook. 604 pages. 1999. 0-7808-0204-7. $78.

■

# Cancer Sourcebook, 1st Edition

*Basic Information on Cancer Types, Symptoms, Diagnostic Methods, and Treatments, Including Statistics on Cancer Occurrences Worldwide and the Risks Associated with Known Carcinogens and Activities*

Edited by Frank E. Bair. 932 pages. 1990. 1-55888-888-8. $78.

Cited in *Reference Sources for Small and Medium-Sized Libraries,* American Library Association, 1999

■

# New Cancer Sourcebook, 2nd Edition

*Basic Information about Major Forms and Stages of Cancer, Featuring Facts about Primary and Secondary Tumors of the Respiratory, Nervous, Lymphatic, Circulatory, Skeletal, and Gastrointestinal Systems, and Specific Organs; Statistical and Demographic Data; Treatment Options; and Strategies for Coping*

Edited by Allan R. Cook. 1,313 pages. 1996. 0-7808-0041-9. $78.

■

# Cancer Sourcebook, 3rd Edition

*Basic Consumer Health Information about Major Forms and Stages of Cancer, Featuring Facts about Primary and Secondary Tumors of the Respiratory, Nervous, Lymphatic, Circulatory, Skeletal, and Gastrointestinal Systems, and Specific Organs*

*Along with Statistical and Demographic Data, Treatment Options, Strategies for Coping, a Glossary, and a Directory of Sources for Additional Help and Information*

Edited by Edward J. Prucha. 1,069 pages. 2000. 0-7808-0227-6. $78.

■

# Cancer Sourcebook for Women, 1st Edition

*Basic Information about Specific Forms of Cancer That Affect Women, Featuring Facts about Breast Cancer, Cervical Cancer, Ovarian Cancer, Cancer of the Uterus and Uterine Sarcoma, Cancer of the Vagina, and Cancer of the Vulva; Statistical and Demographic Data; Treatments, Self-Help Management Suggestions, and Current Research Initiatives*

Edited by Allan R. Cook and Peter D. Dresser. 524 pages. 1996. 0-7808-0076-1. $78.

*SEE ALSO* Breast Cancer Sourcebook, Women's Health Concerns Sourcebook

# Cancer Sourcebook for Women, 2nd Edition

*Basic Consumer Health Information about Specific Forms of Cancer That Affect Women, Including Cervical Cancer, Ovarian Cancer, Endometrial Cancer, Uterine Sarcoma, Vaginal Cancer, Vulvar Cancer, and Gestational Trophoblastic Tumor; and Featuring Statistical Information, Facts about Tests and Treatments, a Glossary of Cancer Terms, and an Extensive List of Additional Resources*

Edited by Karen Bellenir. 600 pages. 2001. 0-7808-0226-8. $78.

*SEE ALSO* Breast Cancer Sourcebook, Women's Health Concerns Sourcebook

# Cardiovascular Diseases & Disorders Sourcebook, 1st Edition

*Basic Information about Cardiovascular Diseases and Disorders, Featuring Facts about the Cardiovascular System, Demographic and Statistical Data, Descriptions of Pharmacological and Surgical Interventions, Lifestyle Modifications, and a Special Section Focusing on Heart Disorders in Children*

Edited by Karen Bellenir and Peter D. Dresser. 683 pages. 1995. 0-7808-0032-X. $78.

*SEE ALSO* Healthy Heart Sourcebook for Women, Heart Diseases & Disorders Sourcebook, 2nd Edition

# Caregiving Sourcebook

*Basic Consumer Health Information for Caregivers, Including a Profile of Caregivers, Caregiving Responsibilities and Concerns, Tips for Specific Conditions, Care Environments, and the Effects of Caregiving*

*Along with Facts about Legal Issues, Financial Information, and Future Planning, a Glossary, and a Listing of Additional Resources*

Edited by Joyce Brennfleck Shannon. 600 pages. 2001. 0-7808-0331-0. $78.

# Colds, Flu & Other Common Ailments Sourcebook

*Basic Consumer Health Information about Common Ailments and Injuries, Including Colds, Coughs, the Flu, Sinus Problems, Headaches, Fever, Nausea and Vomiting, Menstrual Cramps, Diarrhea, Constipation, Hemorrhoids, Back Pain, Dandruff, Dry and Itchy Skin, Cuts, Scrapes, Sprains, Bruises, and More*

*Along with Information about Prevention, Self-Care, Choosing a Doctor, Over-the-Counter Medications, Folk Remedies, and Alternative Therapies, and Including a Glossary of Important Terms and a Directory of Resources for Further Help and Information*

Edited by Chad T. Kimball. 638 pages. 2001. 0-7808-0435-X. $78.

# Communication Disorders Sourcebook

*Basic Information about Deafness and Hearing Loss, Speech and Language Disorders, Voice Disorders, Balance and Vestibular Disorders, and Disorders of Smell, Taste, and Touch*

Edited by Linda M. Ross. 533 pages. 1996. 0-7808-0077-X. $78.

# Congenital Disorders Sourcebook

*Basic Information about Disorders Acquired during Gestation, Including Spina Bifida, Hydrocephalus, Cerebral Palsy, Heart Defects, Craniofacial Abnormalities, Fetal Alcohol Syndrome, and More*

*Along with Current Treatment Options and Statistical Data*

Edited by Karen Bellenir. 607 pages. 1997. 0-7808-0205-5. $78.

*SEE ALSO* Pregnancy & Birth Sourcebook

# Consumer Issues in Health Care Sourcebook

Basic Information about Health Care Fundamentals and Related Consumer Issues, Including Exams and Screening Tests, Physician Specialties, Choosing a Doctor, Using Prescription and Over-the-Counter Medications Safely, Avoiding Health Scams, Managing Common Health Risks in the Home, Care Options for Chronically or Terminally Ill Patients, and a List of Resources for Obtaining Help and Further Information

Edited by Karen Bellenir. 618 pages. 1998. 0-7808-0221-7. $78.

"Both public and academic libraries will want to have a copy in their collection for readers who are interested in self-education on health issues."
—*American Reference Books Annual, 2000*

"The editor has researched the literature from government agencies and others, saving readers the time and effort of having to do the research themselves. Recommended for public libraries."
—*Reference and User Services Quarterly, American Library Association, Spring '99*

"Recommended reference source."
—*Booklist, American Library Association, Dec '98*

∎

# Contagious & Non-Contagious Infectious Diseases Sourcebook

Basic Information about Contagious Diseases like Measles, Polio, Hepatitis B, and Infectious Mononucleosis, and Non-Contagious Infectious Diseases like Tetanus and Toxic Shock Syndrome, and Diseases Occurring as Secondary Infections Such as Shingles and Reye Syndrome

Along with Vaccination, Prevention, and Treatment Information, and a Section Describing Emerging Infectious Disease Threats

Edited by Karen Bellenir and Peter D. Dresser. 566 pages. 1996. 0-7808-0075-3. $78.

∎

# Death & Dying Sourcebook

Basic Consumer Health Information for the Layperson about End-of-Life Care and Related Ethical and Legal Issues, Including Chief Causes of Death, Autopsies, Pain Management for the Terminally Ill, Life Support Systems, Insurance, Euthanasia, Assisted Suicide, Hospice Programs, Living Wills, Funeral Planning, Counseling, Mourning, Organ Donation, and Physician Training

Along with Statistical Data, a Glossary, and Listings of Sources for Further Help and Information

Edited by Annemarie S. Muth. 641 pages. 1999. 0-7808-0230-6. $78.

"Public libraries, medical libraries, and academic libraries will all find this sourcebook a useful addition to their collections."
—*American Reference Books Annual, 2001*

"An extremely useful resource for those concerned with death and dying in the United States."
—*Respiratory Care, Nov '00*

"Recommended reference source."
—*Booklist, American Library Association, Aug '00*

"This book is a definite must for all those involved in end-of-life care." —*Doody's Review Service, 2000*

∎

# Diabetes Sourcebook, 1st Edition

Basic Information about Insulin-Dependent and Non-insulin-Dependent Diabetes Mellitus, Gestational Diabetes, and Diabetic Complications, Symptoms, Treatment, and Research Results, Including Statistics on Prevalence, Morbidity, and Mortality

Along with Source Listings for Further Help and Information

Edited by Karen Bellenir and Peter D. Dresser. 827 pages. 1994. 1-55889-751-2. $78.

". . . very informative and understandable for the layperson without being simplistic. It provides a comprehensive overview for laypersons who want a general understanding of the disease or who want to focus on various aspects of the disease."
—*Bulletin of the Medical Library Association, Jan '96*

∎

# Diabetes Sourcebook, 2nd Edition

Basic Consumer Health Information about Type 1 Diabetes (Insulin-Dependent or Juvenile-Onset Diabetes), Type 2 (Noninsulin-Dependent or Adult-Onset Diabetes), Gestational Diabetes, and Related Disorders, Including Diabetes Prevalence Data, Management Issues, the Role of Diet and Exercise in Controlling Diabetes, Insulin and Other Diabetes Medicines, and Complications of Diabetes Such as Eye Diseases, Periodontal Disease, Amputation, and End-Stage Renal Disease

Along with Reports on Current Research Initiatives, a Glossary, and Resource Listings for Further Help and Information

Edited by Karen Bellenir. 688 pages. 1998. 0-7808-0224-1. $78.

"This comprehensive book is an excellent addition for high school, academic, medical, and public libraries. This volume is highly recommended."
—*American Reference Books Annual, 2000*

"An invaluable reference." —*Library Journal, May '00*

Selected as one of the 250 "Best Health Sciences Books of 1999." —*Doody's Rating Service, Mar-Apr 2000*

"Recommended reference source."
—*Booklist, American Library Association, Feb '99*

". . . provides reliable mainstream medical information . . . belongs on the shelves of any library with a consumer health collection." —*E-Streams, Sep '99*

"Provides useful information for the general public."
—*Healthlines, University of Michigan Health Management Research Center, Sep/Oct '99*

# Diet & Nutrition Sourcebook, 1st Edition

Basic Information about Nutrition, Including the Dietary Guidelines for Americans, the Food Guide Pyramid, and Their Applications in Daily Diet, Nutritional Advice for Specific Age Groups, Current Nutritional Issues and Controversies, the New Food Label and How to Use It to Promote Healthy Eating, and Recent Developments in Nutritional Research

Edited by Dan R. Harris. 662 pages. 1996. 0-7808-0084-2. $78.

"Useful reference as a food and nutrition sourcebook for the general consumer." —*Booklist Health Sciences Supplement, American Library Association, Oct '97*

"Recommended for public libraries and medical libraries that receive general information requests on nutrition. It is readable and will appeal to those interested in learning more about healthy dietary practices." —*Medical Reference Services Quarterly, Fall '97*

"An abundance of medical and social statistics is translated into readable information geared toward the general reader." —*Bookwatch, Mar '97*

"With dozens of questionable diet books on the market, it is so refreshing to find a reliable and factual reference book. Recommended to aspiring professionals, librarians, and others seeking and giving reliable dietary advice. An excellent compilation." —*Choice, Association of College and Research Libraries, Feb '97*

SEE ALSO *Digestive Diseases & Disorders Sourcebook, Gastrointestinal Diseases & Disorders Sourcebook*

# Diet & Nutrition Sourcebook, 2nd Edition

Basic Consumer Health Information about Dietary Guidelines, Recommended Daily Intake Values, Vitamins, Minerals, Fiber, Fat, Weight Control, Dietary Supplements, and Food Additives

Along with Special Sections on Nutrition Needs throughout Life and Nutrition for People with Such Specific Medical Concerns as Allergies, High Blood Cholesterol, Hypertension, Diabetes, Celiac Disease, Seizure Disorders, Phenylketonuria (PKU), Cancer, and Eating Disorders, and Including Reports on Current Nutrition Research and Source Listings for Additional Help and Information

Edited by Karen Bellenir. 650 pages. 1999. 0-7808-0228-4. $78.

"This book is an excellent source of basic diet and nutrition information." —*Booklist Health Sciences Supplement, American Library Association, Dec '00*

"This reference document should be in any public library, but it would be a very good guide for beginning students in the health sciences. If the other books in this publisher's series are as good as this, they should all be in the health sciences collections." —*American Reference Books Annual, 2000*

"This book is an excellent general nutrition reference for consumers who desire to take an active role in their health care for prevention. Consumers of all ages who select this book can feel confident they are receiving current and accurate information." —*Journal of Nutrition for the Elderly, Vol. 19, No. 4, '00*

"Recommended reference source." —*Booklist, American Library Association, Dec '99*

SEE ALSO *Digestive Diseases & Disorders Sourcebook, Gastrointestinal Diseases & Disorders Sourcebook*

# Digestive Diseases & Disorders Sourcebook

Basic Consumer Health Information about Diseases and Disorders that Impact the Upper and Lower Digestive System, Including Celiac Disease, Constipation, Crohn's Disease, Cyclic Vomiting Syndrome, Diarrhea, Diverticulosis and Diverticulitis, Gallstones, Heartburn, Hemorrhoids, Hernias, Indigestion (Dyspepsia), Irritable Bowel Syndrome, Lactose Intolerance, Ulcers, and More

Along with Information about Medications and Other Treatments, Tips for Maintaining a Healthy Digestive Tract, a Glossary, and Directory of Digestive Diseases Organizations

Edited by Karen Bellenir. 335 pages. 1999. 0-7808-0327-2. $48.

"This title would be an excellent addition to all public or patient-research libraries." —*American Reference Books Annual, 2001*

"This title is recommended for public, hospital, and health sciences libraries with consumer health collections." —*E-Streams, Jul-Aug '00*

"Recommended reference source." —*Booklist, American Library Association, May '00*

SEE ALSO *Diet & Nutrition Sourcebook, 1st and 2nd Editions, Gastrointestinal Diseases & Disorders Sourcebook*

# Disabilities Sourcebook

Basic Consumer Health Information about Physical and Psychiatric Disabilities, Including Descriptions of Major Causes of Disability, Assistive and Adaptive Aids, Workplace Issues, and Accessibility Concerns

Along with Information about the Americans with Disabilities Act, a Glossary, and Resources for Additional Help and Information

Edited by Dawn D. Matthews. 616 pages. 2000. 0-7808-0389-2. $78.

"A much needed addition to the Omnigraphics *Health Reference Series*. A current reference work to provide people with disabilities, their families, caregivers or those who work with them, a broad range of information in one volume, has not been available until now. . . . It is recommended for all public and academic library reference collections." —*E-Streams, May '01*

◼

# Domestic Violence & Child Abuse Sourcebook

*Basic Consumer Health Information about Spousal/ Partner, Child, Sibling, Parent, and Elder Abuse, Covering Physical, Emotional, and Sexual Abuse, Teen Dating Violence, and Stalking; Includes Information about Hotlines, Safe Houses, Safety Plans, and Other Resources for Support and Assistance, Community Initiatives, and Reports on Current Directions in Research and Treatment*

*Along with a Glossary, Sources for Further Reading, and Governmental and Non-Governmental Organizations Contact Information*

Edited by Helene Henderson. 1,064 pages. 2000. 0-7808-0235-7. $78.

◼

# Drug Abuse Sourcebook

*Basic Consumer Health Information about Illicit Substances of Abuse and the Diversion of Prescription Medications, Including Depressants, Hallucinogens, Inhalants, Marijuana, Narcotics, Stimulants, and Anabolic Steroids*

*Along with Facts about Related Health Risks, Treatment Issues, and Substance Abuse Prevention Programs, a Glossary of Terms, Statistical Data, and Directories of Hotline Services, Self-Help Groups, and Organizations Able to Provide Further Information*

Edited by Karen Bellenir. 629 pages. 2000. 0-7808-0242-X. $78.

*SEE ALSO Alcoholism Sourcebook, Substance Abuse Sourcebook*

◼

# Ear, Nose & Throat Disorders Sourcebook

*Basic Information about Disorders of the Ears, Nose, Sinus Cavities, Pharynx, and Larynx, Including Ear Infections, Tinnitus, Vestibular Disorders, Allergic and Non-Allergic Rhinitis, Sore Throats, Tonsillitis, and Cancers That Affect the Ears, Nose, Sinuses, and Throat*

*Along with Reports on Current Research Initiatives, a Glossary of Related Medical Terms, and a Directory of Sources for Further Help and Information*

Edited by Karen Bellenir and Linda M. Shin. 576 pages. 1998. 0-7808-0206-3. $78.

◼

# Eating Disorders Sourcebook

*Basic Consumer Health Information about Eating Disorders, Including Information about Anorexia Nervosa, Bulimia Nervosa, Binge Eating, Body Dysmorphic Disorder, Pica, Laxative Abuse, and Night Eating Syndrome*

*Along with Information about Causes, Adverse Effects, and Treatment and Prevention Issues, and Featuring a Section on Concerns Specific to Children and Adolescents, a Glossary, and Resources for Further Help and Information*

Edited by Dawn D. Matthews. 322 pages. 2001. 0-7808-0335-3. $78.

◼

# Endocrine & Metabolic Disorders Sourcebook

*Basic Information for the Layperson about Pancreatic and Insulin-Related Disorders Such as Pancreatitis, Diabetes, and Hypoglycemia; Adrenal Gland Disorders Such as Cushing's Syndrome, Addison's Disease, and Congenital Adrenal Hyperplasia; Pituitary Gland Disorders Such as Growth Hormone Deficiency, Acromegaly, and Pituitary Tumors; Thyroid Disorders Such as Hypothyroidism, Graves' Disease, Hashimoto's Disease, and Goiter; Hyperparathyroidism; and Other Diseases and Syndromes of Hormone Imbalance or Metabolic Dysfunction*

*Along with Reports on Current Research Initiatives*

Edited by Linda M. Shin. 574 pages. 1998. 0-7808-0207-1. $78.

# Environmentally Induced Disorders Sourcebook

*Basic Information about Diseases and Syndromes Linked to Exposure to Pollutants and Other Substances in Outdoor and Indoor Environments Such as Lead, Asbestos, Formaldehyde, Mercury, Emissions, Noise, and More*

Edited by Allan R. Cook. 620 pages. 1997. 0-7808-0083-4. $78.

# Ethnic Diseases Sourcebook

*Basic Consumer Health Information for Ethnic and Racial Minority Groups in the United States, Including General Health Indicators and Behaviors, Ethnic Diseases, Genetic Testing, the Impact of Chronic Diseases, Women's Health, Mental Health Issues, and Preventive Health Care Services*

*Along with a Glossary and a Listing of Additional Resources*

Edited by Joyce Brennfleck Shannon. 664 pages. 2001. 0-7808-0336-1. $78.

# Family Planning Sourcebook

*Basic Consumer Health Information about Planning for Pregnancy and Contraception, Including Traditional Methods, Barrier Methods, Hormonal Methods, Permanent Methods, Future Methods, Emergency Contraception, and Birth Control Choices for Women at Each Stage of Life*

*Along with Statistics, a Glossary, and Sources of Additional Information*

Edited by Amy Marcaccio Keyzer. 520 pages. 2001. 0-7808-0379-5. $78.

*SEE ALSO Pregnancy & Birth Sourcebook*

# Fitness & Exercise Sourcebook, 1st Edition

*Basic Information on Fitness and Exercise, Including Fitness Activities for Specific Age Groups, Exercise for People with Specific Medical Conditions, How to Begin a Fitness Program in Running, Walking, Swimming, Cycling, and Other Athletic Activities, and Recent Research in Fitness and Exercise*

Edited by Dan R. Harris. 663 pages. 1996. 0-7808-0186-5. $78.

# Fitness & Exercise Sourcebook, 2nd Edition

*Basic Consumer Health Information about the Fundamentals of Fitness and Exercise, Including How to Begin and Maintain a Fitness Program, Fitness as a Lifestyle, the Link between Fitness and Diet, Advice for Specific Groups of People, Exercise as It Relates to Specific Medical Conditions, and Recent Research in Fitness and Exercise*

*Along with a Glossary of Important Terms and Resources for Additional Help and Information*

Edited by Kristen M. Gledhill. 646 pages. 2001. 0-7808-0334-5. $78.

# Food & Animal Borne Diseases Sourcebook

*Basic Information about Diseases That Can Be Spread to Humans through the Ingestion of Contaminated Food or Water or by Contact with Infected Animals and Insects, Such as Botulism, E. Coli, Hepatitis A, Trichinosis, Lyme Disease, and Rabies*

*Along with Information Regarding Prevention and Treatment Methods, and Including a Special Section for International Travelers Describing Diseases Such as Cholera, Malaria, Travelers' Diarrhea, and Yellow Fever, and Offering Recommendations for Avoiding Illness*

Edited by Karen Bellenir and Peter D. Dresser. 535 pages. 1995. 0-7808-0033-8. $78.

313

# Food Safety Sourcebook

*Basic Consumer Health Information about the Safe Handling of Meat, Poultry, Seafood, Eggs, Fruit Juices, and Other Food Items, and Facts about Pesticides, Drinking Water, Food Safety Overseas, and the Onset, Duration, and Symptoms of Foodborne Illnesses, Including Types of Pathogenic Bacteria, Parasitic Protozoa, Worms, Viruses, and Natural Toxins*

*Along with the Role of the Consumer, the Food Handler, and the Government in Food Safety; a Glossary, and Resources for Additional Help and Information*

Edited by Dawn D. Matthews. 339 pages. 1999. 0-7808-0326-4. $48.

"This book is recommended for public libraries and universities with home economic and food science programs." — *E-Streams, Nov '00*

"This book takes the complex issues of food safety and foodborne pathogens and presents them in an easily understood manner. [It does] an excellent job of covering a large and often confusing topic."
— *American Reference Books Annual, 2000*

"Recommended reference source."
— *Booklist, American Library Association, May '00*

■

# Forensic Medicine Sourcebook

*Basic Consumer Information for the Layperson about Forensic Medicine, Including Crime Scene Investigation, Evidence Collection and Analysis, Expert Testimony, Computer-Aided Criminal Identification, Digital Imaging in the Courtroom, DNA Profiling, Accident Reconstruction, Autopsies, Ballistics, Drugs and Explosives Detection, Latent Fingerprints, Product Tampering, and Questioned Document Examination*

*Along with Statistical Data, a Glossary of Forensics Terminology, and Listings of Sources for Further Help and Information*

Edited by Annemarie S. Muth. 574 pages. 1999. 0-7808-0232-2. $78.

"Given the expected widespread interest in its content and its easy to read style, this book is recommended for most public and all college and university libraries."
— *E-Streams, Feb '01*

"There are several items that make this book attractive to consumers who are seeking certain forensic data.... This is a useful current source for those seeking general forensic medical answers."
— *American Reference Books Annual, 2000*

"Recommended for public libraries."
— *Reference & User Services Quarterly, American Library Association, Spring 2000*

"Recommended reference source."
— *Booklist, American Library Association, Feb '00*

"A wealth of information, useful statistics, references are up-to-date and extremely complete. This wonderful collection of data will help students who are interested in a career in any type of forensic field. It is a great

resource for attorneys who need information about types of expert witnesses needed in a particular case. It also offers useful information for fiction and nonfiction writers whose work involves a crime. A fascinating compilation. All levels." — *Choice, Association of College and Research Libraries, Jan 2000*

■

# Gastrointestinal Diseases & Disorders Sourcebook

*Basic Information about Gastroesophageal Reflux Disease (Heartburn), Ulcers, Diverticulosis, Irritable Bowel Syndrome, Crohn's Disease, Ulcerative Colitis, Diarrhea, Constipation, Lactose Intolerance, Hemorrhoids, Hepatitis, Cirrhosis, and Other Digestive Problems, Featuring Statistics, Descriptions of Symptoms, and Current Treatment Methods of Interest for Persons Living with Upper and Lower Gastrointestinal Maladies*

Edited by Linda M. Ross. 413 pages. 1996. 0-7808-0078-8. $78.

". . . very readable form. The successful editorial work that brought this material together into a useful and understandable reference makes accessible to all readers information that can help them more effectively understand and obtain help for digestive tract problems."
— *Choice, Association of College and Research Libraries, Feb '97*

**SEE ALSO** *Diet & Nutrition Sourcebook, 1st and 2nd Editions, Digestive Diseases & Disorders Sourcebook*

■

# Genetic Disorders Sourcebook, 1st Edition

*Basic Information about Heritable Diseases and Disorders Such as Down Syndrome, PKU, Hemophilia, Von Willebrand Disease, Gaucher Disease, Tay-Sachs Disease, and Sickle-Cell Disease, Along with Information about Genetic Screening, Gene Therapy, Home Care, and Including Source Listings for Further Help and Information on More Than 300 Disorders*

Edited by Karen Bellenir. 642 pages. 1996. 0-7808-0034-6. $78.

"Recommended for undergraduate libraries or libraries that serve the public."
— *Science & Technology Libraries, Vol. 18, No. 1, '99*

"Provides essential medical information to both the general public and those diagnosed with a serious or fatal genetic disease or disorder."
— *Choice, Association of College and Research Libraries, Jan '97*

"Geared toward the lay public. It would be well placed in all public libraries and in those hospital and medical libraries in which access to genetic references is limited." — *Doody's Health Sciences Book Review, Oct '96*

## Genetic Disorders Sourcebook, 2nd Edition

Basic Consumer Health Information about Hereditary Diseases and Disorders, Including Cystic Fibrosis, Down Syndrome, Hemophilia, Huntington's Disease, Sickle Cell Anemia, and More; Facts about Genes, Gene Research and Therapy, Genetic Screening, Ethics of Gene Testing, Genetic Counseling, and Advice on Coping and Caring

Along with a Glossary of Genetic Terminology and a Resource List for Help, Support, and Further Information

Edited by Kathy Massimini. 768 pages. 2001. 0-7808-0241-1. $78.

"Recommended for public libraries and medical and hospital libraries with consumer health collections."
— *E-Streams, May '01*

"Recommended reference source."
— *Booklist, American Library Association, Apr '01*

"Important pick for college-level health reference libraries." — *The Bookwatch, Mar '01*

## Head Trauma Sourcebook

Basic Information for the Layperson about Open-Head and Closed-Head Injuries, Treatment Advances, Recovery, and Rehabilitation

Along with Reports on Current Research Initiatives

Edited by Karen Bellenir. 414 pages. 1997. 0-7808-0208-X. $78.

## Health Insurance Sourcebook

Basic Information about Managed Care Organizations, Traditional Fee-for-Service Insurance, Insurance Portability and Pre-Existing Conditions Clauses, Medicare, Medicaid, Social Security, and Military Health Care

Along with Information about Insurance Fraud

Edited by Wendy Wilcox. 530 pages. 1997. 0-7808-0222-5. $78.

"Particularly useful because it brings much of this information together in one volume. This book will be a handy reference source in the health sciences library, hospital library, college and university library, and medium to large public library."
— *Medical Reference Services Quarterly, Fall '98*

Awarded "Books of the Year Award"
— *American Journal of Nursing, 1997*

"The layout of the book is particularly helpful as it provides easy access to reference material. A most useful addition to the vast amount of information about health insurance. The use of data from U.S. government agencies is most commendable. Useful in a library or learning center for healthcare professional students."
— *Doody's Health Sciences Book Reviews, Nov '97*

## Health Reference Series Cumulative Index 1999

A Comprehensive Index to the Individual Volumes of the Health Reference Series, Including a Subject Index, Name Index, Organization Index, and Publication Index

Along with a Master List of Acronyms and Abbreviations

Edited by Edward J. Prucha, Anne Holmes, and Robert Rudnick. 990 pages. 2000. 0-7808-0382-5. $78.

"This volume will be most helpful in libraries that have a relatively complete collection of the Health Reference Series."
— *American Reference Books Annual, 2001*

"Essential for collections that hold any of the numerous *Health Reference Series* titles."
— *Choice, Association of College and Research Libraries, Nov '00*

## Healthy Aging Sourcebook

Basic Consumer Health Information about Maintaining Health through the Aging Process, Including Advice on Nutrition, Exercise, and Sleep, Help in Making Decisions about Midlife Issues and Retirement, and Guidance Concerning Practical and Informed Choices in Health Consumerism

Along with Data Concerning the Theories of Aging, Different Experiences in Aging by Minority Groups, and Facts about Aging Now and Aging in the Future; and Featuring a Glossary, a Guide to Consumer Help, Additional Suggested Reading, and Practical Resource Directory

Edited by Jenifer Swanson. 536 pages. 1999. 0-7808-0390-6. $78.

"Recommended reference source."
— *Booklist, American Library Association, Feb '00*

**SEE ALSO** *Physical & Mental Issues in Aging Sourcebook*

## Healthy Heart Sourcebook for Women

Basic Consumer Health Information about Cardiac Issues Specific to Women, Including Facts about Major Risk Factors and Prevention, Treatment and Control Strategies, and Important Dietary Issues

Along with a Special Section Regarding the Pros and Cons of Hormone Replacement Therapy and Its Impact on Heart Health, and Additional Help, Including Recipes, a Glossary, and a Directory of Resources

Edited by Dawn D. Matthews. 336 pages. 2000. 0-7808-0329-9. $48.

"A good reference source and recommended for all public, academic, medical, and hospital libraries."
— *Medical Reference Services Quarterly, Summer '01*

**SEE ALSO** *Cardiovascular Diseases & Disorders Sourcebook, 1st Edition, Heart Diseases & Disorders Sourcebook, 2nd Edition, Women's Health Concerns Sourcebook*

# Heart Diseases & Disorders Sourcebook, 2nd Edition

*Basic Consumer Health Information about Heart Attacks, Angina, Rhythm Disorders, Heart Failure, Valve Disease, Congenital Heart Disorders, and More, Including Descriptions of Surgical Procedures and Other Interventions, Medications, Cardiac Rehabilitation, Risk Identification, and Prevention Tips*

*Along with Statistical Data, Reports on Current Research Initiatives, a Glossary of Cardiovascular Terms, and Resource Directory*

Edited by Karen Bellenir. 612 pages. 2000. 0-7808-0238-1. $78.

**SEE ALSO** *Cardiovascular Diseases & Disorders Sourcebook, 1st Edition, Healthy Heart Sourcebook for Women*

# Immune System Disorders Sourcebook

*Basic Information about Lupus, Multiple Sclerosis, Guillain-Barré Syndrome, Chronic Granulomatous Disease, and More*

*Along with Statistical and Demographic Data and Reports on Current Research Initiatives*

Edited by Allan R. Cook. 608 pages. 1997. 0-7808-0209-8. $78.

# Infant & Toddler Health Sourcebook

*Basic Consumer Health Information about the Physical and Mental Development of Newborns, Infants, and Toddlers, Including Neonatal Concerns, Nutrition Recommendations, Immunization Schedules, Common Pediatric Disorders, Assessments and Milestones, Safety Tips, and Advice for Parents and Other Caregivers*

*Along with a Glossary of Terms and Resource Listings for Additional Help*

Edited by Jenifer Swanson. 585 pages. 2000. 0-7808-0246-2. $78.

# Kidney & Urinary Tract Diseases & Disorders Sourcebook

*Basic Information about Kidney Stones, Urinary Incontinence, Bladder Disease, End Stage Renal Disease, Dialysis, and More*

*Along with Statistical and Demographic Data and Reports on Current Research Initiatives*

Edited by Linda M. Ross. 602 pages. 1997. 0-7808-0079-6. $78.

# Learning Disabilities Sourcebook

*Basic Information about Disorders Such as Dyslexia, Visual and Auditory Processing Deficits, Attention Deficit/Hyperactivity Disorder, and Autism*

*Along with Statistical and Demographic Data, Reports on Current Research Initiatives, an Explanation of the Assessment Process, and a Special Section for Adults with Learning Disabilities*

Edited by Linda M. Shin. 579 pages. 1998. 0-7808-0210-1. $78.

for contacting multiple resources add to the strength of this book as a useful tool." — Choice, Association of College and Research Libraries, Feb '99

"Recommended reference source."
— Booklist, American Library Association, Sep '98

"This is a useful resource for libraries and for those who don't have the time to identify and locate the individual publications."
— Disability Resources Monthly, Sep '98

■

## Liver Disorders Sourcebook

Basic Consumer Health Information about the Liver and How It Works; Liver Diseases, Including Cancer, Cirrhosis, Hepatitis, and Toxic and Drug Related Diseases; Tips for Maintaining a Healthy Liver; Laboratory Tests, Radiology Tests, and Facts about Liver Transplantation

Along with a Section on Support Groups, a Glossary, and Resource Listings

Edited by Joyce Brennfleck Shannon. 591 pages. 2000. 0-7808-0383-3. $78.

"A valuable resource."
— American Reference Books Annual, 2001

"This title is recommended for health sciences and public libraries with consumer health collections."
— E-Streams, Oct '00

"Recommended reference source."
— Booklist, American Library Association, Jun '00

■

## Medical Tests Sourcebook

Basic Consumer Health Information about Medical Tests, Including Periodic Health Exams, General Screening Tests, Tests You Can Do at Home, Findings of the U.S. Preventive Services Task Force, X-ray and Radiology Tests, Electrical Tests, Tests of Blood and Other Body Fluids and Tissues, Scope Tests, Lung Tests, Genetic Tests, Pregnancy Tests, Newborn Screening Tests, Sexually Transmitted Disease Tests, and Computer Aided Diagnoses

Along with a Section on Paying for Medical Tests, a Glossary, and Resource Listings

Edited by Joyce Brennfleck Shannon. 691 pages. 1999. 0-7808-0243-8. $78.

"A valuable reference guide."
— American Reference Books Annual, 2000

"Recommended for hospital and health sciences libraries with consumer health collections."
— E-Streams, Mar '00

"This is an overall excellent reference with a wealth of general knowledge that may aid those who are reluctant to get vital tests performed."
— Today's Librarian, Jan 2000

## Men's Health Concerns Sourcebook

Basic Information about Health Issues That Affect Men, Featuring Facts about the Top Causes of Death in Men, Including Heart Disease, Stroke, Cancers, Prostate Disorders, Chronic Obstructive Pulmonary Disease, Pneumonia and Influenza, Human Immunodeficiency Virus and Acquired Immune Deficiency Syndrome, Diabetes Mellitus, Stress, Suicide, Accidents and Homicides; and Facts about Common Concerns for Men, Including Impotence, Contraception, Circumcision, Sleep Disorders, Snoring, Hair Loss, Diet, Nutrition, Exercise, Kidney and Urological Disorders, and Backaches

Edited by Allan R. Cook. 738 pages. 1998. 0-7808-0212-8. $78.

"This comprehensive resource and the series are highly recommended."
— American Reference Books Annual, 2000

"Recommended reference source."
— Booklist, American Library Association, Dec '98

■

## Mental Health Disorders Sourcebook, 1st Edition

Basic Information about Schizophrenia, Depression, Bipolar Disorder, Panic Disorder, Obsessive-Compulsive Disorder, Phobias and Other Anxiety Disorders, Paranoia and Other Personality Disorders, Eating Disorders, and Sleep Disorders

Along with Information about Treatment and Therapies

Edited by Karen Bellenir. 548 pages. 1995. 0-7808-0040-0. $78.

"This is an excellent new book . . . written in easy-to-understand language."
— Booklist Health Sciences Supplement, American Library Association, Oct '97

". . . useful for public and academic libraries and consumer health collections."
— Medical Reference Services Quarterly, Spring '97

"The great strengths of the book are its readability and its inclusion of places to find more information. Especially recommended."
— Reference Quarterly, American Library Association, Winter '96

". . . a good resource for a consumer health library."
— Bulletin of the Medical Library Association, Oct '96

"The information is data-based and couched in brief, concise language that avoids jargon. . . . a useful reference source."
— Readings, Sep '96

"The text is well organized and adequately written for its target audience."
— Choice, Association of College and Research Libraries, Jun '96

". . . provides information on a wide range of mental disorders, presented in nontechnical language."
— Exceptional Child Education Resources, Spring '96

"Recommended for public and academic libraries."
— Reference Book Review, 1996

317

# Mental Health Disorders Sourcebook, 2nd Edition

Basic Consumer Health Information about Anxiety Disorders, Depression and Other Mood Disorders, Eating Disorders, Personality Disorders, Schizophrenia, and More, Including Disease Descriptions, Treatment Options, and Reports on Current Research Initiatives

Along with Statistical Data, Tips for Maintaining Mental Health, a Glossary, and Directory of Sources for Additional Help and Information

Edited by Karen Bellenir. 605 pages. 2000. 0-7808-0240-3. $78.

"Well organized and well written."
—American Reference Books Annual, 2001

"Recommended reference source."
—Booklist, American Library Association, Jun '00

■

# Mental Retardation Sourcebook

Basic Consumer Health Information about Mental Retardation and Its Causes, Including Down Syndrome, Fetal Alcohol Syndrome, Fragile X Syndrome, Genetic Conditions, Injury, and Environmental Sources

Along with Preventive Strategies, Parenting Issues, Educational Implications, Health Care Needs, Employment and Economic Matters, Legal Issues, a Glossary, and a Resource Listing for Additional Help and Information

Edited by Joyce Brennfleck Shannon. 642 pages. 2000. 0-7808-0377-9. $78.

"Public libraries will find the book useful for reference and as a beginning research point for students, parents, and caregivers."
—American Reference Books Annual, 2001

"The strength of this work is that it compiles many basic fact sheets and addresses for further information in one volume. It is intended and suitable for the general public. The sourcebook is relevant to any collection providing health information to the general public."
—E-Streams, Nov '00

"From preventing retardation to parenting and family challenges, this covers health, social and legal issues and will prove an invaluable overview."
—Reviewer's Bookwatch, Jul '00

■

# Obesity Sourcebook

Basic Consumer Health Information about Diseases and Other Problems Associated with Obesity, and Including Facts about Risk Factors, Prevention Issues, and Management Approaches

Along with Statistical and Demographic Data, Information about Special Populations, Research Updates, a Glossary, and Source Listings for Further Help and Information

Edited by Wilma Caldwell and Chad T. Kimball. 376 pages. 2001. 0-7808-0333-7. $48.

"Recommended pick both for specialty health library collections and any general consumer health reference collection."
—The Bookwatch, Apr '01

"Recommended reference source."
—Booklist, American Library Association, Apr '01

■

# Ophthalmic Disorders Sourcebook

Basic Information about Glaucoma, Cataracts, Macular Degeneration, Strabismus, Refractive Disorders, and More

Along with Statistical and Demographic Data and Reports on Current Research Initiatives

Edited by Linda M. Ross. 631 pages. 1996. 0-7808-0081-8. $78.

■

# Oral Health Sourcebook

Basic Information about Diseases and Conditions Affecting Oral Health, Including Cavities, Gum Disease, Dry Mouth, Oral Cancers, Fever Blisters, Canker Sores, Oral Thrush, Bad Breath, Temporomandibular Disorders, and other Craniofacial Syndromes

Along with Statistical Data on the Oral Health of Americans, Oral Hygiene, Emergency First Aid, Information on Treatment Procedures and Methods of Replacing Lost Teeth

Edited by Allan R. Cook. 558 pages. 1997. 0-7808-0082-6. $78.

"Unique source which will fill a gap in dental sources for patients and the lay public. A valuable reference tool even in a library with thousands of books on dentistry. Comprehensive, clear, inexpensive, and easy to read and use. It fills an enormous gap in the health care literature."
—Reference and User Services Quarterly, American Library Association, Summer '98

"Recommended reference source."
—Booklist, American Library Association, Dec '97

■

# Osteoporosis Sourcebook

Basic Consumer Health Information about Primary and Secondary Osteoporosis and Juvenile Osteoporosis and Related Conditions, Including Fibrous Dysplasia, Gaucher Disease, Hyperthyroidism, Hypophosphatasia, Myeloma, Osteopetrosis, Osteogenesis Imperfecta, and Paget's Disease

Along with Information about Risk Factors, Treatments, Traditional and Non-Traditional Pain Management, a Glossary of Related Terms, and a Directory of Resources

Edited by Allan R. Cook. 584 pages. 2001. 0-7808-0239-X. $78.

*SEE ALSO* Women's Health Concerns Sourcebook

# Pain Sourcebook

Basic Information about Specific Forms of Acute and Chronic Pain, Including Headaches, Back Pain, Muscular Pain, Neuralgia, Surgical Pain, and Cancer Pain Along with Pain Relief Options Such as Analgesics, Narcotics, Nerve Blocks, Transcutaneous Nerve Stimulation, and Alternative Forms of Pain Control, Including Biofeedback, Imaging, Behavior Modification, and Relaxation Techniques

Edited by Allan R. Cook. 667 pages. 1997. 0-7808-0213-6. $78.

"The text is readable, easily understood, and well indexed. This excellent volume belongs in all patient education libraries, consumer health sections of public libraries, and many personal collections."
— *American Reference Books Annual, 1999*

"A beneficial reference." — *Booklist Health Sciences Supplement, American Library Association, Oct '98*

"The information is basic in terms of scholarship and is appropriate for general readers. Written in journalistic style . . . intended for non-professionals. Quite thorough in its coverage of different pain conditions and summarizes the latest clinical information regarding pain treatment." — *Choice, Association of College and Research Libraries, Jun '98*

"Recommended reference source."
— *Booklist, American Library Association, Mar '98*

# Pediatric Cancer Sourcebook

Basic Consumer Health Information about Leukemias, Brain Tumors, Sarcomas, Lymphomas, and Other Cancers in Infants, Children, and Adolescents, Including Descriptions of Cancers, Treatments, and Coping Strategies Along with Suggestions for Parents, Caregivers, and Concerned Relatives, a Glossary of Cancer Terms, and Resource Listings

Edited by Edward J. Prucha. 587 pages. 1999. 0-7808-0245-4. $78.

"A valuable addition to all libraries specializing in health services and many public libraries."
— *American Reference Books Annual, 2000*

"Recommended reference source."
— *Booklist, American Library Association, Feb '00*

"An excellent source of information. Recommended for public, hospital, and health science libraries with consumer health collections." — *E-Streams, Jun '00*

# Physical & Mental Issues in Aging Sourcebook

Basic Consumer Health Information on Physical and Mental Disorders Associated with the Aging Process, Including Concerns about Cardiovascular Disease, Pulmonary Disease, Oral Health, Digestive Disorders, Musculoskeletal and Skin Disorders, Metabolic Changes, Sexual and Reproductive Issues, and Changes in Vision, Hearing, and Other Senses Along with Data about Longevity and Causes of Death, Information on Acute and Chronic Pain, Descriptions of Mental Concerns, a Glossary of Terms, and Resource Listings for Additional Help

Edited by Jenifer Swanson. 660 pages. 1999. 0-7808-0233-0. $78.

"Recommended for public libraries."
— *American Reference Books Annual, 2000*

"This is a treasure of health information for the layperson." — *Choice Health Sciences Supplement, Association of College & Research Libraries, May 2000*

"Recommended reference source."
— *Booklist, American Library Association, Oct '99*

SEE ALSO *Healthy Aging Sourcebook*

# Podiatry Sourcebook

Basic Consumer Health Information about Foot Conditions, Diseases, and Injuries, Including Bunions, Corns, Calluses, Athlete's Foot, Plantar Warts, Hammertoes and Clawtoes, Clubfoot, Heel Pain, Gout, and More Along with Facts about Foot Care, Disease Prevention, Foot Safety, Choosing a Foot Care Specialist, a Glossary of Terms, and Resource Listings for Additional Information

Edited by M. Lisa Weatherford. 400 pages. 2001. 0-7808-0215-2. $78.

# Pregnancy & Birth Sourcebook

Basic Information about Planning for Pregnancy, Maternal Health, Fetal Growth and Development, Labor and Delivery, Postpartum and Perinatal Care, Pregnancy in Mothers with Special Concerns, and Disorders of Pregnancy, Including Genetic Counseling, Nutrition and Exercise, Obstetrical Tests, Pregnancy Discomfort, Multiple Births, Cesarean Sections, Medical Testing of Newborns, Breastfeeding, Gestational Diabetes, and Ectopic Pregnancy

Edited by Heather E. Aldred. 737 pages. 1997. 0-7808-0216-0. $78.

"A well-organized handbook. Recommended."
— *Choice, Association of College and Research Libraries, Apr '98*

"Recommended reference source."
— *Booklist, American Library Association, Mar '98*

"Recommended for public libraries."
— *American Reference Books Annual, 1998*

SEE ALSO *Congenital Disorders Sourcebook, Family Planning Sourcebook*

# Prostate Cancer Sourcebook

*Basic Consumer Health Information about Prostate Cancer, Including Information about the Associated Risk Factors, Detection, Diagnosis, and Treatment of Prostate Cancer*

*Along with Information on Non-Malignant Prostate Conditions, and Featuring a Section Listing Support and Treatment Centers and a Glossary of Related Terms*

Edited by Dawn D. Matthews. 300 pages. 2001. 0-7808-0324-8. $78.

■

# Public Health Sourcebook

*Basic Information about Government Health Agencies, Including National Health Statistics and Trends, Healthy People 2000 Program Goals and Objectives, the Centers for Disease Control and Prevention, the Food and Drug Administration, and the National Institutes of Health*

*Along with Full Contact Information for Each Agency*

Edited by Wendy Wilcox. 698 pages. 1998. 0-7808-0220-9. $78.

**"Recommended reference source."**
— *Booklist, American Library Association, Sep '98*

**"This consumer guide provides welcome assistance in navigating the maze of federal health agencies and their data on public health concerns."**
— *SciTech Book News, Sep '98*

■

# Reconstructive & Cosmetic Surgery Sourcebook

*Basic Consumer Health Information on Cosmetic and Reconstructive Plastic Surgery, Including Statistical Information about Different Surgical Procedures, Things to Consider Prior to Surgery, Plastic Surgery Techniques and Tools, Emotional and Psychological Considerations, and Procedure-Specific Information*

*Along with a Glossary of Terms and a Listing of Resources for Additional Help and Information*

Edited by M. Lisa Weatherford. 374 pages. 2001. 0-7808-0214-4. $48.

■

# Rehabilitation Sourcebook

*Basic Consumer Health Information about Rehabilitation for People Recovering from Heart Surgery, Spinal Cord Injury, Stroke, Orthopedic Impairments, Amputation, Pulmonary Impairments, Traumatic Injury, and More, Including Physical Therapy, Occupational Therapy, Speech/ Language Therapy, Massage Therapy, Dance Therapy, Art Therapy, and Recreational Therapy*

*Along with Information on Assistive and Adaptive Devices, a Glossary, and Resources for Additional Help and Information*

Edited by Dawn D. Matthews. 531 pages. 1999. 0-7808-0236-5. $78.

**"This is an excellent resource for public library reference and health collections."**
— *American Reference Books Annual, 2001*

**"Recommended reference source."**
— *Booklist, American Library Association, May '00*

■

# Respiratory Diseases & Disorders Sourcebook

*Basic Information about Respiratory Diseases and Disorders, Including Asthma, Cystic Fibrosis, Pneumonia, the Common Cold, Influenza, and Others, Featuring Facts about the Respiratory System, Statistical and Demographic Data, Treatments, Self-Help Management Suggestions, and Current Research Initiatives*

Edited by Allan R. Cook and Peter D. Dresser. 771 pages. 1995. 0-7808-0037-0. $78.

**"Designed for the layperson and for patients and their families coping with respiratory illness. . . . an extensive array of information on diagnosis, treatment, management, and prevention of respiratory illnesses for the general reader."**
— *Choice, Association of College and Research Libraries, Jun '96*

**"A highly recommended text for all collections. It is a comforting reminder of the power of knowledge that good books carry between their covers."**
— *Academic Library Book Review, Spring '96*

**"A comprehensive collection of authoritative information presented in a nontechnical, humanitarian style for patients, families, and caregivers."**
— *Association of Operating Room Nurses, Sep/Oct '95*

■

# Sexually Transmitted Diseases Sourcebook, 1st Edition

*Basic Information about Herpes, Chlamydia, Gonorrhea, Hepatitis, Nongonoccocal Urethritis, Pelvic Inflammatory Disease, Syphilis, AIDS, and More*

*Along with Current Data on Treatments and Preventions*

Edited by Linda M. Ross. 550 pages. 1997. 0-7808-0217-9. $78.

## Sexually Transmitted Diseases Sourcebook, 2nd Edition

*Basic Consumer Health Information about Sexually Transmitted Diseases, Including Information on the Diagnosis and Treatment of Chlamydia, Gonorrhea, Hepatitis, Herpes, HIV, Mononucleosis, Syphilis, and Others*

*Along with Information on Prevention, Such as Condom Use, Vaccines, and STD Education; And Featuring a Section on Issues Related to Youth and Adolescents, a Glossary, and Resources for Additional Help and Information*

Edited by Dawn D. Matthews. 538 pages. 2001. 0-7808-0249-7. $78.

**"Recommended pick both for specialty health library collections and any general consumer health reference collection."** — *The Bookwatch, Apr '01*

**"Recommended reference source."**
— *Booklist, American Library Association, Apr '01*

■

## Skin Disorders Sourcebook

*Basic Information about Common Skin and Scalp Conditions Caused by Aging, Allergies, Immune Reactions, Sun Exposure, Infectious Organisms, Parasites, Cosmetics, and Skin Traumas, Including Abrasions, Cuts, and Pressure Sores*

*Along with Information on Prevention and Treatment*

Edited by Allan R. Cook. 647 pages. 1997. 0-7808-0080-X. $78.

**". . . comprehensive, easily read reference book."**
— *Doody's Health Sciences Book Reviews, Oct '97*

***SEE ALSO*** Burns Sourcebook

■

## Sleep Disorders Sourcebook

*Basic Consumer Health Information about Sleep and Its Disorders, Including Insomnia, Sleepwalking, Sleep Apnea, Restless Leg Syndrome, and Narcolepsy*

*Along with Data about Shiftwork and Its Effects, Information on the Societal Costs of Sleep Deprivation, Descriptions of Treatment Options, a Glossary of Terms, and Resource Listings for Additional Help*

Edited by Jenifer Swanson. 439 pages. 1998. 0-7808-0234-9. $78.

**"This text will complement any home or medical library. It is user-friendly and ideal for the adult reader."**
— *American Reference Books Annual, 2000*

**"Recommended reference source."**
— *Booklist, American Library Association, Feb '99*

**"A useful resource that provides accurate, relevant, and accessible information on sleep to the general public. Health care providers who deal with sleep disorders patients may also find it helpful in being prepared to answer some of the questions patients ask."**
— *Respiratory Care, Jul '99*

## Sports Injuries Sourcebook

*Basic Consumer Health Information about Common Sports Injuries, Prevention of Injury in Specific Sports, Tips for Training, and Rehabilitation from Injury*

*Along with Information about Special Concerns for Children, Young Girls in Athletic Training Programs, Senior Athletes, and Women Athletes, and a Directory of Resources for Further Help and Information*

Edited by Heather E. Aldred. 624 pages. 1999. 0-7808-0218-7. $78.

**"Public libraries and undergraduate academic libraries will find this book useful for its nontechnical language."** — *American Reference Books Annual, 2000*

**"While this easy-to-read book is recommended for all libraries, it should prove to be especially useful for public, high school, and academic libraries; certainly it should be on the bookshelf of every school gymnasium."** — *E-Streams, Mar '00*

■

## Substance Abuse Sourcebook

*Basic Health-Related Information about the Abuse of Legal and Illegal Substances Such as Alcohol, Tobacco, Prescription Drugs, Marijuana, Cocaine, and Heroin; and Including Facts about Substance Abuse Prevention Strategies, Intervention Methods, Treatment and Recovery Programs, and a Section Addressing the Special Problems Related to Substance Abuse during Pregnancy*

Edited by Karen Bellenir. 573 pages. 1996. 0-7808-0038-9. $78.

**"A valuable addition to any health reference section. Highly recommended."**
— *The Book Report, Mar/Apr '97*

**". . . a comprehensive collection of substance abuse information that's both highly readable and compact. Families and caregivers of substance abusers will find the information enlightening and helpful, while teachers, social workers and journalists should benefit from the concise format. Recommended."**
— *Drug Abuse Update, Winter '96/'97*

***SEE ALSO*** Alcoholism Sourcebook, Drug Abuse Sourcebook

■

## Transplantation Sourcebook

*Basic Consumer Health Information about Organ and Tissue Transplantation, Including Physical and Financial Preparations, Procedures and Issues Relating to Specific Solid Organ and Tissue Transplants, Rehabilitation, Pediatric Transplant Information, the Future of Transplantation, and Organ and Tissue Donation*

*Along with a Glossary and Listings of Additional Resources*

Edited by Joyce Brennfleck Shannon. 600 pages. 2001. 0-7808-0322-1. $78.

## Traveler's Health Sourcebook

*Basic Consumer Health Information for Travelers, Including Physical and Medical Preparations, Transportation Health and Safety, Essential Information about Food and Water, Sun Exposure, Insect and Snake Bites, Camping and Wilderness Medicine, and Travel with Physical or Medical Disabilities*

*Along with International Travel Tips, Vaccination Recommendations, Geographical Health Issues, Disease Risks, a Glossary, and a Listing of Additional Resources*

Edited by Joyce Brennfleck Shannon. 613 pages. 2000. 0-7808-0384-1. $78.

**"Recommended reference source."**

— *Booklist, American Library Association, Feb '01*

**"This book is recommended for any public library, any travel collection, and especially any collection for the physically disabled."**
—*American Reference Books Annual, 2001*

■

## Women's Health Concerns Sourcebook

*Basic Information about Health Issues That Affect Women, Featuring Facts about Menstruation and Other Gynecological Concerns, Including Endometriosis, Fibroids, Menopause, and Vaginitis; Reproductive Concerns, Including Birth Control, Infertility, and Abortion; and Facts about Additional Physical, Emotional, and Mental Health Concerns Prevalent among Women Such as Osteoporosis, Urinary Tract Disorders, Eating Disorders, and Depression*

*Along with Tips for Maintaining a Healthy Lifestyle*

Edited by Heather E. Aldred. 567 pages. 1997. 0-7808-0219-5. $78.

**"Handy compilation. There is an impressive range of diseases, devices, disorders, procedures, and other physical and emotional issues covered . . . well organized, illustrated, and indexed."** — *Choice, Association of College and Research Libraries, Jan '98*

**SEE ALSO** *Breast Cancer Sourcebook, Cancer Sourcebook for Women, 1st and 2nd Editions, Healthy Heart Sourcebook for Women, Osteoporosis Sourcebook*

## Workplace Health & Safety Sourcebook

*Basic Consumer Health Information about Workplace Health and Safety, Including the Effect of Workplace Hazards on the Lungs, Skin, Heart, Ears, Eyes, Brain, Reproductive Organs, Musculoskeletal System, and Other Organs and Body Parts*

*Along with Information about Occupational Cancer, Personal Protective Equipment, Toxic and Hazardous Chemicals, Child Labor, Stress, and Workplace Violence*

Edited by Chad T. Kimball. 626 pages. 2000. 0-7808-0231-4. $78.

**"Provides helpful information for primary care physicians and other caregivers interested in occupational medicine. . . . General readers; professionals."**
— *Choice, Association of College and Research Libraries, May '01*

**"Recommended reference source."**
— *Booklist, American Library Association, Feb '01*

**"Highly recommended."** —*The Bookwatch, Jan '01*

■

## Worldwide Health Sourcebook

*Basic Information about Global Health Issues, Including Malnutrition, Reproductive Health, Disease Dispersion and Prevention, Emerging Diseases, Risky Health Behaviors, and the Leading Causes of Death*

*Along with Global Health Concerns for Children, Women, and the Elderly, Mental Health Issues, Research and Technology Advancements, and Economic, Environmental, and Political Health Implications, a Glossary, and a Resource Listing for Additional Help and Information*

Edited by Joyce Brennfleck Shannon. 614 pages. 2001. 0-7808-0330-2. $78.